W9-CUF-579

Privacy in Technology

Standards and Practices for Engineers and
Security and IT Professionals

JC Cannon, CIPP/US, CIPT

An IAPP Publication

Copy editor: Sarah Weaver
Compositor: Ed Stevens, Ed Stevens Design
Indexer: Jan Bednarczuk, Jandex Indexing

ISBN: 978-0-9885525-6-2

Library of Congress Control Number: 2014937638

About the IAPP

The International Association of Privacy Professionals (IAPP) is the largest and most comprehensive global information privacy community and resource, helping practitioners develop and advance their careers and organizations manage and protect their data.

The IAPP is a not-for-profit association founded in 2000 with a mission to define, support and improve the privacy profession globally. We are committed to providing a forum for privacy professionals to share best practices, track trends, advance privacy management issues, standardize the designations for privacy professionals and provide education and guidance on opportunities in the field of information privacy.

The IAPP is responsible for developing and launching the only globally recognized credentialing programs in information privacy: the Certified Information Privacy Professional (CIPP), the Certified Information Privacy Manager (CIPM) and the Certified Information Privacy Technologist (CIPT). The CIPP, CIPM and CIPT are the leading privacy certifications for thousands of professionals around the world who serve the data protection, information auditing, information security, legal compliance and/or risk management needs of their organizations.

In addition, the IAPP offers a full suite of educational and professional development services and holds annual conferences that are recognized internationally as the leading forums for the discussion and debate of issues related to privacy policy and practice.

Contents

TABLE LIST

Acknowledgments

The IAPP is pleased to present *Privacy in Technology: Standards and Practices for Engineers and Security and IT Professionals* in support of the Certified Information Privacy Technologist (CIPT) credential. As the global privacy certification for information technology professionals, the CIPT assesses knowledge of privacy practices and the ability to implement privacy in the IT environment.

There are many people who contributed to the development of this program. Harriet Pearson, John Bliss, Linda Betz, Fred Cate, Kim Howell, Jeff Jonas and Mary Gay Whitmer provided early direction on a privacy certification program that would meet the needs of the IT community. Feedback, testing and revisions of the program were provided by Linda Betz, Yim Chan, Lorrie Faith Cranor, Sagi Leizerov, Christine Ravago, Susan Smith, Diane Soloman and Zoe Strickland.

Our certification advisory boards provide critical guidance on the details of our certification programs. I would like to acknowledge these members, past and present, for their important contributions to this certification:

Joseph Alhadeff	David A. Hoffman	Charles Palmer
Chris Arrendale	Jane C. Horvath	Harriet Pearson
Fred Cate	Kim Howell	Douglas Robinson
Linda Betz	John Howie	Javier Salido
Vernon Bush	Jeff Jones	Manoj Kumar Sarangi
Susan Couture	Peter Kosmala	Susan Smith
Ron De Jesus	Ponnurangam Kumaraguru	Zoe Strickland
Michelle Dennedy	Leslie Lambert	Barbra Symonds
Gilles Fourchet	Laura Lazarczyk	Lawrence Tan
Jonathan Fox	Deborah Lohr	Scott Taylor
Dona-Marie Geoffrion	Nandita Jain Mahajan	Mary Gay Whitmer
Kam Golpariani	Mary Morshed	Edward Yakabovicz
Thomas Gross	Sandy Ford Page	

I am grateful to JC Cannon for accepting our request to write this book. With over 30 years' experience in technology—12 of those focused on privacy—he brought an important depth of knowledge to this project. He was a tremendous partner, delivering a final text that successfully balances content and readability.

Many thanks to Adam Shostack, danah boyd and Jeff Chester for their assistance with research and content. Gilles Fourchet, Laura Lazarczyk, Deborah Lohr, Mary Morshed, Javier Salido, Bob Siegel, Jennie Spencer, Ernst Oliver Wilhelm and Ed Yakabovicz provided feedback and guidance on the draft manuscript. I am appreciative for their thoughtful comments that influenced the revision of this text. Thank you to Forrest Carl Peterson and Derek A. Jones for their work in validating the references in this book. To Sarah Weaver and Ed Stevens, thank you for ensuring that the published text is professional in both content and presentation.

This program has benefited from the contributions of so many talented professionals. I am confident that you will find this text an invaluable resource in your preparation for the CIPT exam.

Marla Berry, CIPT
Certification Director
International Association of Privacy Professionals

Introduction

As the profession of privacy has rapidly evolved—the IAPP went from zero to 16,000+ members in 14 short years—one thing has remained the same: The best privacy policies in the world are useless without great practical implementation. Theory and application go hand in hand.

Therefore, while pursuing our mission of improving the privacy profession, we have continued to reach deeper and deeper into organizations to plant the seeds of privacy on the front lines. This is perhaps nowhere better reflected than in *Privacy in Technology*, which not only delivers the core privacy concepts needed to work in the IT field but also answers the most important question of all: How?

Expertly brought together by Microsoft's JC Cannon, CIPP/US, CIPT, who has a decade on the job as a CIPP in the IT department, this text is truly a reflection of the work of a privacy professional in the world of IT. Further, in its coverage of everything from the differences between security and privacy to BYOD and social media, I am confident in saying it will provide you with both the theory and practice needed for greatly enhancing your value to an organization.

Best of all, the book is eminently readable. As you make your way through chapters on the information lifecycle, common privacy techniques and the newest technologies that require privacy considerations, you'll feel a little bit like you're reading the latest stories from the *Wall Street Journal* and *New York Times*. These are the topics everyone is talking about nowadays, from the boardroom to the living room, and you have an opportunity to capitalize on that public fervor.

With this text in hand, you can stop that embarrassing breach, make sure that new app doesn't draw the attention of the Federal Trade Commission and help to prepare your company for truly global commerce.

So, let me be the first to wish you luck on your way to your CIPT certification. Whether you are working at a tech start-up or at a *Fortune* 100 firm, in the healthcare field or financial services, at the head of your department or just starting out, I'm confident that the information herein will be vital and oft-used in your day-to-day job. Terms like "notice," "consent" and "Privacy by Design" will soon be part of your everyday parlance and you'll wonder how you ever got by without them.

J. Trevor Hughes, CIPP
President and CEO
International Association of Privacy Professionals

## CHAPTER 1

Understanding the Need For Privacy in the IT Environment

1.1 Evolving Compliance Requirements

Amy walked down a long narrow hallway toward the data center where she works. Her brow was furrowed as she mulled over the conversation she would soon be immersed in during an emergency meeting with company executives. Amy is the CIO of a large multinational high-tech firm. When she started working there in 2000, there was no LinkedIn, Twitter or Facebook. Her biggest worries back then were minimizing spam, running backups and improving network performance. Viruses and cyber attacks were few and far between.

In recent months, she has had to update her IT plans to account for the firm's bring your own device (BYOD) program, e-Privacy Directive updates, Children's Online Privacy Protection Act (COPPA) rule changes and possible Do Not Track requirements from the Tracking Protection Working Group of the W3C (World Wide Web Consortium).[1] In addition, the recent National Security Agency data-gathering scandal brought several high-tech companies under greater scrutiny.[2] Even though Amy's company was not involved in the scandal, she has had to spend time preparing statements, briefing executives about the issue and confirming that their company was clear of any involvement.

Regulatory activities, security threats, advances in technology, new software releases and the increasing proliferation of social networks can have serious impacts on an IT department's approach to compliance. Not only must IT professionals be able to respond to the needs of their organization, but they must also be able to predict how events might impact the products, security and privacy readiness of the organization.

More than ever, privacy controls have become an integral part of a comprehensive IT compliance program. Additionally, having good internal privacy procedures can help to attract and retain good employees. Prospective employees will be reluctant to work at a company that has an undesirable privacy reputation because such a reputation is likely to damage their professional career. Moreover, they may be concerned that their employee data could be released to the wrong person, causing financial or reputation issues.

Having good external privacy procedures can also help attract and retain customers, business partners and investors. Conversely, doing business with a company with a bad privacy reputation can be seen as a general risk. Having a relationship with such a company could taint one's own reputation.

Bill is an IT compliance professional who works for Amy. He uses the COBIT 5 Framework to help him perform a risk assessment of the company's IT systems, develop controls by which to measure the systems and validate that the controls are helping the company reach its compliance goals.[3] Bill knows that having a formal process in place will help to minimize informational risk.

Carrie is a privacy compliance professional who works for Amy. She works with Bill to help ensure the privacy compliance of systems that host employee and customer data. She follows the NCASE rules as set out by the Federal Trade Commission's (FTC's) Fair Information Practice Principles (FIPPs) as she goes about her daily duties.[4] NCASE is the acronym for the five privacy principles:

- **Notice.** Consumers should be given notice of an entity's information practices before any personal information is collected from them. Without notice, a consumer cannot make an informed decision as to whether and to what extent to disclose personal information.

- **Choice.** At its simplest, choice means giving consumers options as to how any personal information collected from them may be used. Specifically, choice relates to secondary uses of information—that is, uses beyond those necessary to complete the contemplated transaction.

- **Access.** Access refers to an individual's ability both to access data about him- or herself—that is, to view the data in an entity's files—and to contest that data's accuracy and completeness. Both are essential to ensuring that data is accurate and complete.

- **Security.** Both managerial and technical security measures are needed to protect against loss and the unauthorized access, destruction, use or disclosure of data. Technical security measures to prevent unauthorized access include encryption in the transmission and storage of data; limits on access through use of credentials, implementation of role-based access controls (RBAC) and other techniques; and the storage of data on secure servers or computers.

- **Enforcement.** It is generally agreed that the core principles of privacy protection can only be effective if there is a mechanism in place to enforce them. Absent an enforcement and redress mechanism, a fair information practice code is merely suggestive rather than prescriptive, and does not ensure compliance with core Fair Information Practice Principles.

Amy opened the door and walked into an unusually crowded conference room. There were too many suits being worn for all the occupants to be company employees. She overheard comments about WikiLeaks, foreign governments and a major breach that had to be contained. Amy could feel the blood flowing from her face and her knees weakening as she started to go through all the system checks in her head, wondering what could have gone wrong. "Amy, I hope you cleared your calendar today," said the chief operating officer as he walked up to her. "This is going to be a long meeting."

1.2 IT Risks

Like all IT professionals, Amy has to be ever vigilant about threats to the environment for which she is responsible. She gets numerous calls and e-mails throughout the day describing various problems being experienced by individuals or entire departments. The real issue could be a hardware or software failure, setting misconfiguration, cyber attack or simply user error. Amy does not have the luxury to assume that an issue is innocuous. Each issue could cause sensitive data to be leaked, permanently damage computer systems or the network, or adversely impact a company's reputation.[5]

Amy is responsible for all of the company's client machines, which can be desktop workstations, laptops, tablets or even mobile devices. Additionally, there are hundreds of servers, networks, devices, applications and installations that she has to maintain and protect. Not only does she need to ensure that all the systems under her purview are running smoothly, she has to be certain she is complying with all of the regulatory requirements, industry obligations and corporate policies. Each type of system has its own set of requirements that must be addressed. Failure to address the requirements could cause privacy incidents such as a data breach and improper use of personal data. IT risks include improper access controls or application of retention policies, leaving corporate documents exposed to the wrong people. Failure to meet industry commitments could result in a loss of accreditation, leading to a loss in customers. In the worst-case scenario, the company could be fined, forced to change its practices and have its executives jailed.

1.2.1 Client Side

The client side represents the computers typically used by company employees. These computers normally connect to the company's server-side systems via wireless and hardwired networks. The client side can represent a significant threat to the company's systems as well as sensitive data that may be on the client computers. Employees often download customer files, corporate e-mails and legal documents to their computer for processing. Employees may even store their personal information on company computers. Even more concerning is that the client computer can access resources across the company that could have vast amounts of planning documents that might be of great interest to competitors or corporate spies. For that reason, client computers should be protected from possible threats.

Protecting client computers from all of the possible threats is a daunting task for IT professionals. There are many threats to the contents of client computers. The computer itself could be stolen; a virus could make the computer unusable or send data outside the company; poor access control policies or lack of an auto-lock policy could leave data on the computer exposed to an intruder. At the same time, employees must be able to use their computers to complete their daily tasks. For that reason, IT professionals must make sure that their decisions maintain a healthy balance between protecting corporate systems and minimizing the impact on employee productivity.

Even when an employee's computer is protected from known threats, there is still more to be done to address client-side privacy issues. When accessing data from client computers, employees should be made aware of their privacy obligations. Employees should be required to take privacy training before accessing personal data. Initial accesses to data should display a reminder of the privacy policies for the data as well as a link to those policies.

1.2.2 Server Side

Organizational servers can share the same vulnerabilities as their client counterparts, though those risks can be minimized. Many client applications do not need to be on a server and most users have less of a need to access servers directly. Social, office productivity and communications software are examples of the types of applications that are typically not needed on servers and should be kept off of them. Reducing the number of applications on a computer reduces the surface area that can be vulnerable to attack. The more applications that exist on a server, the greater the chance that one could harbor a virus or contain a vulnerability that could be exploited, leaving the server exposed to attack. Reducing the number of applications running on a server can also boost the performance of the server and, by extension, the client machines that connect to it. One way to limit applications on a server is to use a bastion server—a server that has one purpose and only contains software to support that purpose.[6] A proxy server, printer server, database server and e-mail server are all examples of bastion servers.

Many servers do not need access to the Internet and can be placed on isolated networks that do not have Internet connections, thus minimizing the inherent risks of the Internet. Using that approach can help protect servers from cyber attacks, phishing exploits and Internet-based malware.

When computers do have to be connected to the Internet, a firewall can be used to block unwanted network traffic from reaching the corporate network. The firewall can screen incoming network data packets and block undesirable ones based on the IP address, port number or protocol used. Another approach to protecting corporate servers is to use a screening host at the Internet boundary.[7] These types of servers or network devices block unwanted accesses and network data packet types from accessing the internal network or frontline servers.

Where possible, all data on a server should be classified based on its category, origin, sensitivity and purpose. This will help ensure that employees know which privacy policies apply to the treatment of the data. Efforts must be made to ensure that retention, usage and de-identification policies are applied to data. For example, it may be a requirement that data used for research contain no personally identifiable information or that data for use by marketing contain no personal data. Care must be taken to ensure that the linkage between datasets does not break any of the organization's privacy rules. For example, a database may use IDs to avoid the use of personal data. However, if those IDs map to personal data in another database, then the privacy policies could be easily circumvented without the right protections in place.

1.2.3 Security Policy and Personnel

It could be said that a company with no security policy has no security at all. Privacy cannot be assured unless practical security measures have been established. Likewise, a security policy with no accountability or people to enforce it is of little value. Each company should have a security policy in place along with compliance and security personnel to enforce it. This policy will help employees understand what their security responsibilities are. The compliance personnel can create a set of security controls to help enforce accountability with security policy objectives. Security personnel will help ensure that security policies are being followed.

When determining the appropriate security policy to protect personal information, a privacy impact assessment (PIA) can help find any gaps in coverage and determine security requirements to address them. While there will be several internal corporate obligations to consider, all security policies should also include external requirements, such as:

- **Corporate.** A company stores data from consumers, partners, vendors and employees. This data needs to be protected based on its sensitivity and in accordance with any contracts, agreements or privacy policies. Organizations also need to ensure that data is kept secure to protect their own interests.

- **Regulatory.** Government entities often place privacy requirements on organizations. These requirements can present themselves in the way of laws from local, state, federal and even foreign governments. Regulations can even come from government agencies such as the U.S. Federal Trade Commission, Office of the Information and Privacy Commissioner of Ontario and the UK Information Commissioner's Office.

- **Industry.** Companies will want to comply with different industry groups to show their commitment to certain industries and their principles. This is one way to avoid the creation of new legislation and regulatory scrutiny, not only in the United States, but also in Europe, Canada and other regions where there is a close relationship between industry groups and regulatory bodies. These industry groups include the Better Business Bureau, Interactive Advertising Bureau, TRUSTe and the Entertainment Software Rating Board.

Once completed, the security policy will drive the processes and procedures that an organization can follow for implementing the policy. Several industry standards can provide guidance on creating security policies, processes and procedures.[8] Below are examples of security measures that should be included in a security policy to help protect data:

- **Encryption.** Encryption is one of the best means to protect data during transmission and storage. The type of encryption used should be based on how the encryption's performance and complexity may impact company systems. The National Institute of Standards and Technology has developed a Cryptographic Toolkit to assist organizations with the selection of cryptographic security components and functionality for protecting their data, communications and operations.[9]

- **Software protection.** Different types of software can be used to protect sensitive data from privacy threats. Antivirus software can detect malicious software that may grab data from an employee's computer. Software can help to ensure that client computers accessing the network are properly configured. Packet filtering can help ensure that inappropriate communications packets do not make it onto the company's network.

- **Access controls.** Most computers, websites and data storage applications provide a programmatic means for preventing unwanted access to the data they host. This control usually comes from an access control list. These lists should be continually verified to ensure that they include only the appropriate people with only the approved type of access.

- **Physical protection.** Protecting sensitive systems from physical access is one of the most important things an organization can do. Very few security measures can protect against a person who has physical access to a machine. For that reason all computers should have a minimum level of physical security to prevent outsiders from getting access. Computers with sensitive data should have cameras watching them, a guard in place to restrict access and strong physical security to prevent unauthorized access. If strong physical security is cost prohibitive or cannot be achieved because of operational needs, the data stored on these computers should be encrypted.

- **Social engineering prevention.** Data thieves posing as legitimate vendors or customers can mislead company personnel and convince them to inadvertently release data to the wrong people. The ChoicePoint data breach, which caused the leakage of over 100,000 customer records, was one of the most high-profile cases of social engineering.[10] This breach was not caused by hackers who broke into ChoicePoint computers, but by criminals posing as legitimate companies. It brought awareness to the risks of social engineering and data breaches and probably single-handedly did the most to instigate data breach legislation.

Employees should be properly trained to detect exploits where individuals pretend to represent a company or person in order to inappropriately gain access to data.

- **Auditing.** System and application administrators often have access to sensitive data even when company policy requires that they do not access it. Since the administrators control most security mechanisms, auditing is one of the few ways to mitigate this type of threat. The auditing system should be configured so that logs are sent to a remote auditing machine outside the control of the system and application administrators. A modification to the audit log configuration should send an alert to the remote monitoring system as well to help prevent the disruption of the audit logs.

Once a security policy has been developed, employees should be periodically trained so they understand the processes and procedures necessary to help ensure proper privacy protection of personal data.

1.2.4 Application

Most company employees depend on applications to get their jobs done. However, it is prudent to restrict the number and types of applications that are deployed on a company's computers. The more applications that exist on a user's computer, the more opportunities for one of them to carry malware or be exploited by an adversary. Office productivity software is probably the most commonly used type of application. But even these applications can harbor viruses, key loggers, data gatherers or other types of malware. The market for security vulnerabilities has escalated to the point that hacking is becoming a full-time job for some programmers, which increases the need to validate all applications.[11] Some legitimate applications may openly collect data as part of their terms of use, which should be understood before the applications are permitted for use within the company. Here are some important steps to consider to avoid privacy-invasive applications:

- **Privileged access.** Restrictions can be placed on who can install or configure software on a user's computer. For example, a person on each team could be assigned the responsibility for administering the software on each person's computer. The software administrator can provide personalized service to employees while relieving them of the responsibility for knowing the software installation or configuration policies.

- **Software policy.** Each company should have a policy in place that describes the requirements and guidelines for applications used on company computers. Companies can manage application usage in one of the following ways:
    1. Have the company's IT department mandate the software that can be installed on each employee's computer.
    2. Use a product standards board or third-party application to approve software that can be installed on each computer.

3. Distribute a list of approved applications to employees that they must follow.

4. Give employees guidelines on the types of applications that they can install on their computers. While this option provides the greatest flexibility, it also carries the greatest risk and should be avoided.

- **Privacy links.** Where possible, each application should have a link to a privacy policy that explains the privacy obligations to data that may be accessible via the application.

- **Application research.** In general, companies should perform research to determine which applications are the most appropriate for their employees, computers and networks. They should also determine and document the proper versions, settings, computer configuration and install procedures for each application within the environment where it will be installed. IT personnel should monitor security bulletins for information that will help identify application vulnerabilities and potential mitigation strategies, as well as newly released/discovered malware.

- **Employee training.** All employees should be periodically trained on the company's software policy. The training should include the threats to privacy that can come from the inadvertent installation of malicious applications or improper configuration of legitimate applications. All the IT safeguards in the world will not protect the privacy of sensitive data the way properly trained employees will. Where appropriate, reminders should be presented to employees about special handling that might be required for data. Requiring yearly privacy training is also a good practice.

- **IT involvement.** The IT department must be an integral part of any application management strategy. IT professionals should be trained to identify privacy threats and work with the organization's privacy team to adequately manage application deployment across the company. IT personnel will also serve as advisors to employees and therefore should be well versed in the variety of productivity applications so they can instruct employees on the most appropriate application to complete a specific task. Based on the company's software policy, the IT department can have any of the following types of application deployment strategies:

  o **IT controlled.** The IT department of each company can enforce a policy that only the IT department can set up each computer, ensuring that only specific applications are installed. The IT department can also ensure that all applications have the proper version, patches and upgrades.

  o **IT monitored.** Company computers can be periodically scanned to validate that each installed application is on the approved list of applications and has the right version and proper configuration set. Ensuring that an up-to-date antivirus program is installed on each computer will also help prevent malware.

○ **Employee controlled.** Companies can choose to let employees manage their own computer systems based on corporate policy. If this approach is taken, each employee should be given training on the company's software policy and encouraged to use approved anti-malware software. This approach is the riskiest and should be avoided, as harm from malicious applications may not be limited to a single user's computer but may spread to the company's network, servers and other employee computers.

1.2.5 Network

A company's network is one of the most challenging systems for IT professionals to protect because of its pervasiveness and the number of possible connection points, both ephemeral and permanent. The network is connected to client machines, servers, routers, hubs, load balancers, packet filters, wireless endpoints and the Internet, to name just a few connections. Traffic over the network can come from employees, vendors or customers connected to the network via a direct, wireless, VPN or cellular connection. Many of the applications running on client and server computers, network devices and smartphones can also access the network. Any one of these devices, individuals or applications, which have a legitimate reason to be on the network, could cause a data breach. A breach can cause a loss of personal data, trade secrets or sensitive plans, which can lead to lawsuits, fines and loss of customers. There are several ways to mitigate these types of network risks:

- **Keep computers clear of malware.** Malicious software running on a computer system can read network traffic and send it to a remote computer or store it locally for later download by someone who has access to the computer. To avoid this risk, all company computers should be running the latest anti-malware software with up-to-date signatures.

- **Apply smartphone policies.** Smartphones represent a higher level of risk as they are more vulnerable to theft. Phone passwords, auto-device lock and remote wiping mechanisms should be enforced for smartphones connecting to network resources.

- **Validate network devices.** Each device attached to the network must come from a reputable vendor, have the proper configuration and have the most recent updates from the manufacturer. Even though network devices aren't considered to be computers, they can harbor viruses that could steal sensitive data off the network.

- **Write secure code.** Developers who create a line of business applications for the company that access the network should follow guidelines on how to write software that avoids the risk of exposing data over networks. *Writing Secure Code* is a good book for learning how to avoid writing code that could inadvertently expose sensitive data over a network.[12] The Open Web Application Security Project is an organization that can be of great assistance to individuals desiring to keep up-to-date on the latest security trends.[13]

- **Validate applications.** All applications running on computers or smartphones should be restricted from accessing network services unless they are on a safe list set up by the IT department. They of course should have the most recent updates and be properly configured.

Besides threats posed by all of the legitimate connections to the company network, many risks to a network come from devices, individuals and applications that should not be on a network; these include inappropriate access to resources, scanning of network data and deployment of malware. This type of threat prevention requires going beyond the mitigations listed above.

- **Strong authentication practices.** Would-be data thieves will often attempt to log in to company networks to access data. Attacks can come from individuals or from automated software that runs authentication attacks against network computers. Having strong password rules, authentication rules (maximum tries, account lockout, progressive response, etc.) and IP blocking set up can mitigate these types of attacks. Each employee should have login credentials to connect to the network and know the proper way to configure his or her computer to get on the network. Where possible, make the network setup for computers an automated process.

- **Network monitoring.** Malware can infect a company's network and travel from computer to computer, gathering data. Network monitoring software can look for known virus signatures or use other means to find and cleanse network infestations. Network-level data loss prevention technologies can monitor data that has been tagged as private and prevent it from leaving the company. Network-based zero-day threat detection systems can look for signatureless advanced malware and take targeted actions.

- **Network encryption.** Data thieves don't need to have legitimate access to a company's network in order to access data flowing across it. Using a network sniffer, anyone can view or copy unprotected data from a company's wireless network. A legitimate visitor to a company could also connect a device to a network outlet using a cable and copy all unencrypted data from the network. This becomes especially important when discussing VoIP technologies, where voice communications are traveling across the data network. Using strong encryption on wireless and wired networks at the transportation layer will help mitigate this threat.

1.2.6 Storage

Companies store sensitive data in many locations, each with its own pros and cons. It's important to have policies that cover each of the following storage mechanisms and to continually train employees on their proper use to minimize the risk of improper access to data, a data breach or the placement of malware.

- **Files.** Storing data in files provides both flexibility and challenges when it comes to protecting sensitive data. Access to files can be restricted using the security of an operating system or document management systems. However, once the files are removed from the system, the protection goes away. Files can be protected outside of their storage system using password-based encryption or digital rights management (DRM), each system having its own benefits and limitations. Passwords must be shared among everyone who has access to the data and if the password is lost, access to the files will be lost. DRM-protected files must be connected to a policy server in order for them to be accessed. DRM also limits a person's flexibility in regard to what she can do with a file, even if she has proper access to it.

  Preventing the proliferation of files is another challenge. Files can be protected during storage in company systems. Disk-based encryption can also be used to protect files while they are stored on disk. However, in each case the protection ceases once the files are removed from storage. Once that happens, an employee has the ability to copy files to offline storage or e-mail them to a personal e-mail account.

  Data loss prevention technologies can be used to categorize files with sensitive data and apply policies that prevent files from being copied, printed or otherwise shared in a manner that is inconsistent with the configured policies.

- **Websites.** Organizations' websites often hold sensitive data, such as product plans, design documents, customer contact information, patent filings or even personal data such as credit card numbers. In general, employees can have access to internal websites, but that access should be limited due to the risk of data falling into the wrong hands. Each website should have a privacy policy link so employees know their privacy obligations with regard to processing of data accessible via the website.

  Content stored on an internal website can be protected at several levels across the website to ensure that employees have access only to data appropriate to their jobs. Using individual or group access control lists, access can be restricted to an entire website or just to portions of the site. The website can be organized by category to help protect sensitive content that is at the same sensitivity level. Files can also be stored on a website where each file can have its own individual access control. This provides greater granularity of protection, but can require more time to maintain.

Websites can also be used to provide web pages that host formatted access to data that is stored in a database in the back end. For these types of pages, access control can be managed by the website or the database itself. The data from each web page can still be copied, but the process can be made a lot more tedious depending on how the web page is constructed.

- **Databases.** Much of the sensitive data stored by a company is kept in databases. Databases have many features that make them attractive for storing sensitive data, such as general access control, role-based access control, various types of encryption, data categorization, retention management and auditing. In addition, applications can be written on top of the database to provide an extra layer of control over the data that is presented to a user. Even with all of those features, it is difficult to prevent a database administrator from gaining access to sensitive data. However, technology like the SELinux operating system, role-based access control and remote auditing can help to mitigate that threat by providing the ability to restrict an administrator's access to sensitive data.[14]

- **Cloud storage.** Organizations often use cloud storage for several reasons, such as to provide better access to data for customers, to lower operational costs and to limit regulatory risks from cross-border transfer of customer data. However, using a hosting company for cloud storage can introduce additional risks. Steps must be taken to ensure that the hosting company follows the organization's data storage policies. For this reason a contract should be in place between the organization and the hosting company. Risks can come from inappropriate access by companies that share a data center in a multitenant configuration or from the country where the data is hosted. Encryption can be used to protect organizational data, but care should be taken not to share the encryption keys with the hosting company.

  A company sometimes acts as a hosting company for organizations and individuals in cloud data centers. ("Cloud data center" simply means servers that are accessible over the Internet.) This causes additional requirements for companies as they must help organizations comply with policies that may conflict with their own. For example, a company may not collect credit card data, but may need to help another company meet Payment Card Industry or Basel III compliance.[15] Hosting data for others can also increase data breach risks, as a company that holds data for multiple companies or individuals can be seen as a more valuable target.

- **Applications.** Many applications, such as accounting, HR and financial systems, store sensitive data that can be accessible to anyone who has authorization to use the application. Make sure to use applications that have strong role-based access controls. Those controls should be continually verified to ensure that the right people are in the right roles. An employee's membership in an application's roles or access control lists should be reviewed as part of any transition plan or termination process.

- **Backup tapes.** Backup tapes are often overlooked as a source of data leakage. Tapes don't have an access control list and can easily be read by anyone who has a tape reader unless the data on the tapes is properly encrypted. Remember that just because the data is encrypted while on disk or in a database doesn't mean the data will be encrypted after the backup process completes. Ensure that backups are encrypted and stored in a safe place. Backups should also be segregated into those that need to be part of a retention process and those that don't. Data that has a specific retention period should only be backed up to tapes that are eventually destroyed or overwritten in order to comply with retention policies. Of course, you would not want to dispose of data that you feel should be kept forever, such as the recipe for Coca-Cola or blueprints for building a production car. Backup tapes should be properly degaussed or wiped with an approved software deletion product before disposal.

- **Hardware.** When storage hardware is replaced, it is important that any data is completely destroyed or made unreadable before recycling or disposing of the old hardware. This includes but is not limited to printer or copy machine hard drives, simple cell phones or smartphones, removable media cards and server or desktop hard drives. IT should have documented hardware disposal procedures in place.

1.3 Stakeholders' Expectations for Privacy

According to the *Business Dictionary*, a stakeholder is "a person, group or organization that has interest or concern in an organization. Stakeholders can affect or be affected by the organization's actions, objectives and policies."[16] Managing stakeholders' expectations can be a huge responsibility for organizations with regard to protecting privacy even when the organization does not hold stakeholders' data. An organization can have many stakeholders who are concerned about the organization's privacy practices—some inside the company and some outside.

Expectations around privacy often go beyond what the law allows or what a company may state in its privacy policy. When consumers make online purchases or vendors do business with a company, they expect their personal data to be treated a certain way. They don't want to be compelled to read a long privacy statement in order to feel that their privacy will be respected. As a matter of course, most people do not read privacy statements.[17] Here is a list of some stakeholders and expectations that companies should be aware of:

- **Consumers.** On average, web consumers are one of the biggest sharers of personal information on the Internet. They share information with social, shopping, search, banking and healthcare sites, to name just a few. Very few of them read a website's privacy policy, but they have expectations for their privacy nonetheless. Most consumers expect a website to see and retain their browsing habits or the information they give the website. Consumers don't expect a website to share that data with other sites across the Internet unless it is to fulfill a transaction, such as sharing an address with UPS for shipping purposes.

- **Regulators.** Several U.S. regulators monitor privacy issues for consumers. Agencies such as the Federal Trade Commission, Federal Communications Commission and Federal Reserve Board are responsible for different aspects of consumer privacy. These agencies enforce regulations such as COPPA, the Fair Credit Reporting Act and the Right to Financial Privacy Act. In the European Union, the Data Protection Directive requires individual member states to establish national regulatory bodies.[18] The institutions of the EU itself (such as commission, council, parliament, etc.) are monitored by the European Data Protection Supervisor.[19] The European Free Trade Association (EFTA) has much the same system, in which member states establish independent national regulatory bodies and the EFTA institutions are monitored by the EFTA Surveillance Authority.[20] As in Europe, each province in Canada has its own privacy commission with a national body known as the Office of the Privacy Commissioner of Canada.[21] Regulators work to ensure that companies follow privacy regulations and fine them when they don't. For example, the company Path was fined $800,000 for collecting personal information without permission.[22]

- **Industry groups.** There are many industry groups that work to protect consumer privacy via self-regulation. The Better Business Bureau, Interactive Advertising Bureau and TRUSTe are examples of organizations that represent companies for specific industries, such as consumer advocacy, advertising and online privacy. One of their main goals is to encourage companies to follow self-regulatory principles that they set up and avoid costly legislation, which can have a chilling effect on online business.

- **Researchers.** Many academic and corporate researchers conduct studies that aim to improve consumer safety, find cures for diseases and increase the yield and nutrition of food. Much of this research requires the use of personal information from lots of people. While there is enormous support for these types of research from a broad set of stakeholders, there is an expectation that the work will be done in a way that will preserve the privacy of those providing the personal information. Those responsible for collecting and storing the information must ensure that proper privacy and security procedures are in place to minimize the risk of a data breach or improper use of the data. Technological means have been developed to help protect sensitive data used for research while preserving its utility.

- **Employees.** Depending on their perspective, employees are either concerned about how the privacy of their personal data within the company is protected or how they should be protecting personal data for which they are responsible. For that reason, even internal websites should have a link to a privacy statement so employees can be assured that their privacy expectations are being met. Accordingly, employees should know where to find the appropriate privacy training based on their role in the company. They should also understand the company's expectations of them in regard to protecting the personal data of others.

1.4 Mistakes Organizations Make

Amy sits at a table with Bill, Carrie, David, Euan and Filo, the organization's privacy council. Collectively, they represent privacy, compliance, legal, business, security and PR teams. "Hello, everyone," says Amy. "I hope you all enjoyed your long weekend off. I assure you privacy incidents did not take a break this weekend. I'm going to forgo our normal monthly update and get right to the issue at hand. An employee in the new Widgets group inappropriately shared personal data with a third party and now we have a European Commission inquiry to deal with. Once again it was a case of no privacy representation in the group. Even if it is only part time, every team in the company that manages personal data has to have privacy representation. Until now, executives have been reluctant to mandate privacy representation because they thought it was heavy handed. Now I think we have a strong case for it. I need each of you to provide your perspectives of the risks involved with not having broad privacy representation. Your input along with this new inquiry should encourage the executives to be more accountable for supporting privacy. Please send your input by end of day so I can get this in front of the executives as soon as possible."

Organizations are often entrusted with personal information from customers and other entities. This data can come from different parts of the company and be brought in using multiple means. This disjointed set of systems can be a recipe for disaster for companies that do not manage data policies consistently across their organization. When multiple teams across an organization are managing personal data, care must be taken to ensure that they are all following organizational policies to avoid situations where misuse of data against policy causes lawsuits, fines or lost business. For this reason, management must see privacy as a strategic imperative that is expressed across the organization.

Privacy policies and internal standards governing the use of the data must cover each point of collection, transfer and use. The following types of mistakes can happen when managing personal data:

- **Insufficient policies.** Before the first byte of data is collected from or about individuals, a set of internal standards should be in place to cover the proper classification, collection, storage, usage, sharing and disposal of the data. This will help to ensure that proper access controls, encryption and processing of data occur, helping the organization to avoid legal, brand and financial risks. There should also be a public policy that informs those providing the data about how the data will be handled. New companies are often slow to implement these types of practices. However, improper standards can lead to mishandling of data, regulatory fines and a loss of trust, and so should not be neglected.[23] Assessments need to be performed against the policies on a regular basis to ensure compliance. Having a policy is a good start, but ensuring that the policy is followed is key to overall success.

- **Improper training.** All the privacy standards, processes and guidelines in the world will not make a bit of difference if employees aren't trained to use them. Training should cover proper notification, collection, storage, access, processing, sharing and retention procedures for data. All employees, from the janitor to the CEO, must have basic privacy training to understand their obligations when it comes to handling personal data. The level of training given should reflect each employee's level of data management. Employees should see themselves as privacy ambassadors and be able to point to the company's privacy policy as well as the top three ways that the company protects customers. Multiple training formats are available. The organization should utilize the methods that best deliver the message in a manner that is clear, concise and understood.

- **Disjointed practices.** Companies often have multiple departments that maintain relationships with the same customers. Problems arise when cross-team sharing of data happens. Commitments made to users about how their data will be handled do not always follow the data as it moves to different teams. Likewise, employees are rarely trained on privacy practices from other teams. Without the proper practices in place, employees may mishandle data, share it with the wrong entities and inappropriately contact the owners of the data. Even when there is a high level of trust in employees, their practices should be verified in order to minimize the risk of a data breach that damages that trust.

- **Complacency.** Companies may feel that because they are small, have minimal web presence or never had a privacy incident, they don't have to be vigilant about their data-handling practices. As a company grows or matures, its data practices can evolve even though the standards and policies are not updated to reflect the changes in practices. Having periodic internal or external audits can help a company maintain adequate privacy controls and avoid complacency.

- **Third-party contracts.** A company can be doing all the right things in regard to privacy protections but be lax in the way it monitors how vendors treat their data. A company's responsibility to its customers' information does not end when it hands off the data to a third party. The same commitments that were made to users persist after the data leaves the company. Companies should use contracts and other agreements to help ensure that data is processed in a consistent fashion, from collection to disposal, no matter how many hands it might pass through. Where possible, third-party data processors should be monitored or periodically audited to help ensure that they are following their contractual obligations.

1.5 Privacy vs. Security—What's Alike and What's Different

Though privacy and security are inexorably linked, they are by no means interdependent. It is also not necessary to give up one to have the other. To help ensure privacy, it is important to employ security mechanisms. Guards, locks, cameras, access controls and encryption are types of security mechanisms that can be deployed to help ensure privacy. It is not just the perimeter that should be protected but the data items themselves, such as individual rows or columns in a database. Even with the strongest security measures possible, an employee who has legitimate access to data can mishandle it if he or she does not have a thorough understanding of the privacy policies that govern the processing of the data. Proper auditing can help provide after-the-fact detection of breaches, but that is not without its challenges. For these reasons one cannot rely on security or privacy alone to protect data. They offer the best protection when used together.

New advances in encryption have provided a means to protect sensitive data while maintaining its utility. Homomorphic encryption, multiparty computation and differential privacy are examples of technology that prevent the raw data from being accessed, but still provide the ability to perform analysis on the data.[24] Trusted third parties, such as credit reporting companies, can also be used to provide information on users without exposing unnecessary personal data. There will be cases where privacy practitioners will be asked to give up privacy in order to ensure security, sometimes going against stated policies or contractual agreements. Instead of taking the path of least resistance and releasing sensitive data against company commitments, privacy-preserving solutions should be sought that support the desired analysis without relinquishing sensitive data.

Privacy and security have a shared goal of protecting personally identifiable information (PII). In that manner they are very much alike. However, they have different approaches for achieving the same goal. Privacy governs how PII should be used, shared and retained. Security restricts access to the sensitive data and protects it from being viewed during collection, storage and transmission. In that way they have a symbiotic relationship. Privacy policies can inform security systems about the security that is needed to protect data, and the security systems can accordingly enforce those privacy policies. For example, one policy could state that only payroll administrators can view employee salaries, and database access controls could enforce that policy. The eXtensible Access Control Markup Language (XACML) is an example of a policy language that permits the definition of policies that can be programmatically enforced via security controls.[25] Microsoft's SQL Server's Policy-Based Management System permits the definition of user and group policies that can be programmatically enforced by the database.[26] There is no silver bullet and no one fix to ensure both privacy and security. Rather, it takes continual education, awareness and the application of appropriate controls in accordance with statute, standards and policies.

The essential challenge around privacy and security for privacy practitioners is to be steadfast and express how to preserve both in an environment of escalating data collection and security threats without negatively impacting business operations. While privacy and security are not the same, our commitment to each should be. When requests are made to lower the privacy bar for the sake of security, the response should not be "no," but the start of a conversation on how to achieve the desired goals while preserving privacy.

1.6 IT Governance vs. Data Governance

IT governance focuses on the systems, applications and support personnel that manage data within a company. For the most part IT governance is managed by the IT department. The key performance indicators (KPIs) or IT controls for IT governance should be based on access control, physical and technical security measures, encryption, software inventory, computer and network device configurations, database schemas, backups and retention management. Proper IT governance is the foundation for great data governance. It is through the proper application of IT policies such as access control, encryption and auditing that proper data handling can be enforced. IT governance can be achieved through business alignment, consistency and common frameworks such as COBIT 5.

Data governance focuses on the proper management of data within a company. Data governance is a shared responsibility for all teams across a company. IT governance is an important element in reaching data governance, but it is not all that is needed. Beyond the IT requirements are mandates for providing transparency to users and honoring commitments to manage data in accordance with published policies. KPIs or privacy controls for data governance should be based on transparency of data practices, user data control, and principles for data usage, sharing of data, data retention, vendor contracts and customer contact. One way to view the differences in the two models is by using a plumbing metaphor. IT governance is about governing the way the pipes are built, maintained and protected. Data governance is about governing how water flows through the pipes.

1.7 The Role of the IT Professional and Other Stakeholders in Preserving Privacy

"How did Hua have access to the data in the first place?" asked Amy. "The security team forgot to remove her from the database's access control list when she moved departments," Bill explained.

"Don't blame security," said Carrie, agitated. "The privacy policies were not updated to cover the usage of the Widget data. It's always been within policy to share our data with advertisers. However, the Widget application uses precise location data instead of less granular regional data."

"Using the more precise data increases our revenues, and we should understand the financial risk before ending the program," added David.

"Filo, what's the PR hit if we change our privacy notice to reflect the new data sharing?" asked Amy.

"As long as we can update the consent mechanism we should be okay. We'll have to delete all the data captured before consent was collected, though," replied Filo.

"That's going to cost us some revenue and development resources that were dedicated to another project," said David. "Considering the alternative, I don't see where we have a choice. Let's put a plan together to address this issue and get it before the executives for sign off right away," stated Amy.

IT professionals are responsible for laying the technical foundation for an effective privacy program. They ensure that the computers, networks, applications, websites, databases and security are maintained at levels that protect data privacy in accordance with company policy, regulatory requirements and industry standards. If the company's technical infrastructure is properly set up, it is easy for other employees to follow the company's privacy policies. For example, by encrypting the data that flows through networks, employees won't have to worry about the secure transfer of data. By creating incident response processes, it is easier for employees to record privacy incidents in a consistent and efficient manner. Though the IT professional is not responsible for a company's privacy program, their work in laying a good technical foundation makes the effectiveness of a program more attainable.

A small company might be able to deploy a successful privacy program without the assistance of IT professionals, but it wouldn't be as effective, and this is a bad practice. When an IT department is not involved in a company's privacy program, it makes everyone else less efficient and opens the company up to increased risk. Likewise, a privacy program will not be effective without the involvement of personnel throughout the company, including the following roles:

- **Privacy professionals.** These employees are responsible for a company's overall privacy program. They define the policies, standards, guidelines, auditing controls, training and internal and external relationships. It is through their leadership that they stimulate a company's dedication to privacy and inspire employees to uphold its importance.

- **Company executives.** A company's privacy group must feel that it has the sponsorship of executives to create a meaningful privacy program that it can mandate to employees. Accordingly, employees must feel that they are empowered to devote time to such programs. It is the duty of executives to support privacy programs through their words and actions.

- **Lawyers.** The legal department is responsible for creating privacy statements, writing contracts, ensuring compliance with laws and regulations and addressing formal inquiries from regulators. If they do their jobs properly, the legal staff are the ones who keep the company out of trouble and employees out of jail.

- **Marketers.** The marketing team is involved in marketing campaigns, e-mail campaigns, contests, product registrations and conference booths. Each of these events provides an opportunity to collect information from users or contact them via some form of communication. Marketers must be sure that they are following the company's privacy practices in these exchanges. For example, if a user signs up for one product's marketing campaign, it doesn't mean that marketers can send material for other products.

- **Public relations.** A great privacy program will not benefit a company if no one knows about it. The PR team can be a great resource for promoting a company's commitment to privacy. The PR team can also help to respond to privacy incidents in a way that enforces the company's privacy position while minimizing any backlash from the incident.

- **Other employees.** Though other employees may not be on the front line of the fight for an effective privacy program, they are no less important to its success. All employees must see themselves as privacy ambassadors and help to ensure compliance with the company's privacy policies.

While IT and privacy professionals are responsible for the creation and deployment of effective IT and data governance, it is the organizational executives who are accountable for their success. Without the right funding, personnel and mandate from the top, employees will not be empowered to follow privacy policies, especially where there is tension between business goals and privacy protection.

1.8 Conclusion

Amy held the coffee cup to her lips without taking a drink. Lost in her thoughts about the recent privacy issue, she wondered how she would have made it through the day without the privacy council in place. This time they didn't dodge the bullet, but at least the wound wouldn't be fatal. It's unfortunate that it takes a privacy incident for executives to agree to provide adequate resources when it would have been much cheaper to provide the resources up front. Suddenly, Amy was pulled away from her thoughts by a phone call. "Amy, Bill here. It appears the CEO received an inquiry this morning from the FTC on the same privacy issue the European Commission is asking about. He said it got lost in his inbox."

"No problem. Send it my way and copy the council. It appears that this is one issue that is not going to go away soon, and neither is this long day."

IT departments are continually under pressure to ensure that systems under their control stay in compliance. Items such as computers, network devices and applications must have different privacy controls applied to them to validate their compliance. The ever-evolving landscape of cyber attacks, privacy regulations and self-regulatory requirements makes privacy compliance challenging. The proliferation of smart devices and use of social networks in the workplace add to the spectrum of privacy risks that exacerbates the difficulty of keeping IT systems in compliance.

Employees outside of the IT department have a part to play in compliance as well. By taking the appropriate training and following company policies, standards and guidelines, employees can help to simplify the job of IT compliance.

Maintaining the privacy of personal data is an important element of reaching compliance that goes far beyond IT governance. Providing transparency, control and retention management of personal data stored by a company helps not only to attain compliance but also to increase a company's trust quotient, which will attract customers and employees alike.

Endnotes

1 Tom Bradley, "Pros and Cons of Bringing Your Own Device to Work," *PC World*, December 20, 2011, www.pcworld.com/article/246760/pros_and_cons_of_byod_bring_your_own_device_.html; see Council Directive 2009/136/EC, 2009 O.J. L 337 p. 11, available at http://eur-lex.europa.eu/LexUriServ/LexUriServ.do?uri=OJ:L:2009:337:0011:0036:en:PDF; "FTC Strengthens Kids' Privacy, Gives Parents Greater Control Over Their Information by Amending Children's Online Privacy Protection Rule," Federal Trade Commission, December 19, 2012, www.ftc.gov/opa/2012/12/coppa.shtm; Tracking Protection Working Group, W3C, accessed September 6, 2013, www.w3.org/2011/tracking-protection/.

2 Glen Greenwald and Ewen MacAskill, "NSA Prism Program Taps in to User Data of Apple, Google and Others," *The Guardian*, June 6, 2013, www.guardian.co.uk/world/2013/jun/06/us-tech-giants-nsa-data.

3 "COBIT 5: A Business Framework for the Governance and Management of Enterprise IT," ISACA, accessed September 9, 2013, www.isaca.org/cobit/Pages/default.aspx.

4 "Staff Report: Public Workshop on Consumer Privacy on the Global Information Infrastructure," Chapter II, Federal Trade Commission, December 1996, www.ftc.gov/reports/staff-report-public-workshop-consumer-privacy-global-information-infrastructure.

5 Sensitive data can have many meanings. It could relate to personal data, sensitive PII, corporate secrets or the contents of e-mail. The definition of sensitive data can vary among people, industry groups, privacy practitioners and countries. In this book it is used to relate to any data that the company or its customers might consider sensitive.

6 Kurt Dillard, "Intrusion Detection FAQ: What Is a Bastion Host?" Sans, accessed September 9, 2013, www.sans.org/security-resources/idfaq/bastion.php.

7 John Wack, "Screened Host Firewall," Telstra, February 3, 1995, www.vtcif.telstra.com.au/pub/docs/security/800-10/node57.html.

8 One of these industry standards is the ISO 27000 series of standards, available at www.27000.org/index.htm.

9 The NIST Computer Security Division's Security Technology Group Cryptographic Toolkit is available at http://csrc.nist.gov/groups/ST/toolkit/index.html.

10 "ChoicePoint: More ID Theft Warnings," CNN Money, February 17, 2005, http://money.cnn.com/2005/02/17/technology/personaltech/choicepoint/.

11 Nicole Perlroth and David E. Sanger, "Nations Buying as Hackers Sell Flaws in Computer Code," New York Times, July 13, 2013 (detailing how computer hackers find and sell flaws in code to nations seeking to exploit the flaws for national security purposes), http://mobile.nytimes.com/2013/07/14/world/europe/nations-buying-as-hackers-sell-computer-flaws.html?pagewanted=all&_r=0&; Nicole Perlroth, "Hackers in China Attacked The Times for Last 4 Months," New York Times, January 30, 2013 (detailing how Chinese hackers attacked the New York Times stealing passwords from every Times employee), www.nytimes.com/2013/01/31/technology/chinese-hackers-infiltrate-new-york-times-computers.html?pagewanted=all&_r=0.

12 Michael Howard and David LeBlanc, Writing Secure Code: Practical Strategies and Proven Techniques for Building Secure Applications in a Networked World, 2nd ed. (Redmond, WA: Microsoft Press, 2004).

13 The Open Web Application Security Project is an organization focused on improving the security of software. Open Web Application Security Project (OWASP), last modified January 31, 2014, www.owasp.org/index.php/Main_Page.

14 "Red Hat Enterprise Linux 4: Red Hat SELinux Guide," Red Hat Inc., 2005, https://access.redhat.com/site/documentation/en-US/Red_Hat_Enterprise_Linux/4/html/SELinux_Guide/selg-preface-0011.html.

15 The PCI Security Standards Council, www.pcisecuritystandards.org; Basel iii Compliance Professionals Association (BiiiCPA), www.basel-iii-association.com.

16 BusinessDictionary.com, www.businessdictionary.com/definition/stakeholder.html.

17 James Temple, "Why privacy policies don't work—and what might," SFGate, January 29, 2012, www.sfgate.com/business/article/Why-privacy-policies-don-t-work-and-what-might-2786252.php.

18 For a comprehensive list of data protection authorities of the member states of the European Union, see www.dataprotection.eu/pmwiki/pmwiki.php?n=Main.EUAuthorities.

19 "The European Data Protection Supervisor," European Union, http://europa.eu/about-eu/institutions-bodies/edps/.

20 For a comprehensive list of data protection authorities of the member states of the European Free Trade Association, see www.dataprotection.eu/pmwiki/pmwiki.php?n=Main.EFTAAuthorities; information about the European Free Trade Association Surveillance Authority can be found at EFTA Surveillance Authority, www.eftasurv.int.

21 Office of the Privacy Commissioner of Canada, last modified February 19, 2014, www.priv.gc.ca/index_e.asp.

22 Grant Gross, "FTC fines maker of Path app $800,000 for privacy violations," PC World, February 3, 2013, www.pcworld.com/article/2026985/ftc-fines-maker-of-path-app-800-000-for-privacy-violations.html.

23 "Google Will Pay $22.5 Million to Settle FTC Charges it Misrepresented Privacy Assurances to Users of Apple's Safari Internet Browser," Federal Trade Commission, August 9, 2012, www.ftc.gov/opa/2012/08/google.shtm.

24 Larry Hardesty, "Securing the Cloud: New Algorithm Solves Major Problem with Homomorphic Encryption," Phys.org, June 10, 2013, http://phys.org/news/2013-06-cloud-algorithm-major-problem-homomorphic.html; Christopher P. Andrews, "Craig Gentry honored for encryption breakthrough," IBM Research, last updated June 29, 2010, http://researcher.watson.ibm.com/researcher/view_project.php?id=1820; "Multi-Party Computation," Microsoft Research (providing a definition of multiparty computation and a list of relevant articles), http://research.microsoft.com/en-us/projects/mpc/default.aspx; Cynthia Dwork, "The Promise of Differential Privacy: A Tutorial on Algorithmic Techniques," Microsoft Research, October 2011 (providing a discussion of differential privacy from the 52nd Annual IEEE Symposium on Foundations of Computer Science), http://research.microsoft.com/apps/pubs/default.aspx?id=155617.

25 "OASIS eXtensible Access Control Markup Language (XACML) TC," OASIS, accessed September 6, 2013, www.oasis-open.org/committees/tc_home.php?wg_abbrev=xacml.

26 "Administer Servers by Using Policy-Based Management," Microsoft, accessed September 6, 2013, http://msdn.microsoft.com/en-us/library/bb510667.aspx.

## CHAPTER 2

Core Privacy Concepts

When Amy joined her company, its privacy program was in its infancy. No company privacy policies governed the work of the IT department. The company's privacy notice was a generic one that was created by a law firm and covered only their practices as they had existed several years before. They used vendors extensively to manage some of their data for them, but the contracts had no privacy provisions. She was concerned that the company's lack of privacy maturity could be detrimental to the company's fiscal future. At that moment, Bill knocked on her door.

"Amy, I'm so glad you joined our team," stated Bill. "We've had a few lingering issues that we held on the back burner that we were hoping you could help us with."

"Okay, let me hear them," responded Amy.

"Well, our developers run tests of their new code on our customer data to make sure it's working okay. One of our developers was debugging an issue on his laptop at a Starbucks and lost it. It wasn't encrypted, and we haven't heard about any of the credit card data being used so we believe we are safe—though we feel we should send a breach notice to someone. Next we received an FTC inquiry because they feel we may be in violation of the CAN-SPAM Act because we started sending e-mails to our cosmetics customers for our new spa products even though they opted out of cosmetic e-mails. We thought we were okay. We are also being sued by a Hollywood actress."

Bill asked the question written on Amy's face. "Why would a Hollywood actress be suing us? One of our sales guys got her phone number from the spa she goes to in exchange for a discount on our products. When she complained, he replied that her opt-out didn't apply to us because we didn't have an agreement with her. She became enraged and hung up. The next day we received a letter from her lawyer. I should probably stop there. You're not looking too good."

"You mean there's more?" Amy asked. Bill nodded while Amy placed her hand to her head. "That's enough, Bill. Get the team together. I want everyone on my team to clear their calendars next week because they will be taking privacy boot camp. The time for lax privacy practices has ended."

2.1 Foundational Elements for Embedding Privacy in IT

Without privacy policies in place and proper training for employees, it is extremely difficult to ensure that employees are following proper privacy practices. An organizational privacy policy is the first essential piece of collateral material needed for an effective privacy program. The privacy policy must come before a privacy notice is created as the notice is a reflection of a company's privacy policy. Likewise, setting up privacy training is not practical until a policy is in place. As important as the privacy policy is, its creation should not be taken lightly.

Within this book, to avoid confusion, the term "privacy notice" will be used to denote the external privacy statement and "privacy policy," the internal privacy standards.

2.1.1 Organizational Privacy Notice

The privacy notice is an external instrument that informs the outside world about an organization's privacy practices. It is a reflection of the organization and its commitment to privacy and can affect its brand. It provides transparency for consumers and comfort for privacy advocates; in some jurisdictions, it's a legal requirement. To avoid legal entanglements and preserve its brand, an organization must ensure that its privacy notice is based on the organization's internal privacy policies.

The sheer size of a privacy notice can be daunting to the average website visitor. Having a privacy notice that fits on one page and covers the most important aspects of an organization's privacy practices will go a long way toward setting the website visitor at ease. This will also set the organization apart from most Internet sites. For example (as of press time), Facebook's privacy notice achieves both of those goals.[1] It also provides "Learn More" links that permit site visitors to get access to more detailed information along with videos and privacy settings. Naming it their Data Use Policy is also more descriptive of the content.

2.1.1.1 Outline of a Privacy Notice

Below is a list of sections that should exist in a privacy notice. They include information that consumers as well as privacy advocates and regulators will want to know about. Organizations with fewer or more complex data-handling practices may require fewer or more sections.

- **What data is collected.** This is one of the most important pieces of the privacy notice, as it lets everyone know what data is collected and, by extension, what data is not collected. A distinction should be made between what data is received by web servers and the data that is processed and used within the organization. This declaration should include data that is observed, inferred and declared directly from users as well as data collected from third parties.

- **How collected data is used.** This section describes how collected data is used across the organization. It should provide a general description of data usage, including how the data may be used by all groups across the organization. This description should also include any third-party usage of the data.

- **How collected data is shared.** This section should cover how data is shared not only outside the organization but with which teams across the organization. Any law enforcement or regulatory requirements to share data should be described here as well. Individuals should be provided with controls to manage the sharing of their data where possible.

- **User control over collected data.** This section should describe how users can control the collection and use of their data. There should be a description of any preference or configuration management system that will help users manage how their data is collected or used. While it may not be possible to discontinue the normal transmission of data logs to web servers during a website visit, users should have some control over how their data is used.

- **Controlling marketing contact.** Users should be able to control how and when an organization contacts them. Service and transactional e-mails are expected when an individual creates a relationship with an organization or purchases a product. However, those same individuals should not have to be subjected to marketing e-mails in order to receive service e-mails. In addition, if an individual has a relationship with one product group within an organization, other product groups within the company should not take the liberty to contact the individual without first obtaining consent. For example, if an individual purchases Duracell batteries from Procter & Gamble, he or she shouldn't expect to receive marketing e-mails from the Pampers division. Even after consent has been granted, individuals should have the ability to opt out of receiving unwanted e-mails that are not required for their continued relationship with the organization.

- **Use of cookies and other tracking mechanisms.** Cookies are the main mechanisms by which organizations keep track of visitors to their websites. However, companies may use Flash cookies, locally stored objects, HTML5 storage, fingerprinting or some other means to track users. A description should be provided to users about the tracking mechanisms an organization uses as well as some ability to limit their use.

- **Gaining access to data.** The notice should explain how users can access the data an organization holds on them. This access should be provided online where possible, but can be provided in a file format or printout as a last resort. This access can be limited to just the information collected while the user is in an authenticated state in order to avoid delivering the data to the wrong person.

- **Resolving privacy issues.** This section should describe how users can resolve privacy issues they may have with an organization. This can be handled via an online form, e-mail address, phone number or postal address. Users should also have the option of contacting a third-party organization to address any issues as needed, via either arbitration or a self-regulatory organization.

- **Date of privacy notice.** The date the privacy notice was released should be prominently displayed as part of the privacy notice. If the privacy notice was recently updated, that should be stated.

- **Changes to privacy notice.** Users should be made aware of how often a privacy notice may be changed and how they will be informed of changes. Users should also be provided with a means to see previous versions of a privacy notice. Organizations should track which privacy notice was in effect when any data was collected or processed.

2.1.1.2 Creative Formatting

Formatting can make a privacy notice easy to read and navigate. Microsoft's updated privacy notice (Figure 2-1) uses large colored tiles and a layered design that delivers on both capabilities and makes their notice engaging.[2]

Figure 2-1: Microsoft.com Privacy Statement

Used with permission from Microsoft.

2.1.1.3 Consolidation

Consolidating multiple privacy notices into a single one can make it easier to find the desired privacy information. Google consolidated more than sixty disparate privacy notices into a single notice (see Figure 2-2), making it easier to find the privacy information of interest without having to go to multiple web pages.[3]

Figure 2-2: Google Privacy Policy

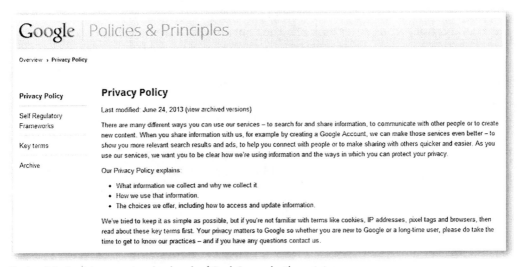

Google and the Google logo are registered trademarks of Google Inc.; used with permission.

2.1.1.4 Multilayered Notices

Multilayered privacy notices provide an abbreviated form of an organization's privacy notice while providing links to more detailed information when required by the reader. The U.S. Postal Service was one of the early organizations to implement a multilayered privacy notice.[4] An approach to the creation of multilayered notices was introduced back in 2007 in a paper published by The Center for Information Policy Leadership at Hunton & Williams LLP.[5] Since then, many companies have deployed variations of the idea. Layered notices offer brevity at one level, making an overview of an organization's privacy practices accessible to site visitors who are looking for a simple notice, while a detailed notice is just a click away for those who want more in-depth information. Those wishing to implement a layered notice should be certain to give readers enough information at the overview level to make an informed decision about the site and the organization without having to look at details.

2.1.1.5 Privacy Icons

Privacy icons provide visual cues to a company's or application's privacy characteristics. The icons can be shown on a website's homepage or in the footer of each page for easy viewing by site visitors. Applications can show the icons at startup, during install or within a privacy interstitial, application policy or settings dialog. The icons can be useful as part of a just-in-time privacy consent notice because the data being collected is often very specific. They are less practical when used for a company's entire privacy notice, as a company can have multiple data collection, usage, sharing and retention practices. For this reason privacy icons never took off. The Center for Internet and Society at Stanford Law School held a privacy icon hackathon at Mozilla's headquarters. During the event, participants found it difficult to decide which set of icons would be most appropriate based on the privacy notices selected from the Internet.

Disconnect created a set of privacy icons (shown in Figure 2-3) that have been in use since June 2011.[6] The Association for Competitive Technology created a set of privacy icons for developers.[7] However, adoption has been slow. One of the concerns with using such a system is that if the icons are too broad, they give the impression that all data is collected, shared with everyone and kept forever. Alternatively, if the icons are too specific and do not accurately cover all privacy practices, the company can leave itself susceptible to litigation.

Figure 2-3: Disconnect Privacy Icons

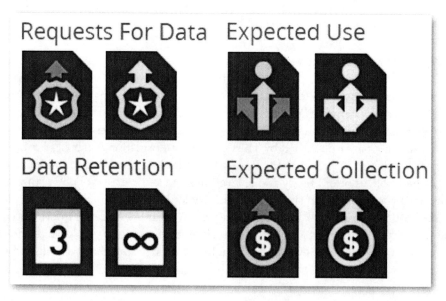

Used with permission from Disconnect, Inc.

2.1.1.6 Privacy Nutrition Label

A privacy nutrition label is similar to the nutrition labels seen on products in a store. Instead of listing the nutritional value of a product, the labels provide the abbreviated form of a company's privacy practices. The privacy nutritional label is more informative than the privacy icons, though it is only practical as part of the company's privacy notice or a privacy notice for a newly installed application. However, like the privacy icons, it is difficult for one label to provide a clear, unambiguous view of a large firm's privacy practices when there could be multiple collection, usage, sharing and retention practices across the company. A sophisticated privacy nutrition label was defined by Carnegie Mellon University's CyLab Usable Privacy and Security (CUPS) Laboratory (see Figure 2-4).[8] The CUPS Laboratory also sponsors a yearly event, Symposium on Usable Privacy and Security (SOUPS), which takes place in different cities across the United States.[9]

Figure 2-4: Bell Group Privacy Nutrition Label

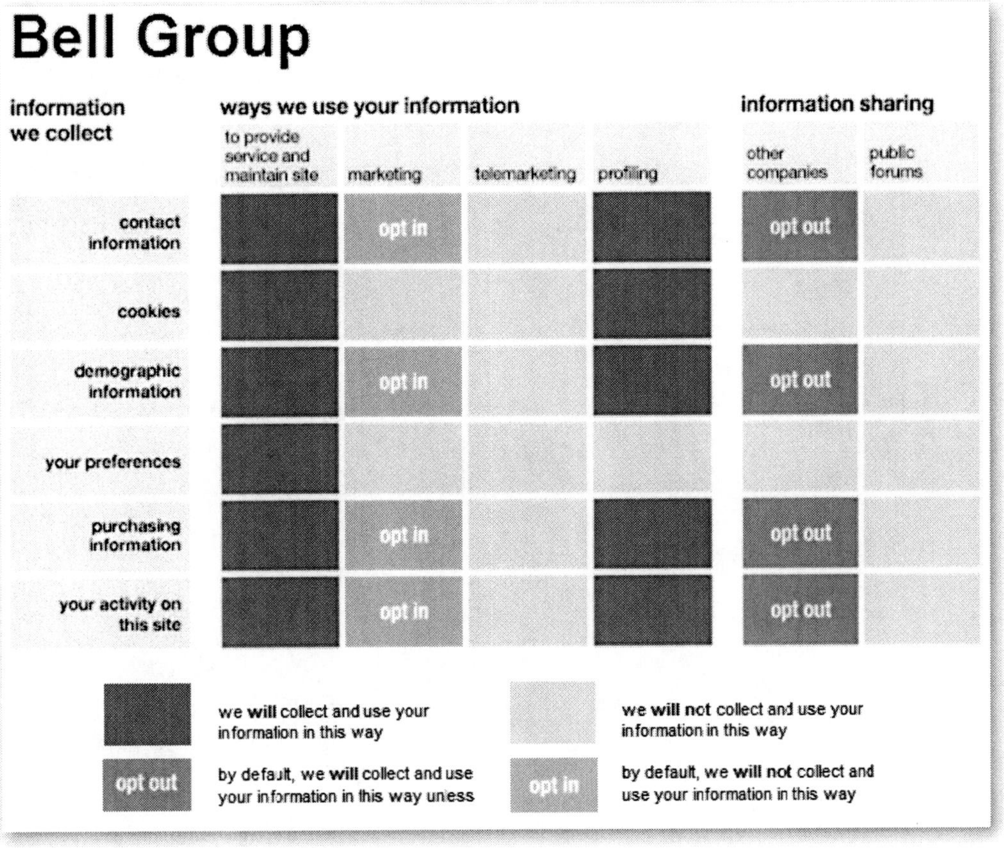

Used with permission from CyLab Usable Privacy and Security Laboratory, Carnegie Mellon University.

2.1.1.7 Combination Privacy Statement

Some companies, like TRUSTe, have combined several simplification techniques to create a privacy notice where icons and short descriptions make it easy to find and grasp the company's privacy content (see Figure 2-5).[10]

Figure 2-5: TRUSTe Privacy Statement

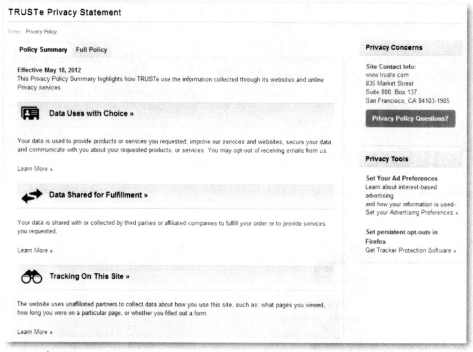

Image courtesy of TRUSTe.

2.1.1.8 Blended Mobile Statements

PrivacyChoice created Policymaker, which is a combination of icons and a nutrition label.[11] TRUSTe has also created a program to provide mobile applications with a privacy statement that contains icons and a layered notice (Figure 2-6).[12]

Figure 2-6: TRUSTe Privacy Policy Optimized for Mobile Devices

Image courtesy of TRUSTe.

2.1.1.9 Privacy Notice Services

One way to simplify the task of creating, hosting and supporting a privacy notice is to outsource the effort to another company. There are several companies that have a legal staff to guide companies through the process of a privacy evaluation (different from a privacy impact assessment), in which they determine an organization's data collection, usage, sharing, retention and disposal practices in order to create a privacy notice with the appropriate content.

Websites such as www.freeprivacypolicy.com provide an online tool for the creation of a privacy policy. Companies such as TRUSTe provide privacy notice creation, localization and hosting services, which can be expensive for small companies to manage on their own.[13] In addition, a privacy notice service can act as a privacy response center for an organization and respond to privacy inquiries from its website visitors.

2.1.2 Organizational Privacy Policies

The privacy policy is the guiding set of privacy principles used by teams within an organization to help them understand their privacy obligations as they develop software and services, create marketing campaigns, work with vendors and engage the general public. A privacy policy also serves as a guide for all organizational activities and drives the commitments made within the privacy notice. Even though an organization might be a sprawling global enterprise with dozens of business groups, it should have a single overall policy that sets the tone for privacy across the entire organization. There can still be separate privacy policies that cover specific groups, products or programs, but they should align with the overall organizational policy. The importance of the privacy policy dictates that its creation should involve members from all major business groups across the organization.

Because of the eventual impact of the privacy policy, those creating it should be careful not to make the policy overly prescriptive and/or restrictive as this could limit the business potential of some groups. The organizational privacy policy should provide general guidelines while leaving business groups the flexibility to provide more prescriptive rules that support their business goals. An organization's privacy policy should at a minimum cover the following topics:

- **Types of data classification.** To identify data and the rules that may apply to it, a classification system should be defined. A classification system can be a simple set of sensitivity levels or a complex taxonomy, understanding that complexity can be a barrier to adoption and accuracy.

- **Data collection principles.** The policy should describe when and how data should be collected as well as list obligations for data collection. The description should indicate the notification, control, protection required, minimization requirements and sharing limits for collected data.

- **Protection of data.** The privacy policy should indicate how data is to be protected during collection, storage and handling. The type of protection required, be it encryption or access control, will typically vary based on the classification of the data collected and regulatory requirements.

- **Data retention period.** All data should have an associated retention period. This period will vary based on regional regulatory requirements. The retention period may be indefinite, but there should always be a justification for the period selected. The policy should also describe what happens to the data once the retention period expires.

- **Treatment of sensitive data.** The definition of sensitive data can be elusive, as everyone has a different idea of what is sensitive, and that can change with context. Most jurisdictions agree that specific medical and financial data is sensitive. However, religion, political views, ethnicity, sexual preference and entertainment choices can be considered sensitive to certain people and locales. An organization should decide which categories of data are sensitive, how they should be handled and the type of consent, if any, that should accompany the use of sensitive data.

- **Sharing of data across groups.** A policy should describe the management of data as it is shared across groups within an organization. It is important that the policy take into account the privacy commitments made at the time by the group originally collecting the data. This includes complying with the retention commitment based on when the data was originally collected. The organization's sharing policy should eventually be covered in the privacy notice.

- **Sharing of data with partners and vendors.** Privacy policies should cover how and when data can be shared with external parties like partners and vendors. Contracts can help to ensure that third parties process the data they receive in a way that does not conflict with the organization's privacy policies. The organization's retention policies should be reflected in the sharing policy. The privacy notice should describe any third-party sharing that might occur as well as a mechanism to opt out of this sharing where appropriate.

- **Creation of departmental privacy policies.** Groups within an organization will often create a privacy policy that covers their specific processing of collected data. These policies must not conflict with the organizational policy. The organizational privacy team should be involved in the sign off of departmental privacy policies. As the organization's privacy policy evolves, departmental policies must be updated to reflect any changes that might impact those policies.

- **Performance of privacy reviews.** A privacy policy should outline when and how privacy reviews should occur. This description should cover how privacy reviews apply to both new and completed projects to ensure that they maintain the level of privacy protection mandated by privacy policies as they evolve.

- **Participation in a privacy response center.** All organizations should have a privacy response center in place that responds to external privacy incidents. The privacy policy should detail how groups within the organization should be involved in the privacy response center and indicate the obligations of each group in response to a privacy incident. The policy should also describe how the organization should be integrated with the response programs of external organizations such as the Better Business Bureau.

- **Responding to privacy inquiries.** Privacy inquiries can be received by an organization that are not caused by a privacy incident. Regulators, consumer advocates or journalists may have general questions about an organization's privacy practices, notifications or plans. The privacy policy should describe how privacy inquiries will be handled and who should be involved in the response to privacy inquiries.

- **Responding to data requests.** Data requests can come from users who own the data, law enforcement agencies or third parties wishing to have access to data. An organization's privacy policy should indicate the conditions under which data requests will be honored and outline the process for verifying the rightful owner of the data. The policy also needs to describe the management of takedown requests and should cover whether the organization should handle the request or pass the request on to the person who posted the content to be taken down.

2.1.2.1 Data Classification

Data classification is key to effective and efficient data inventories and policy-based data management. While the idea of data classification may sound simple, it can be very complex. A data record may contain a simple user ID, date and a web address. What would be the classification of each field and the entire record? What if the user ID is an index in a table with personally identifiable information (PII)? What if the web address points to a user's Facebook account? Now imagine that a new record contains a person's birth date, gender and zip code. How would each field be classified? How would the record be classified? Research done by Latanya Sweeney shows that 87 percent of the U.S. population have reported characteristics that likely make them unique based only on a five-digit zip code, their gender and date of birth.[14] Furthermore, 53 percent of the U.S. population are likely to be uniquely identified using only a person's city, gender, date of birth. How does the record classification change when a record is split up or combined with other data? How do the retention, access and usage policies change? These are all questions that must be worked out before a data classification system can be implemented.

The approach to classifying data should not be rushed or taken lightly. The chosen classification system will have a long-term effect on the processing of data by the organization. There will be a desire to classify the data at a granular level unnecessarily. The data classification system should not be any more granular than the rules developed to regulate it. For example, a database table may include phone number, postal address and e-mail address. These three different types of data will probably be treated the same in regard to privacy. Therefore, they should be given the same classification, such as PII.

There are several ways to classify data. Research should be done to determine the best approach for the organization. It should not be so complex that it is difficult to understand or discourages adoption. There should also be clear rules about how each category should be treated. Classification can be as simple as high, medium and low; can be based on data sensitivity; or can be as sophisticated as a system based on multilevel security (MLS) used by various militaries.[15] MLS makes it easy to develop a strong role-based or attribute-based access control system. These provide a great means for programmatically protecting data based on policy, though they require a lot of maintenance, which can lead to out-of-date and inconsistent classifications.

One error that organizations make is having different classifications for the same data or different rules for processing the same classification of data. These disparities can occur when teams create classifications in isolation, data is collected because of an acquisition or local laws or contractual agreements influence classification rules. Until the disparities can be rectified, organizations should be careful to ensure that the treatment of the data matches the commitments made at the time that the data was collected. This may mean an extra classification value to allow for the application of different rules to certain pieces of data in the same category.

2.1.2.2 Data Retention

All data should have a retention period associated with it based on the data's classification and regulatory requirements. When data hasn't been classified or where no retention period has been applied to the classification, an agreed-upon maximum period should be applied. Organizations should resist simply stating "as long as needed for business purposes." We all know how frustrating it can be when repair people give us vague time frames for when they will show up, possibly disrupting our plans for the day.

Sometimes a set of data will have a retention period of several years due to regulatory requirements; however, not all of the data in a class may be subject to the same requirements. As a result, data in a class may need to be stored for different periods of time.

Once a retention period has been reached, the organization needs to determine what to do with the data. It can be deleted, de-identified or aggregated.

- Data deletion requires the complete removal of data once the retention period has passed. This can be a difficult task depending on the access controls on the data. If data is allowed to be shared across teams, copied to personal computers or external devices or shared with third parties, it will be nearly impossible to be certain that all the data has been deleted.

- De-identification is the process of removing all items from the data record that could lead to the identification of an individual. Care should be taken that identifiers or other data within the record cannot be combined with other data to permit identification of an individual.

- Data aggregation is the process of combing data from multiple records so that the combined data reflects the attributes of a group versus an individual. Care should be taken that there are enough records in the collection to avoid the identification of an individual.

Once again, organizations should harmonize their policies across teams to ensure that retention polices are applied consistently to the same data. Custom agreements will always override organizational policies; however, they should not conflict with commitments made in privacy notices to users.

2.1.2.3 Data Deletion

Deleting unneeded or expired data is one of the best ways to remove the risk that can come from having too much data. The less data an organization holds, the lower its privacy risk. Data can be deleted by deleting files, formatting the storage medium or removing specific entries from a database or other data store. When to delete data can be based on the data's retention period, which can be determined by the data record's timestamp or file creation date when the data was collected. These dates should persist as the data moves throughout the company. Data deletion can also be triggered by the termination of a contract, acquisition by another organization, completion of a transaction, a regulatory requirement or a deletion request by the data owner. Upon deletion care must be taken to ensure that copies of the data do not exist in offline storage or in backup media. Backup procedures should include regular rotation of backup media such that expired data is removed or the backup media are destroyed.

2.1.2.4 Data Inventory

"Bill, how is privacy boot camp going?" asked Amy.

"So far so good. We're learning a lot. As a matter of fact, the more we learn, the more worried I get," responded Bill.

"I feel if we are going to get a better handle on our privacy we need to better understand what data we have. Our three-level privacy categorization for data is great for understanding how to protect it, but it doesn't help much with understanding our regulatory requirements for the data or our commitments to data that we collect from users. When you get back to boot camp, let me know what you can find out about data classification schemes," said Amy.

"I like your idea. Validating compliance has been tough for teams since they weren't sure when to apply policies to data. I'll let you know what I find out."

Understanding the risk to data requires that organizations know what data exists under their control. Answering questions like "Do you have any data of type X?," "Have you complied with your data retention policies?" and "Who has access to data of type X?" is difficult unless there is a clear idea of where all the data of type X is stored. Better yet, if the data is classified, finding it and applying policies can be much simpler and even automated.

Problems can arise when data is stored off of the organization's network. When an organization's data is placed in removable storage, personal devices or transferred to third parties, it is difficult to validate that it is being managed in accordance with organizational policy. In addition, those scenarios increase the risk of data breach, which can be a major liability for an organization. Guidelines for effecting a meaningful inventory include:

- Have rules governing where data can be placed.

- Minimize the use of offline storage. An exception can be made for backups.

- Data placed on thumb drives and personal devices should be encrypted and short lived.

- Contracts should be in place to govern the use of organizational data by third parties.

- Classify data to simplify the discovery of data and the application of appropriate policies.

- Create data flows and list all data stores in a data inventory.

Scripts can be written to help simplify the data inventory process. To make this job easier, field and column names for data should be made consistent across data stores. Adding metadata to the column and record definitions will make it easier to find a certain class of data. For example, within a database, the table and column attributes could contain a classification designation. XML attributes can be used to indicate the data classification for an element.[16] For example:

```
<DataItem Classification="SensitivePII">
  <Name Classification="PII">John Smith</Name>
  <Religion Classification="Sensitive">Catholic</Religion>
</DataItem>
```

Once the data classification has been completed, performing a data inventory can be easier and more complete. Scripts can be created that can scan databases and other data stores to not only find data but also to classify it into an inventory table.[17] Once a data inventory is complete it can be placed in a database where it can more easily be accessed via web pages, database tools and scripts. Compliance tools can be run against data stores as well to verify compliance with retention, de-identification and access policies. A data inventory can also simplify audits and record retrievals to respond to data inquiries. Table 2-1 provides an example of what a data inventory might look like.

Table 2-1: Example Data Inventory

Title	Description
Name	Name of the data item.
Description	A description of the data item.
Classification	The overall class of the data item.
Source	The origin of the data item.
Governing policy	A link to the policy that applies to the data.
Owner	The team or title for the data controller.
Compliance	A link to the compliance obligations for this data item.
Location	The path to the data. If there are multiple locations, there should be a separate entry for each location.

2.1.3 Organizational Security Policies

Organizational security policies help to protect an organization's infrastructure and vital resources. It is the security policies that help maintain an organization's privacy policies. An organization should go through a security review to determine where its risks are. Performing a privacy impact assessment, which will be discussed in more detail in section 2.1.8, can help identify where security practices will need to be applied in order to mitigate privacy risks.

An evaluation should be done for every data source to understand what security measures need to be in place to protect it. Sometimes simply putting in adequate access control is enough. At other times more advanced access controls, password protection, encryption and isolation techniques may have to be deployed. Intrusion detection should also be implemented to combat any external risks.

2.1.3.1 Access Control

Access control is a mechanism by which access permission to a resource is managed. A resource can be a file, database, website, device or type of electronic medium. The type of access can vary depending on the resource type or operating system that hosts it. Types of access permission include read, write, delete, execute, print and audit.

An access control list (ACL) consists of a series of access control entries (ACE). Each entry contains the name of an entity and the type of access the entity has to a particular resource. An entity can be a user, group, device or service. Figure 2-7 is a screenshot of an ACL from the Windows operating system, containing three ACEs. Each ACE can indicate if an entity is granted or denied a specific access right to a resource. An ACL can also be used to indicate whether access to a resource should be audited.

Figure 2-7: ACL Screenshot in Windows

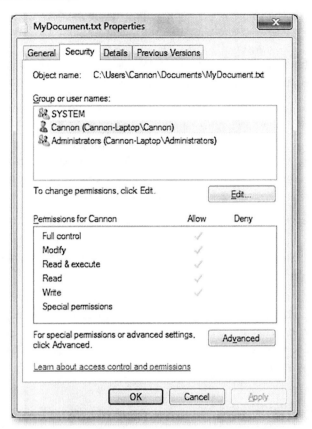

Used with permission from Microsoft.

ACL entries should be validated on a regular basis to ensure that the entries are still appropriate. This should include the verification of group memberships. Each time an individual changes roles within an organization, the individual's group memberships should be reviewed to ensure that they reflect the change in role. Following are the types of access control that may be implemented on a system.

- **Discretionary access control.** Discretionary access control is a mechanism by which a user has complete control over all the resources he or she owns. The user also has the ability to determine the permissions other users have to resources she owns. Note that if an ACE granting a user access to a resource appears before an ACE denying access, then access will be granted to the user. When groups are used, it is not always evident if an individual has access to a resource or not. It is important to review group memberships and the permission inheritance that may apply to a resource to ensure that only appropriate individuals have access to a resource. The owner of a resource and the system administrator will always have full rights to a resource. Microsoft Windows is an example of an operating system that supports discretionary access control.

- **Mandatory access control.** Mandatory access control is a mechanism where only the administrator can assign access rights to a resource. This mechanism protects access to resources by default and can even prevent an administrator from accessing a resource. The one downside to this type of control is that it is possible to clear a resource's ACL and permanently lose access to the resource. SELinux is an example of an operating system that supports mandatory access control.

- **Role-based access control (RBAC).** RBAC manages an entity's access to resources based on organizational roles. An RBAC ACL will contain a set of security roles that map to the physical roles in an organization, such as chief financial officer or accounts payable clerk.

- **Attribute-based access control (ABAC).** ABAC is an extension of RBAC in that it permits the addition of attributes to refine an entity's description. For example, an attribute can indicate the time, location, nationality or age required to access a resource. The extensible access control markup language (XACML) is a standard that can be used to implement ABAC systems.[18]

2.1.3.2 Encryption

Encryption is an important tool for protecting sensitive data. Two examples of encryption, secure sockets layer (SSL) protocol and transport layer security (TLS), help to protect data that is transmitted from client to server machines and server to server machines.[19] SSL is commonly used to protect communications between a browser and web server. TLS is often used to protect e-mail as it is transmitted between e-mail servers.[20]

For protecting data at rest, symmetric and asymmetric encryption can be used. Symmetric encryption uses a single cryptographic key for encryption and decryption. It is an efficient means for protecting data that needs to be accessed by multiple people. One difficulty in using symmetric encryption is the safe distribution of the cryptographic key. A loss of a cryptographic key will allow anyone who has it to decrypt protected data.

Asymmetric encryption uses a set of cryptographic keys, one for encryption and one for decryption. This method provides a safe means for sharing cryptographic keys. Asymmetric encryption is also a safe means for distributing symmetric cryptographic keys. The downside to asymmetric encryption is that it functions more slowly and it is more complicated to share encrypted data between more than two people.

Hashing is a method of protecting data that uses a cryptographic key to encrypt data but does not allow the data to later be decrypted. This method permits the use of sensitive data while protecting the original value. For example, a credit card number can be hashed and used as index for an individual's credit card transactions while preventing the hashed value from being used for additional transactions. For additional protection, salting, which shifts the encrypted value, can be used.

2.1.3.3 Password Control

Access to computers, files, databases, websites, networks and other resources containing sensitive data can be controlled by a password. Each resource can be accessed using a separate user account with its own ID and password, or a single sign-on (SSO) mechanism can permit access to multiple resources using a single user account. Using separate accounts for multiple resources often encourages people to use simple, similar passwords or to write the passwords on a piece of paper or easily accessible file. Both alternatives are risky for protecting access to sensitive data. Using SSO simplifies password management, though if the user's password is compromised it gives an interloper access to multiple resources. Conversely, using SSO offers the ability to centrally lock a person out of multiple resources as needed.

IT administrators should enforce the need for passwords on all systems that hold sensitive information. Likewise, a policy mandating strong passwords should be enforced to mitigate the risk of weak passwords, leaving sensitive resources susceptible to dictionary attacks or other exploits. Forcing passwords to expire on a regular basis mitigates the risk that compromised passwords could continually be used or compensates for an administrator who forgot to revoke the password of someone leaving the company.

2.1.3.4 Machine Access Restriction

Some operating systems provide the ability to limit which computers can access another computer based on a computer identifier or an IP address. This is a useful feature if only a small number of computers need to access a specific computer. This is a good way to restrict access to a database or document server that contains sensitive content. For example, access to a payroll database could be limited to a set of computers in the payroll department. In that case, if a network account ID and password were compromised, an intruder would also need direct access to a computer with privileges on the computer storing the sensitive data.

2.1.3.5 Intrusion Detection

Attacks on data can come from external entities wishing to gain access to an organization's network resources. Organizations big and small are constantly under attack from outsiders desiring access to organizational data. The famous infiltration of Google by Chinese hackers educated the public to the extent of attacks on organizations.[21] Intrusion exploits can happen through attempts to log in to users' accounts, denial of service attacks, phishing e-mails, malware infestation and other means. All of these exploits can cause threats to an organization's privacy resilience. To protect themselves from external threats, organizations should deploy intrusion detection systems.

2.1.4 Other Commitments Made by the Organization—Contracts and Agreements

In the era of big data, an organization can receive data from many sources. That data can flow in via various entry points and throughout the organization, eventually landing at an external data processor. The question for the data processor is which actions can be performed on the data. The group within the organization that transferred the data to the external data processor may not even know what commitments were made to the owners of the data. This represents not just a breakdown in communication, but a possible liability for the organization.

Whenever data is transferred out of an organization, there should be a contract in place that governs how the data should be handled. The contract should cover the access, processing, sharing, retention and disposition rights of the data. Any group within the organization that discloses data to a third party must do so in accordance with the commitment made to the owner of the data. If the commitment with the data owner came from another group, then those commitments must persist as the data flows from group to group.

2.1.5 Incident Response—Security and Privacy Perspectives

Having a mature incident response program is an important part of any privacy program. Sometimes it is the only way that an organization's customers can submit a privacy issue. The incident response program should consist of an incident response center, web form, e-mail address, phone number, and representatives from public relations, legal, privacy and security.

The privacy response form should be easily accessible from the organization's privacy notice as well as easy to use. Providing a selection setting with privacy categories is one way to simplify the request. Categories can include things such as data breach, data access request and account takeover. A simple response should be sent to the user right away to give the sense that the issue is being taken seriously. A description of the incident should be placed in an incident tracking system and a tracking number assigned to it. Members of the incident response team should review the incident and contact the appropriate person in the business group affected by the incident.

One innovative way to address a user's privacy questions is to create a form that guides the user to the answers they need without having to fill out a form or send an e-mail and wait for a response. Google provides a great example of this technique in their Privacy Troubleshooter. Figure 2-8 is an example of how Google's Troubleshooter works.

Figure 2-8: Google Privacy Troubleshooter

Google and the Google logo are registered trademarks of Google Inc.; used with permission.

Privacy incidents tend to occur because of misuses of data or a user's desire to gain access to his or her data or change his or her privacy settings. Privacy and security are different concepts, though they are interrelated. Privacy incidents can happen due to poorly applied security controls. For example, improper access controls can permit inappropriate access to data by people inside or outside the company. The lack of encryption can leave data susceptible to data breaches and interception during transmission.

2.1.6 Security and Privacy in the Systems Development Lifecycle

The systems development lifecycle (SDLC) consists of several phases, from project initiation to maintenance or disposal. Including security and privacy evaluations at each phase in the SDLC helps to streamline the process and save time overall. For privacy, Privacy by Design should be incorporated into the process.[22] Also, the collection, processing, sharing and retention practices of the data should be analyzed. To ensure security risks are mitigated, an analysis of access control, intrusion detection and resource protection measures should be made.

Upon completion of each phase of the SDLC, a security and privacy review should be performed to identify and mitigate possible risks before moving to the next phase. Outcomes of the reviews should be recorded as part of the SDLC documentation.

2.1.7 Enterprise Architecture and Data Flows, Including Cross-Border Transfers

According to Gartner, "Enterprise architecture (EA) is a discipline for proactively and holistically leading enterprise responses to disruptive forces by identifying and analyzing the execution of change toward desired business vision and outcomes. EA delivers value by presenting business and IT leaders with signature-ready recommendations for adjusting policies and projects to achieve target business outcomes that capitalize on relevant business disruptions. EA is used to steer decision making toward the evolution of the future state architecture."[23] EA involves managing the data flows across an organization in order to minimize privacy risk and support business growth.

Data flows should be designed such that they maximize utility of organizational data while maintaining compliance with organizational responsibilities. A data flow diagram (DFD) provides a graphical means to illustrate the flow of data across an organization.[24] The DFD can show the origin of data, indicating whether the origin was an individual, external entity, internal group or process. It can show which processes and data stores are involved in a data flow, how the data may evolve as it flows across processes and even where data might flow across geographic borders. If a data dictionary is used, the makeup of the data at each point in the data flow can be determined.

Once a DFD is completed, the flow and processing of data can be mapped to organizational policies, privacy notices and external agreements to ensure they are in compliance. Sophisticated DFD systems can have a link associated with each data flow that connects it to the policy that governs the use of the data contained in the data flow. Care must be taken with cross-border data flows to ensure that the data transfers occur in accordance with local laws at each end of the data flow. For example, Argentina, the European Union, New Zealand and South Korea all have restrictions that cover the transfer of data outside the country as well as access to a citizen's data from outside the country. IT departments should work with their legal departments when access to foreign data is involved.

2.1.8 Privacy Impact Assessments

The privacy impact assessment (PIA) is one of the most important parts of a privacy program. It helps an organization identify its privacy risks and measure the criticality of each risk. The results of the PIA can facilitate an action plan for addressing each risk. In a small organization, the privacy team can perform the risk assessment. In large organizations the risk assessment responsibilities may have to be spread out across teams. Using the assistance of an external party can help to streamline the process.

The importance of performing a PIA is reflected in the mandate that all government agencies, such as the Federal Trade Commission (FTC), are required by the E-Government Act of 2002 to perform PIAs.[25] Under the Treasury Board of Canada Secretariat's Directive on Privacy Impact Assessment, Canadian government departments are required to conduct a PIA.[26] The European Union does not currently have PIA legislation. However, the Madrid Resolution of the 31st International Conference of Data Protection and Privacy includes guidance to EU member states on the importance of PIAs.[27]

The PIA should occur at least yearly across the organization. A higher rate may be prudent depending on the level of privacy risk that exists across the organization. For example, social networking companies such as Facebook are likely to have greater privacy risks than a blogging site.

The PIA should not take the place of privacy reviews that should accompany all new development, marketing and vendor activities. Consequently, privacy review statistics should be captured as part of the PIA process.

The PIA should be as thorough as possible in order to capture as many privacy risks as possible that might exist within an organization. It should be understood that an organization will probably not be able to address every identified risk during an assessment period, but they should be identified and recorded all the same.

A person should be identified within each major team to work with the organizational privacy team to develop a coordinated PIA.

2.1.8.1 Performing a Privacy Impact Assessment

For complex global companies, performing a PIA can be equally complex. Regulations, contracts, industry agreements, the number of internal projects handling data and extensive privacy notices will all impact the privacy risk of an organization. Several events can trigger a PIA:

1. The creation of a new product or service

2. A new or updated program for processing data

3. A merger or acquisition

4. Creation of a new data center

5. Onboarding of new data

6. Movement of data to a different country

7. Changes in regulations governing data use

The following factors should be taken into account when a PIA is performed:

1. With which sets of privacy regulations must the organization comply? For example, the EU Data Protection Directive, the Canadian Personal Information Protection and Electronic Documents Act (PIPEDA) or Children's Online Privacy Protection Act (COPPA)?[28]

2. Which standards, such as the Better Business Bureau's Code of Business Practices, is the organization obligated to uphold as a result of industry memberships?[29]

3. Which third-party contractual obligations does the organization have?

4. What commitments has the organization made in its privacy notices?

5. What commitments has the organization made in its internal privacy policies?

6. What data is being collected, processed and shared by the organization?

7. What are the gaps between policies and practices?

8. What controls are in place to validate privacy practices?

Privacy risks identified by the PIA should be categorized by area and prioritized by severity. The prioritization should be measured based on the possible harm to users, liability to the organization, cost to mitigate the risk and likelihood that the risk will occur. Formulas can be used to measure risk, though they are only a rough gauge of how much a privacy incident might impact an organization. A breach may be innocuous at one company while devastating at another. Having a trusted brand and mature incident response team can go a long way toward minimizing the effects of a privacy incident.

Risks can be addressed in several ways: avoid, mitigate, accept or transfer. Let's use the possibility of a breach exposing credit card numbers as an example of how to address a privacy risk.

- **Avoid risk.** The organization can decide that it will no longer process credit card transactions. Instead, it will rely on a third-party service to process them.

- **Mitigate risk.** The organization can decide to encrypt the credit card number during collection and storage, and place tight restrictions on access to credit card data.

- **Accept risk.** The organization can decide that it would be too costly to use a third party to process its credit card transactions or to modify systems to encrypt the numbers. It may instead rely on current practices to protect the credit card data and hope for the best.

- **Transfer risk.** The organization can purchase business insurance to cover the firm in the case of a data breach.

Once risks have been identified and prioritized, they should be entered into an issue tracking system and assigned owners. Each incident should be monitored for progress and tracked to closure. Even if the organization determines that it must resolve a risk, it may need to postpone the resolution until enough resources become available to do so. A yearly review of privacy incidents and closures should be made to identify negative trends that may need to be addressed.

2.1.8.2 Resources for Guidelines on Performing Privacy Impact Assessments

While procedures are similar, different countries will have their own guidance for performing a privacy impact assessment. Below are some of the guidelines provided by different locales:

- New Zealand Privacy Commissioner, "Privacy Impact Assessment Handbook"[30]

- Office of the Australian Information Commissioner, "Privacy Impact Assessment Guide"[31]

- Office of the Privacy Commissioner for Personal Data, Hong Kong, "Privacy Impact Assessments"[32]

- Treasury Board of Canada Secretariat, "Privacy Impact Assessment Guidelines: A Framework to Manage Privacy Risks Guidelines"[33]

- U.K. Information Commissioner's Office, "Privacy Impact Assessment Handbook"[34]

- U.S. Department of Homeland Security, "Privacy Impact Assessments Official Guidance"[35]

2.1.9 Privacy and Security Regulations with Specific IT Requirements

Several regulations have been created over the years that place requirements for IT departments. While most organizations are only impacted by regulations within their jurisdiction, global organizations will be impacted by regulations in each locale where they do business and thus must understand those regulations. Below is a list of some of the regulations and how they impact IT departments:

- **Canada: Personal Information Protection and Electronic Documents Act (PIPEDA).**[36] This law applies to any company doing business in Canada. The regulation consists of the following principles: accountability; identifying purposes; consent; limiting collection; limiting use, disclosure and retention; accuracy; safeguards; openness; individual access; and challenging compliance. At a minimum, organizations must obtain opt-out consent from data subjects in order to collect, use or disclose personal information.

- **EU Data Protection Directive.**[37] This directive applies to European companies as well as non-European companies that transfer data from European citizens. The directive contains the following principles: notice, purpose, consent, security, disclosure, access and accountability. The directive applies to processing of all online and offline data, and to all organizations holding personal data.

- **Hong Kong: Personal Data Ordinance.**[38] This law applies to organizations doing business in Hong Kong. It contains six principles that apply to the collection, use, accuracy and security of personal information. Data subjects must be provided the right to access, correct or delete their personal information.

- **Mexico: Law on the Protection of Personal Data Held by Private Parties.**[39] This law requires Mexican companies and companies doing business in Mexico to comply with the privacy principles of legality, consent, notice, quality, purpose limitation, fidelity, proportionality and accountability as well as a retention requirement. The gathering and processing of data require the prior consent of each person involved.

- **United States: Children's Online Privacy Protection Act (COPPA).**[40] COPPA applies to commercial websites and online services targeted at children under 13 that collect, use or disclose personal information from children. It also applies to general audience websites or online services with actual knowledge that they are collecting, using or disclosing personal information from children under 13. The rule also applies to websites or online services that have actual knowledge that they are collecting personal information directly from users of another website or online service directed to children.

2.1.10 Common Standards and Framework of Relevance

The Code of Fair Information Practices (FIPs) formed the first privacy framework to be developed. They were first proposed in 1973 by a U.S. government advisory committee. The original codes were as follows:[41]

1. There must be no personal data record-keeping systems whose very existence is secret.

2. There must be a way for an individual to find out what information about him is in a record and how it is used.

3. There must be a way for an individual to prevent information about him obtained for one purpose from being used or made available for other purposes without his consent.

4. There must be a way for an individual to correct or amend a record of identifiable information about himself.

5. Any organization creating, maintaining, using, or disseminating records of identifiable personal data must assure the reliability of the data for their intended use and must take reasonable precautions to prevent misuse of the data.

In 1980, the Organisation for Economic Co-operation and Development (OECD) used these practices as a basis for its set of privacy principles, which in turn became the basis for privacy principles and practices of countries and organizations across the globe.[42] The OECD's privacy principles are not only essential to privacy protections but also help to reduce an organization's legal risk and improve its trust quotient. They are as follows:

1. Collection Limitation Principle

2. Data Quality Principle

3. Purpose Specification Principle

4. Use Limitation Principle

5. Security Safeguards Principle

6. Openness Principle

7. Individual Participation Principle

8. Accountability Principle

The OECD's work influenced the FTC's Fair Information Practice Principles, the Asia-Pacific Economic Cooperation (APEC) Privacy Framework, the Australian Privacy Principles and many other public and private organizations around the world.[43] By creating a set of privacy principles that are commonly accepted, organizations can streamline the process of sharing data with each other and across national borders. To simplify the process of creating a set of privacy principles and to show their commitment to commonly accepted privacy principles, organizations often join global industry groups that have a set of mandated privacy principles, such as the Interactive Advertising Bureau Privacy Principles.[44]

2.2 The Information Lifecycle: An Introduction

The information lifecycle (ILC) is the process data goes through, starting with its acquisition and ending with its disposition. All information must go through specific ILC phases: collection, use, disclosure, retention and destruction.

- **Collection.** Collection covers the receipt of data into an organization. The data can come directly from the user, indirectly from the user via a third party, via an aggregation service or other means. Sometimes data is collected by a company via its web server, but the data is never processed and so may never be used.

- **Use.** Use of data occurs when an organization processes the data in any way. It could be to perform research, improve the website, provide personalized content, better understand the user or many other purposes.

- **Disclosure.** Disclosure is the sharing or onward transfer of data to third parties.

- **Retention.** Retention is the persistence of data beyond initial collection. Retention covers the data in logs as well as data that has been processed and stored in databases or other data stores.

- **Destruction.** Destruction of data can occur by deletion, but may also occur through modification of the data via truncation, hashing or perturbation.

2.3 Common Privacy Principles

Each organization should govern itself by a core set of privacy principles that cover how personal information under its control is processed. These principles can serve as a framework for employees to follow as they develop their internal policies.

2.3.1 Collection Limitation

This principle covers the restraint from the excessive collection of personal information. Organizations should limit the amount of data they collect in order to minimize privacy risk and legal liability that can come from excessive data collection. The less personal information collected and stored by an organization, the less chance that the information will be inappropriately accessed by an employee, shared with the wrong person or accidentally leaked to the general public.

2.3.2 Data Quality

This principle covers the idea that organizations that collect personal information should make efforts to maintain the quality of the information. When collecting personal information, organizations should ensure that they have collected all the information that was requested and that the information is not modified during transmission or storage. Individuals should also be provided the ability to access their information and correct it as needed.

2.3.3 Purpose Specification

This principle covers the expression of purpose for which personal information is collected. Whenever personal information is collected, the purpose for its collection should be expressed to the individual. This notification should be provided to the user before the collection. Once the data has been collected, the purpose for its collection should not change without providing notice to the user and obtaining consent to apply the new purpose to the previously collected information.

2.3.4 Use Limitation

This principle covers the idea that the use of personal information should be limited within an organization. Any usage should be covered by the privacy notice in effect at the time the personal information was collected. Furthermore, organizations should strive to limit the number of teams that process the personal information.

2.3.5 Security Safeguards

Organizations have an obligation to provide security for the data they collect from users. The level of security should match the sensitivity of the data being collected. For aggregate data that simply lists the number of site visitors and the pages they viewed, a low level of security is probably okay unless it is critical business data; then the organization should have an elevated level of security on the data to keep it out of the hands of competitors. Unfortunately, determining the threshold for data sensitivity can be difficult. As Helen Nissenbaum explains it, "What people care most about is not simply restricting the flow of information but ensuring that it flows appropriately, and an account of appropriate flow is given here through the framework of contextual integrity."[45]

2.3.6 Openness

This principle encourages organizations to be open about the personal information they collect and the privacy principles that govern their treatment of such information. Every organization should provide a privacy notice that is easy to find and easy to read, covering all aspects of its personal information handling practices.

2.3.7 Individual Participation

This principle provides the ability for an individual to receive confirmation from an organization that the organization holds data collected from or relating to the individual. If such data exists, the individual should have the right to request and receive such data from the organization in a timely manner and at a reasonable cost. Upon granting the data request, the organization should deliver the data to the individual in a format that is intelligible to that person. If the request for the information is denied, the individual should have the right to challenge the denial. Furthermore, if upon receipt of the data the individual determines that the data is incorrect, the individual should have the right to have the data corrected, amended or deleted.

2.3.8 Accountability

This principle covers the idea that whenever an organization plans to transfer an individual's personal information, it should obtain consent from the individual or exercise extreme care in handling the personal information. The organization should also ensure that the recipient of the personal information will protect it in a manner that is consistent with commonly held privacy principles.

2.4 Conclusion

A great house starts with a great foundation. The bigger the house, the better the foundation must be. If a company wants to be great at privacy, it must begin with the foundational elements of privacy. Companies must invest in privacy if they want to get the returns that come from a mature privacy program. Training, policies and programs focused on privacy are a worthwhile investment. It is important for all employees to participate in a training program that teaches privacy principles. Creating privacy policies will help employees understand their privacy obligations. Developing an information lifecycle program around a data classification system will make privacy compliance more attainable.

Performing privacy impact assessments will help mitigate privacy mishaps that can occur in new projects. Developing an incident response program will help a company respond to privacy incidents as they occur and build trust with privacy advocates, regulators and consumers. Providing transparency via a privacy notice is another way that a company can build trust and head off privacy inquiries. While an investment in privacy may not result in a direct increase in revenues, it can mitigate the risk of revenue loss as a result of a privacy incident.

Endnotes

1 "Data Use Policy," Facebook, www.facebook.com/about/privacy/, accessed March 28, 2014.

2 Brendon Lynch, "Microsoft Privacy Statements: A New Look," Microsoft, *Trustworthy Computing* (blog), July 11, 2012, http://blogs.technet.com/b/trustworthycomputing/archive/2012/07/11/privacy-statements.aspx.

3 "Google's New Privacy Policy," Google, *Official Blog*, February 29, 2012, http://googleblog.blogspot.com/2012/02/googles-new-privacy-policy.html.

4 "Privacy Policy Highlights," United States Postal Service, accessed September 12, 2013, http://about.usps.com/who-we-are/privacy-policy/privacy-policy-highlights.htm.

5 "Ten Steps to Develop a Multilayered Privacy Notice," Center for Information Privacy Leadership, March 2007, www.hunton.com/files/Publication/37a71d77-14c4-4361-a62b-89f67feb544f/Presentation/PublicationAttachment/e7ffca9d-da66-4ed6-a445-f8fdc0b97e22/Ten_Steps_whitepaper.pdf.

6 Disconnect, Inc., https://icons.disconnect.me/icons.

7 Scott Reyburn, "ACT Debuts the App Privacy Icons," Inside Mobile Apps, October 4, 2012, www.insidemobileapps.com/2012/10/04/act-debuts-the-app-privacy-icons/.

8 "Privacy Nutrition Labels," Cylab Usable Privacy and Security Laboratory, Carnegie Mellon University, accessed September 12, 2013, http://cups.cs.cmu.edu/privacyLabel/.

9 "Symposium on Usable Privacy and Security," Cylab Usable Privacy and Security Laboratory, Carnegie Mellon University, accessed September 12, 2013, http://cups.cs.cmu.edu/soups/.

10 Travis Pinnick, "Privacy Short Notice Design," *Truste Blog*, February 17, 2011, www.truste.com/blog/2011/02/17/privacy-short-notice-designpart-i-background/.

11 Jim Brock, "Introducing Policymaker: Making mobile privacy easier (and better)," Privacy Choice, August 15, 2011, http://blog.privacychoice.org/2011/08/15/introducing-policymaker-making-mobile-privacy-easier-and-better/.

12 "Free Privacy Policy for Mobile Apps," Truste, accessed September 12, 2013, http://www.truste.com/free-mobile-privacy-policy/.

13 "Website Privacy Services," Truste, accessed September 12, 2013, http://www.truste.com/products-and-services/enterprise-privacy/TRUSTed-websites.

14 Latanya Sweeney, "Simple Demographics Often Identify People Uniquely," Data Privacy Working Paper 3 (Pittsburgh: Carnegie Mellon University, 2000), http://dataprivacylab.org/projects/identifiability/index.html.

15 Fred B. Schneider, lecture notes by Michael Clarkson, "Multi-level Security," Cornell University Department of Computer Science, accessed September 12, 2013, http://www.cs.cornell.edu/courses/CS5430/2012sp/mls.html.

16 Definition: XML (Extensible Markup Language), Search SOA, http://searchsoa.techtarget.com/definition/XML.

17 Shayak Sen, Saikat Guha, Anupam Dutta, Sriram Rajamani, Janice Tsai, and Jeannette Wing, "Bootstrapping Privacy Compliance in Big Data Systems," in *Proceedings of the 35th IEEE Symposium on Security and Privacy* (San Jose, CA, May 18-21, 2014), http://research.microsoft.com/apps/pubs/default.aspx?id=208626.

18 "OASIS eXtensible Access Control Markup Language (XACML) TC," Oasis, accessed September 12, 2013, www.oasis-open.org/committees/tc_home.php?wg_abbrev=xacml.

19 Definition: Secure Sockets Layer (SSL), Search Security, last updated March 2007, http://searchsecurity.techtarget.com/definition/Secure-Sockets-Layer-SSL.

20 "Transport Layer Security for Inbound Mail," Google Postini Services, accessed September 12, 2013, www.google.com/support/enterprise/static/postini/docs/admin/en/admin_ee_cu/ib_tls_overview.html.

21 Charlie Osborne, "Chinese cyberattack on Google exposed spy data: US officials," ZD Net, May 21, 2013, www.zdnet.com/chinese-cyberattack-on-google-exposed-spy-data-us-officials-7000015653/.

22 Ann Cavoukian, "About PbD," Privacy by Design, www.privacybydesign.ca/index.php/about-pbd/.

23 "Enterprise Architecture (EA)," Gartner IT Glossary, accessed September 12, 2013, www.gartner.com/it-glossary/enterprise-architecture-ea/.

24 For an example of a data flow diagram, see "What are Data Flow Diagrams?," SmartDraw, www.smartdraw.com/resources/tutorials/data-flow-diagrams/.

25 "Federal Trade Commission Privacy Impact Assessments," Federal Trade Commission, accessed September 12, 2013, www.ftc.gov/ftc/privacyimpactassessment.shtm.

26 "Privacy Impact Assessments," Office of the Privacy Commissioner of Canada, accessed September 12, 2013, www.priv.gc.ca/resource/fs-fi/02_05_d_33_e.asp.

27 For the text of the Madrid Resolution, see "Internacional Standards on the Protection of Personal Data and Privacy, the Madrid Resolution," www.gov.im/lib/docs/odps/madridresolutionnov09.pdf.

28 Council Directive 1995/46/EC, 1995 O.J. L 281 p. 31, http://eur-lex.europa.eu/LexUriServ/LexUriServ.do?uri=CELEX:31995L0046:EN:HTML;
Personal Information Protection and Electronic Documents Act (PIPEDA), S.C. 2000, c. 5, http://laws-lois.justice.gc.ca/eng/acts/P-8.6/index.html; Children's Online Privacy Protection Act of 1998, 15 U.S.C. §§ 6501-6505, http://business.ftc.gov/privacy-and-security/childrens-privacy.

29 "BBB Code of Business Practices (BBB Accreditation Standards)," Council of Better Business Bureaus, accessed September 12, 2013, www.bbb.org/council/for-businesses/about-bbb-accreditation/bbb-code-of-business-practices-bbb-accreditation-standards/.

30 "Privacy Impact Assessment Handbook," Privacy Commissioner Te Mana Matapono Matatapu, July 16, 2008, www.privacy.org.nz/news-and-publications/guidance-notes/guidance-notes/privacy-impact-assessment-handbook/.

31 "Privacy Impact Assessment Guide," Australian Government, Office of the Australian Information Commissioner, May 2010, www.oaic.gov.au/privacy/privacy-resources/privacy-guides/privacy-impact-assessment-guide.

32 "Privacy Impact Assessments," Office of the Privacy Commissioner for Personal Data, Hong Kong, July 2010, www.pcpd.org.hk/english/publications/files/PIAleaflet_e.pdf.

33 "Privacy Impact Assessment Guidelines: A Framework to Manage Privacy Risks Guidelines," Government of Canada, Treasury Board of Canada Secretariat, May 2010, www.tbs-sct.gc.ca/pol/doc-eng.aspx?id=12451&section=text.

34 "Privacy Impact Assessment Handbook," Version 2.0, Information Commissioner's Office of the United Kingdom, (accessed February 25, 2013), http://ico.org.uk/pia_handbook_html_v2/html/0-advice.html.

35 "Privacy Impact Assessments Official Guidance," U.S. Department of Homeland Security, May 2007, www.dhs.gov/xlibrary/assets/privacy/privacy_pia_guidance_may2007.pdf.

36 Personal Information Protection and Electronic Documents Act (PIPEDA), S.C. 2000, c. 5, http://laws-lois.justice.gc.ca/eng/acts/P-8.6/index.html.

37 Council Directive 95/46/EC, 1995 O.J. L 281 p. 31, http://eur-lex.europa.eu/LexUriServ/LexUriServ.do?uri=CELEX:31995L0046:EN:HTML.

38 Personal Data (Privacy) Ordinance, CAP 486, The Laws of Hong Kong as amended by Personal Data (Privacy) (Amendment) Ordinance A2129 Ord. No. 18 of 2012, www.pcpd.org.hk/english/ordinance/ordglance.html.

39 "Law on the Protection of Personal Data Held by Private Parties," Official Diary of the Federation (DOF), July 5, 2010, www.dof.gob.mx/nota_detalle.php?codigo=5150631&fecha=05/07/2010.

40 Children's Online Privacy Protection Act of 1998, 15 U.S.C. §§ 6501-6505, http://business.ftc.gov/privacy-and-security/childrens-privacy.

41 Secretary's Advisory Committee on Automated Personal Data Systems, *Records, Computers and the Rights of Citizens,* Department of Health, Education, and Welfare [now Health and Human Services], July, 1973.

42 For a list of these principles see "OECD Privacy Principles," Organisation for Economic Co-operation and Development, July 20, 2010, http://oecdprivacy.org/.

43 "Privacy Online: Fair Information Practices in the Electronic Marketplace," Federal Trade Commission, May 2000, www.ftc.gov/reports/privacy3/fairinfo.shtm; "APEC Privacy Framework," Asia-Pacific Economic Cooperation, December 2005, http://publications.apec.org/publication-detail.php?pub_id=390; "Australian Privacy Law and Practice" (ALRC Report 108), chapter 18, Australian Government, Australian Law Reform Commission, January 10, 2013, www.alrc.gov.au/publications/18.%20Structural%20Reform%20of%20the%20Privacy%20Principles/development-current-australian-privacy-.

44 "Privacy Principles," Interactive Advertising Bureau, February 24 2008, www.iab.net/guidelines/508676/1464/.

45 Helen Nissenbaum, *Privacy in Context: Technology, Policy, and the Integrity of Social Life* (Stanford, CT: Stanford University Press, 2009), http://www.sup.org/book.cgi?id=8862.

## CHAPTER 3

Privacy Considerations in the Information Lifecycle

Amy powered up the projector and paused to let the title slide appear on the screen. "Welcome back, everyone. I'm excited to hear about how your privacy boot camp went. But, before we get to that, I want to show you how you are going to apply your new skills. While you were away, I reviewed some of our document libraries and noticed that half of them don't have a classification or a retention policy. So your first order of business will be to develop a formal information lifecycle program for our company. So roll up your sleeves and be prepared to deliver a world-class information lifecycle program."

Amy's challenges are indicative of those many companies face. A lot can happen to data from the moment it first enters a company until it is eventually disposed of. Even the definition of "information lifecycle" will change depending on the type of data to which it applies. Data can take the form of files, database records, DVDs, web logs or even paper documents from prospective employees. Companies should define a lifecycle plan for each type of data. Even to not define a plan defines one by default, albeit a plan that would bring great risk to an organization.

In this chapter, we will look at the information lifecycle from the viewpoint of collection, use, disclosure, retention and destruction. Each step in the lifecycle should be described in your plan. Having no information lifecycle plan means unneeded data could be around indefinitely. The longer a company keeps data, the greater the risk of mishandling. Lack of a plan can also mean little thought is given for where data is stored and who has access to it.

3.1 Collection

Amy stood in front of her staff and paced a bit, bouncing the fingertips of each hand together. "Team," she announced, "our privacy notice's description of collection is a bit convoluted. Sure, globally our web servers receive lots of data every time someone visits our websites, but most of that data we don't even process. Logs are kept for thirty days to support operational activities such as intrusion detection, fraud prevention, network continuity and the like. The data that runs our business is a small percentage of the log data, and furthermore, it doesn't contain PII. At least, that is our corporate policy. First, we need to make sure that all departments are complying with our policy. Second, we need to update our privacy notice to ensure that it reflects our practices so people are clear about the data we collect and how we use it."

Collection, in the context of this chapter, is the process of receiving data from a user, device or entity. For the most part, collection occurs via an organization's web server, though it can occur via download from a third-party site or media shipped to the organization. Proper collection practices can minimize privacy risks by helping to ensure that only the necessary data is collected and only the appropriate people access it. When collecting data from users, they should be provided with notice, choice, control and consent as needed. There should be limits on the data being collected, and it should be secured from inappropriate access.

3.1.1 Notice

Notice is the act of informing others about a topic that might impact them. We see notices everywhere: for road closures, store closures, flood warnings, buildings going up, buildings coming down, warnings that a dog is around. And we see notices about an organization's privacy practices.

More often than not, notices warn of possible danger. When one considers the potential harm that might result from the use of data collected at a website, it seems appropriate to provide users with a privacy notice that explains the organization's privacy practices. In general, the privacy notice should provide the following information:

- What data is being collected

- The mechanisms by which data is collected

- How the data is used

- Who has access to the data

- With whom the data may be shared or disclosed

- How long the data is kept and its disposition at expiration

- What control the user has over the collection, usage and persistence of the data

- How the data is protected

- How users can access and export their data as appropriate

- How users can contact the organization with questions or concerns about their privacy

While browsing the Internet or using or installing software, take note of the privacy statements you see, not just the content, but their look and feel. Compare them to the ones that your organization uses and look at ways to improve them.

In life, many warning signs explicitly state what people should do: "Sidewalk closed. Use other side." Others provide a warning that readers intuitively know how to respond to: "Beware of dog!" When a privacy notice states that it collects personal information and shares it with third parties, it usually provides no additional information about how users are supposed to protect themselves, nor do most users intuitively know how to do so.

Even when a privacy notice does provide guidance, such as how to manage cookies or how to opt out of certain data usages, it is buried in text containing thousands of words. Imagine walking through the woods and seeing a thousand-word, small-font sign ending with, "A bear may eat you," with no information about how to avoid bears.

The privacy notice should be informative in a way that is useful to the reader, who will for the most part be a consumer and not a lawyer or regulator. Gritty details still need to be available to provide all audiences with the detailed information if they desire to access it.

Notices can come in different flavors. The help text pop-up on a dialog can provide information about a button or icon without the user having to click on it. See the example in Figure 3-1. Hovering the mouse over the icon that looks like a mouse informs users that clicking on it will take them to the homepage.

Figure 3-1: Pop-up Dialog Text as Shown in Chrome

Google and the Google logo are registered trademarks of Google Inc.; used with permission.

A simple pop-up or banner can inform users about cookie usage without disrupting their browsing experience. A "learn more" link can provide additional information as needed. Yahoo's UK homepage provides such a banner.[1]

Placing a lot of important information in front of the user during install or setup may be inappropriate, as a different person may be performing those functions or the user may not have the time or interest to digest it all. A pop-up in context when an application or feature is being used can be more timely and practical. While a standalone notice can be a powerful tool when displayed at the right time, the same information should be available and easy to find whenever the user needs a refresher on the information. Color codes or icons can help the user connect the dots between a just-in-time notice and a full help page.

Layered privacy notices are a good way to provide transparency in a simplified format.[2] Carnegie Mellon University has performed research on another approach—privacy notices in the form of nutrition labels (see Figure 2-4).[3]

3.1.2 Choice

Choice provides consumers with the opportunity to have input regarding their privacy preferences. It can provide users with a say in how their data is managed by an organization. Many will agree that choice is an important tenet of privacy. However, many will argue that choice suffers similar failings as notice.[4] While there is an expectation that websites, services and application developers will provide consumers with a privacy notice as well as adequate privacy choices, the difficulty lies in the execution of those choices. Many applications and services provide a simple set of privacy settings, but they are often difficult to find. Though the setting may only be a couple of clicks away on an Options menu, consumers are typically reluctant to go in search of an application's privacy settings.

The PrivacyChoice.org site provides a privacy indicator in plain view on the left side of the page. Clicking on it provides an easy-to-follow, layered notice on the organization's privacy practices. Browser plug-ins such as Abine's DoNotTrackMe and MaskMe are visible to the user at all times in the browser toolbar and provide quick access to privacy settings at the click of a button.

Problems can arise when there are too many choices. Bruce Schneier stated that complexity is the enemy of security.[5] The same holds true for privacy. If you want users to engage your privacy settings, make it easy for them. A *New York Times* article describes why too many choices can have a chilling effect on a person's ability to make a decision.[6] The LinkedIn privacy settings provide an example where there are lots of choices to make. The settings are spread across a series of links. As can be seen in Figure 3-2, the links are easy to understand, but a user would have to go through several links to manage all of her privacy settings.

Facebook goes further by providing a list of privacy links across several dialogs. While the granularity is great for people who enjoy having that level of control over their privacy settings, for those who prefer a simpler mechanism, it can be daunting. To a lot of people, too many choices is no choice at all.

Choice is often conflated with control or consent, when in fact the three are all very different. The fact that choice is distinct from control and consent warrants a deeper discussion.

Figure 3-2: LinkedIn™ Privacy Settings

Profile	Privacy Controls	Settings
Communications	Turn on/off your activity broadcasts	Manage your Twitter settings
	Select who can see your activity feed	Helpful Links
Groups, Companies & Applications	Select what others see when you've viewed their profile	Edit your name, location & industry »
	Select who can see your connections	Edit your profile »
		Edit your public profile »
Account	Change your profile photo & visibility »	Manage your recommendations »
	Show/hide "Viewers of this profile also viewed" box	

3.1.2.1 Control

According to *Merriam-Webster*, control is "an act or instance of controlling; *also*: power or authority to guide or manage."[7] In privacy terms, that means users have the ability to manage how data about them is used. Many privacy settings give consumers choice, but not real control. Users can opt out of behavioral advertising, but can't control the collection of their data. Users can disable tracking of location data, but then mapping is disabled. Do Not Track is implemented in the major browsers. Users can turn it on or off as much as they like, but today it gives them no control whatsoever.[8] For choice to be relevant it has to be meaningful. It has to give users true control over their data.

3.1.2.2 Consent

Consent in this context is an agreement from the user for an organization to process her data in a certain fashion. Consent is usually provided by users at the time they are presented with a choice. Most consent from users is *implied consent*, meaning the user never provides specific consent or says no to a particular data-handling practice. Going to a website and browsing around is implicit consent of the website's privacy policy or terms of use. Not opting out of behavioral advertising is implicit consent to receive targeted advertisements.

Explicit consent is when the user provides a positive, verifiable acknowledgment to a specific data-handling practice. Agreeing to the collection of location services for a mapping application or agreeing to accept a software update is an example of explicit consent.

There is a natural tension between the explicit consent regulators would like to see, the implied consent online companies would like to provide and the amount of disruption in browsing consumers are willing to tolerate. Most websites rely on implied consent for their privacy notice and use of cookies. To obtain explicit consent would require that website visitors leave the page they are on, be presented with a privacy notice and provide consent. This is something website visitors would probably be reluctant to do on every web page they visit. To address that concern, EU regulators asked that companies provide enhanced notice on the homepage of their websites that links to more detailed information. However, instead of embracing these notices, consumers have complained that they are annoyed by even the smallest of the notices.[9] Consent is important, but must be given in the context of data collection so that it is meaningful for users and practical for websites to deploy.

3.1.3 Collection Limitations

A privacy notice or terms of use should not be seen as a license to collect as much data as possible. In fact, organizations should work hard to minimize the data they collect. The European Data Protection Supervisor defines a *data minimization principle*, which states, "The principle of 'data minimization' means that a data controller should limit the collection of personal information to what is directly relevant and necessary to accomplish a specified purpose."[10]

Some would argue that the more data an organization collects, the greater the benefits that can be realized from it. The benefits of big data are indisputable.[11] However, across universities, governments and businesses, the same question is being asked: How much data is too much?[12] There are just as many risks as benefits from the use of big data.[13]

Despite all we know about data breaches, they continue to happen.[14] Consider the possibility of a data breach from collected credit card numbers. According to a recent Ponemon Institute study, the cost of data breaches is constantly increasing, with the average global cost per record for 2012 at $136, up from $130 in 2011. The average number of breached records in 2012 was 23,647.[15] The best way to defend against data breaches is to not have the data in the first place.

3.1.4 Secure Transfer

Whenever data is transferred, it should be done in a secure manner that is proportionate with the sensitivity of the data. Using a high level of security such as encryption for all data transfers can place an unnecessary burden on organizations because it decreases the speed of data transfers and adds complexity to the management of data transfers.

For nonsensitive data, unencrypted transfer may be fine. For sensitive data being transported between different sites of the same company, encrypting the transmission link may be sufficient. Several mechanisms exist that permit the protection of data during transmission. When transmitting data over the Internet, secure sockets layer (SSL) and transport layer security (TLS) can be used to encrypt the data during transmission. Encrypted e-mail can also be used to protect data from point to point.

For more sensitive data, it may be necessary to encrypt the file where the data is stored. Files can be encrypted before transmission using native features such as those that come with Microsoft Office 13.[16] Files of all types can also be encrypted by readily available third-party encryption programs such as those from NCH Software.[17] Databases such as IBM Informix support encryption of data transmissions between databases.

3.1.5 Reliable Sources—Collection from Third Parties

One of the tenets of privacy is data quality. It is important that data collected by an organization be accurate before it is used. When collecting data from a third-party organization, it is crucial that the company be reputable. Even when the company is reputable, steps must be taken to ensure that the data is accurate. When an organization receives a hundred records for a hundred different people named John Smith, how is it to know which record belongs to which John Smith? Furthermore, how can a company ensure that the data is accurate? According to a recent study, over 40 million people in the United States have a mistake on their credit reports.[18]

To help ensure the accuracy of data received from third parties:

- Validate the company's data collection and verification practices.

- Insist that the organization be a member of the Better Business Bureau or similar organization.

- Ensure that all necessary fields in a user's record have been filled.

- Contact the user periodically and ask for a verification of his or her data.

- Provide access control and auditing of data to be able to track changes.

3.1.6 Collection of Information from Individuals Other Than the Data Subject

Organizations should be more cautious when collecting information from individuals rather than companies, whose reputation is easier to validate. An individual can easily provide inaccurate or malicious information that may place a company at risk if used. However, when the person providing the information is the data subject, there is less chance of inaccurate information being given causing a dispute. When building a business that relies on consumer information, one of the main goals is providing products and services that match the customer's interests and attributes. This is difficult to do if your customer data is inaccurate. One of the best ways to get it right is to validate the identity of the user. This can be done by temporarily capturing the user's credit card number for validation or using a third-party service.

3.2 Use

"Team," Amy said, "I've been performing a gap analysis with departments across the company to measure the difference between what our privacy notice says we do and our actual practices. I have to tell you that I found some alarming discrepancies. We need to make it clear that it is not okay to share data across the company unless our policies support that. In addition, there may be contractual obligations on the data that limit how we can use it."

"I could start locking down data sources until we get this ironed out," suggested Euan.

"No, that would be too drastic," replied Amy. "I don't want to disrupt our day-to-day operations. Bill, let's get together and make sure that our policies are up-to-date. Filo, I want you to look at creating some training around proper data handling. I'm going to call a meeting tomorrow of all our privacy managers later this week so we can start addressing the problems right away. We will go department by department until we get this problem addressed. I want all of you involved in this process as it covers every discipline and I need your expertise to make sure I am not missing anything."

Use is the processing or sharing of information for any purpose beyond simple storage and deletion. Even the processing of data for security or fraud purposes is a use. Any access of data by an individual who reads the data is performing a use, as the person could take an action on the data based on what is read.

While there are hard, fast rules that can come from an organization's privacy policies, other factors will drive how data is used in an organization as well. For example:

- **According to privacy policies.** An organization's practices must reflect the commitments made in its public privacy policies. In large organizations it is possible that many employees will not be aware of their own firm's privacy policies. And even when they are aware of the policies' restrictions, they may be tempted to ignore them to meet a pressing business need. Accordingly, an organization may change its notice to reflect a change in the policies.

- **According to regulations.** The limitation of data use is called out in Article 6 of the EU Data Protection Directive and has been incorporated into laws such as Principle 3 of the United Kingdom's Data Protection Act.[19] Sectoral regulations also place limits on how data may be used. For example, banking institutions in the EU are subject to the Third Basel Accord (Basel III) regulatory standard, while medical institutions in the United States are subject to the Health Insurance Portability and Accountability Act (HIPAA).[20]

- **According to commitments.** An organization's data usage policy should reflect contractual agreements made with the suppliers of the data. Contractual agreements must always be followed; thus it is important that groups within the organization are aware of them so they can abide by their usage obligations. Obligations must follow data as it moves to different teams in an organization. Care must be taken to determine when one set of data has records that fall under different agreements. Even though the data may be the same, it may have been collected from different organizations and have distinct obligations.

- **Too many data elements.** The *data minimization principle* described by the European Data Protection Supervisor applies to the use of data as well as collection. An evaluation of the actual data use should be made to ensure that all collected data is indeed used by the organization. The collection points should then be updated to reflect the results of the evaluation. Keeping excess data or expanding its use could result in unnecessary compliance obligations for an organization. For example, keeping financial data unnecessarily could make a company responsible for Basel III, PCI or GLBA compliance.

- **Outdated data elements.** Data elements should occasionally be eliminated to keep them current and relevant. Over time data elements can become outdated or unneeded. A person's license plate, credit card and passport are things that expire over time. Interests change as a person progresses through high school, college, marriage, parenthood and retirement. Addresses, phone numbers and names can change over the course of a person's life. It's expected that the person's record within an organization will be updated to reflect those changes. When updated values are not known, they should be removed to avoid using inaccurate data. Applying a retention policy to data can help automate these types of policies.

- **Internal sharing.** Even after collection an effort should be made to limit the use of data by an organization's internal teams to those elements needed to fulfill a specific business purpose. For example, a consumer may fill out a form to purchase a product online. The contents of the form in its entirety will probably be stored in a database for processing. When it comes time to ship the product, the shipping department should get only the name and address of the recipient and not the entire database record, which may have additional information (such as a credit card number) that is not needed for shipping. When sharing customer data across an organization, it is important that each team using the data understand the obligations surrounding its use. For example, some data may be restricted from use for advertising based on a contractual obligation, or a customer who signed up for product news from Product A may not want to receive information on Product B.

3.2.1 Secondary Uses

Data is usually collected from individuals to fulfill a primary purpose that is typically expressed in the privacy notice or terms of use. To use data for a purpose other than the primary use generally requires prominent notice and explicit consent. Be certain that usage data collected by your organization is restricted to the primary purpose. For example, data collected to improve your company's blog cannot be used to improve the mail service or research unless explicit consent is given by the user. Secondary usage can sometimes mean use by a third party. In some jurisdictions, any secondary usage of collected data must be accompanied by explicit consent from the user.

3.2.2 User Authentication

Authentication is the validation that a person has been provided with access to a resource such as a network, computer or application. Resources containing sensitive data can be protected by an authentication mechanism that requires an ID and password to access the data. One ID can be assigned per user for identification purposes, and a strong password can be mandated to reduce the risk of account hijackers. The use of multifactor authentication can also reduce the risk of undesired access to resources.

3.2.3 Access Control

Access controls are a great way to restrict access to sensitive data. Each organizational privacy policy should have a section on security. That section should reflect the security practices in place to protect sensitive data. While the idea of a browser log may sound innocuous, it can contain embarrassing or private information depending on the sites a user has visited. From a web address, one can infer someone's medical condition. For example, if the user is visiting a cancer research site, one could infer that the person has cancer. Similarly, if the user visits a payday loan site, one could deduce that the person is having financial difficulties.

Using access controls to restrict access to server logs or other potentially sensitive data is prudent. It will help to limit liability, reduce risk of data breaches and preserve the privacy of the organization's customers. Access to all resources in an organization should be treated with a right-to-know policy. Having a default policy of giving everyone access to a resource is a bad practice.

3.2.4 Audit Trails

Audit trails can be applied to resources to monitor accesses to the resource by company personnel. Auditing is a useful tool when there is concern that employees may be inappropriately accessing sensitive data. Audit logs can be used during privacy reviews and compliance audits to validate that internal policies and compliance controls have been followed.

3.2.5 Restricting Use with Digital Rights Management

The preceding mechanisms can limit access to content, but not necessarily how it is used. Digital rights management (DRM) is a technology used to limit the distribution of digital content to those with a legitimate right to it. It can also limit what assigned users can do with the content. For example, a person may be permitted to read a document, but not allowed to print it, e-mail it to others, copy content from it or modify it. Organizational DRM should be treated separately from the DRM used to protect music. The former helps to restrict access to and usage of sensitive data under the organization's control.

3.2.6 Securing Hard Copies

Securing hard copies of content can be difficult because of the ease with which they can be copied, photographed and just carried away. Proper policies and training are important first steps to encourage proper document use. Marking documents with their usage and copy limitations is also a good practice, but does not enforce proper usage. Sensitive documents should be locked up when not in use and destroyed once they expire. When it is important that the use of documents be restricted, they can be stored in a locked room where their access and use are monitored by security personnel.

3.2.7 Using Personally Identifiable Information in Testing

Companies that collect personally identifiable information (PII) generally have applications that process it. Membership applications, product purchases and room reservations all require that individuals provide PII. The many applications used to collect the data in such scenarios need to be tested using realistic data. Many companies will be tempted to run tests using real data. However, that greatly increases the possibility of a data breach or misuse of information.

As a general rule testers and developers should not have access to PII. PII should only be accessible by employees who have a legitimate reason to process the information. When there is a need to test an application that uses PII, several steps can be taken to minimize risk to the real data.

1. A program can be developed that takes the raw PII data, anonymizes it and creates a test dataset from it. Dummy data should be used to test the anonymization program. The difficulty with this approach is ensuring that a good enough job is done anonymizing the data while maintaining its utility.

2. A program can be created that generates random data similar to the real data. The downside of this approach is that it's hard to simulate all the possibilities that might arise from the real data entered by a human being.

3. Use one of the free data generation programs available on the Internet.[21] While this approach can save time and money over the other ones, these programs are limited in the type of data they can generate.

4. When real data is needed to perform tests, they should be done on a limited basis, the data should be protected during use and the data should be deleted as soon as possible, including backups.

3.2.8 Limitations on Use When Sources of Data Are Unclear

Usage of data should always align with an organization's policies as well as its contractual obligations. Data held by the organization should always be linked to such obligations.

When such a link does not exist, the data should not be used, so as to avoid the risk of misuse or liability to the company. If the data is aggregated or anonymized, it may be used as long as there are no policies against it.

3.3 Disclosure

"Carrie, this is Amy. A quick call to let you know that the marketing team has been sharing our customer lists with marketers without a contract. I don't care if it has been working well for years, we need verifiable assurances that they are following our policies around use, onward transfer and retention. Could you see to it that they have the right contracts in place? This may mean that we will have to have them destroy any data they received from us and start over, but it's better to be prudent than litigated."

"I am completely in agreement with you there. I'll get right on it and send you an update by end of day on Wednesday."

Disclosure is typically viewed as the sharing of information external to an organization collecting it. This is also known as **onward transfer**. It's rare for organizations to collect data and not put it to practical use. The act of putting the data to use has to involve sharing at some level. Otherwise, the data would remain on the collection servers unused. Disclosure can happen internally across groups or externally with service providers, clients, partners, law enforcement or consumers.

Only data needed for legitimate, identified business practices should be collected. Likewise, only data needed by the recipient should be disclosed. Where possible, data should be anonymized before disclosure. Organizations sometimes have a habit of sending all data in a dataset or giving groups access to an entire database or table when only a subset of the data is needed. Creating a data flow diagram of the data being transferred between groups will make it easier to identify the information that is needed and limit the transfer of excessive data. Data described in the data flow diagram should tie into the company's data inventory. That is, data should not be transferred throughout the organization if the data is not yet documented in an inventory.

3.3.1 Internal Disclosure

Internal disclosure of data should be documented by a data flow diagram. The metadata associated with the diagram should point to the privacy policies of the groups sharing and receiving the data. The groups receiving the data should not share it with others unless prior arrangements were made. Instead, requests for data should be passed on to the original collectors of the data.

3.3.2 External Disclosure

Each act of external disclosure should be covered by a contract that expresses the limits of processing the data and the retention and destruction policy for the data. The terms of the contract should reflect any commitments made around third-party or first-party sharing in regard to service providers who are working on behalf of the organization collecting the data. The contracts should also comply with any privacy notices. When validating contracts it is important to note not only the type of data being disclosed but also the group within the organization disclosing the data. Even if the same data is being shared with the same external party, the commitment made about the processing of the data at the time it was collected may be different.

Each external data flow should be documented on a data flow diagram that points to the contract as well as other descriptive information about the data flow, such as a data inventory. Each company's data-handling practices should be reviewed to ensure that they align with the organization's policies.

3.3.3 According to Legal Obligations

Organizations should be clear about their obligations to disclose information to law enforcement authorities or government officials. Where possible, any requests for data should be made public.

3.3.4 According to Notice

Any data disclosure by an organization should be described in its privacy notice, even if that disclosure is only expected to happen between internal groups. An organization should not be disclosing data to entities unless it is stated in its privacy notice. This type of transparency is often overlooked by organizations and is the source of angst for privacy advocates. Where possible and practical, organizations should provide information in their privacy notice about who will have access to their data. This is an important means of building trust.

3.3.5 Minimization and Anonymization, Aggregation

The *data minimization principle* applies to the disclosure of information and can be more critical for disclosure than for other principles, as once data leaves the control of an organization there is no way to know with certainty what will happen to it. For that reason it is always important to have a contract that covers any disclosure of data to a third party. The size of the dataset should not dictate what data is disclosed to a third party. The data disclosed should always be limited to the data legitimately needed by the third party.

Disclosure of data to third parties is more acceptable when it can be done in a way that does not reveal any information about the data subject. Two ways to safely disclose data to third parties in a manner that protects the data owner's identity are to anonymize the data beforehand or to share the data only as an aggregate of the entire dataset. Neither of these methods is foolproof, so care must be taken when using either one.

3.3.6 Define Use and Limitations

Privacy policies should express the limitations of use for data that is collected, understanding that contractual agreements may override internal policies. When the internal disclosure of data is found to be necessary, an organization should ensure that the teams receiving the data understand the limitations of it use, from either policies or contractual agreements. When data is disclosed to third parties, a contract should be in place that describes how the data can be used by the third party and its limitations in onward transfer.

3.3.7 Vendor Management Programs

To formalize relationships with vendors, organizations should create a program that outlines the engagement model for vendors. The plans for the disclosure of data to vendors must be thoroughly reviewed as this disclosure does not relieve the organization of any responsibility from commitments it made in its privacy notice or in contracts with external providers of data. The organization can still be liable for mistreatment of the data by the vendor.

Before engaging vendors for sharing of information, organizations must perform an inventory to be certain of what data will be sent. The organization must also decide how it will transfer the data; a secure means should be used to transfer data to vendors. Alternatively, an organization could provide a vendor with remote access to the data. In such a case a secure connection should be used to access data.

No matter what means is used to provide the vendor with access to the data, the vendor and its data protection capabilities should be reviewed before engaging the vendor. The organization must review the vendor's data access, storage and handling practices to ensure that they are aligned with its practices.

3.3.8 Using Intermediaries for the Processing of Sensitive Information

Often, an organization will not have the capabilities to perform the necessary processing of the data. In those cases an intermediary can be used. The arrangement with the intermediary must be covered by a contract. The intermediary must have a clear understanding that it must apply the same usage and security policies as the organization with regard to the treatment of the data. Furthermore, the intermediary must never use the data for its own purposes. The rules that apply to vendors must be applied to intermediaries as well.

3.4 Retention

Retention refers to the persistence of data by an organization after its collection. All organizations should have policies that govern the retention of data to comply with regulatory requirements, reduce the risks that come from holding too much data for too long and show their trustworthiness. All data that is stored by a company should be assigned a minimum and maximum retention period. The remainder of this section looks at specific aspects of data retention.

3.4.1 Working with Records Management

Records management has to do with all aspects of managing records, from creation to final disposition. Records can include database records, e-mails, server logs, documents, periodicals, media, contents of files and the files themselves.[22] Records coming from individuals might be job applications, resumes, sales receipts or complaints. Records coming from external organizations could be contracts, nondisclosure agreements or purchase orders. Records can of course be generated by any number of employees in an organization.

Proper handling of records is important to managing risk in an organization. The handling of records will change depending on the type of record and the phase of the lifecycle it is in. Enabling audit trails throughout the lifecycle will help to ensure that record management policies are being followed. The lifecycle of a record should include the following phases:

- **Receipt or creation.** This is the point at which a record comes into existence within an organization. The first steps that must be taken are to identify the record and determine if it should even remain in the organization. Remember, the more records that exist within an organization, the greater the risk for an incident to occur. If a record appears in the organization that shouldn't be there, it should be returned immediately to the sender or destroyed.

- **Storage.** Once a record has been identified as something that should be kept, it should be classified and put away for safekeeping depending on its classification. A record's classification should be based on its type, contents and sensitivity. The classification can also help to determine the appropriate access rules and retention policy. Once classified, the record must be stored in a way that makes it easy to retrieve when needed and eventually disposed of. Using metadata attached to records can help to automate the different records management phases.

- **Usage.** During its lifetime a record may be accessed many times. Great care must be taken to ensure that records are accessed only by the proper personnel or customers and that they are processed in accordance with organizational policies. If copies are made of the records, they need to be tracked to ensure that the records management policies are being followed.

- **Maintenance.** Records may need to be updated over their lifetime. Think about tax rates, product pricing, address changes or updates to policies. Whenever changes occur to records, their versions need to be managed and copies of the records must be found and updated as needed. Periodically, maintenance means the culling of expired records.

- **Disposition.** Once records have reached the end of their useful life they must be disposed of. A record could be disposed of by deletion, destruction, recycling, selling, rights management expiration or returning it to the original owner.

3.4.2 Regulatory Limitations on Retention

Limiting the retention of sensitive data is a good practice to help minimize organizational liability. Managing retention periods is also a regulatory requirement in many jurisdictions. For example, Clause 4.5 of the Personal Information Protection and Electronic Documents Act (PIPEDA) requires organizations to develop guidelines for minimum and maximum retention periods.[23] Section V.B.1 of the FTC privacy report, "Protecting Consumer Privacy in an Era of Rapid Change: A Proposed Framework for Businesses and Policymakers," requests that organizations develop sound retention practices.[24]

3.4.3 Provide Data Subject Access

When an organization collects personal data on individuals, it has an obligation to provide them with access to their data. The Greater Transparency principle of the FTC's privacy framework asks that companies provide reasonable access to the consumer data they maintain. Section 3.4.3 of the proposed changes to the e-Privacy Directive will require that organizations give data subjects greater access to the data an organization has on them.[25]

Providing access to personal data should not be viewed simply as a regulatory requirement, but as a way to build trust. People feel more comfortable when they can gain access to their data. Facebook and Google, which have received complaints about holding a lot of data on users, both provide a way for their users to download their data from the services.

Providing an online means for users to access their data is the best approach. The ability to access one's data should include the ability to export or download it. In cases where providing online access is not possible, there should be a mechanism for users to have their data sent to them in electronic or printed form. These types of requests should be possible via an organization's privacy incident site or customer support service.

When processing requests, great care should be taken to validate the requestor of the data. Users often provide data to websites in an active or passive fashion that does not uniquely identify them. If a user has not signed in to a service, then an IP address or cookie is probably the only way to identify that visitor. However, multiple people sharing the same computer could be identified by those same mechanisms. Requiring an account ID and password to access user data and only data that was created while the user was signed in is the only safe way to handle data access requests. When requests are made by phone or e-mail, proper identification procedures that have requestors validate their account information must be followed to ensure that sensitive data is not released to the wrong person.

3.4.4 Secure Transfer to Archiving, Secure Storage of Information and Metadata

Retention requirements often mandate that data be kept for long periods. Instead of keeping the data online where it can take up valuable network resources, data can be stored offline. This can be challenging when storing sensitive data. While data can be protected in many ways on network resources, storing the data offline, maybe even at a third-party storage facility, can be risky. To support adequate disaster recovery and business continuity practices, it is more prudent to store important organizational data off premises to protect against a building being destroyed or a persistent power outage. The following are ways to protect the data:

- **Network encryption.** Even though data may be encrypted while resting in a database or on a hard drive, it may be unencrypted during transmission. To reduce the risk of the data being intercepted on its way to the backup device, the network carrying the data should be encrypted.

- **Storage encryption.** Offline storage such as tapes and DVDs don't have integrated access control systems or support native encryption. Some flash drives offer encryption, but their small size and poor write endurance make them a poor choice for long-term, offline storage.[26] Encrypting the data itself is the best way to protect it offline. Decryption keys should be stored separately to prevent local recovery and support retrieval in case the original backup system becomes unusable.

- **Using metadata.** Metadata can assist with the retrieval of data from offline storage, especially when the data is encrypted. Metadata can be used to determine the type of data being stored on backup media without exposing the contents of the data. For example, the metadata could provide categorization information, sensitivity level or even the index to the encryption keys used to encrypt the contents of the backup.

3.4.5 Considerations for Business Continuity and Disaster Recovery

Retention management can play a big role in a business' continuity plan. Retention is often viewed as the maximum length of time data must be kept within an organization. Retention policies should also cover the minimum amount of time data should be maintained in order to support disaster recovery contingencies. Lost data can ruin even the most successful companies. Consider what would happen if Coca-Cola lost its formula for Coke, Toyota lost the blueprints for its new car models or Facebook lost all of its member account data. Losing purchase orders, contracts, product designs or customer contact lists could all have a devastating effect on an organization.

Business continuity and disaster recovery are iterative processes that must be continually reviewed. The process starts with an assessment of business risks. A plan should be put in place to mitigate the risks. Execute the plan, test the plan, fix gaps and then start again with a new assessment. Part of the planning should include identification of business-sensitive data that must be retained to support a disaster recovery scenario. The International Organization for Standardization created standard ISO 22313:2012 to provide guidelines on business continuity planning.[27]

3.4.6 Portable Media Challenges

The days of floppy disks, CDs and DVDs are all but a faded memory. Still, portable media can take many forms, though laptops, mobile devices, flash drives and USB drives are the most common. Though these types of devices can provide great flexibility as well as data protection via encryption, they share a common flaw—lack of accountability. Retention rules that may apply to content residing on an external drive cannot be enforced if the drive is not attached to the organization's network. The only real mitigation to this risk is disabling USB ports. However, creating strong policies and training employees about the risks of using portable media may be more practical.

3.4.7 Persistent and Transient Storage

Persistent storage is where most content is placed, such as on a hard drive. Persistent storage can also be devices such as tapes, DVDs or flash drives. When retention management plans are created, they usually target data in persistent storage, though transient storage may also have data worth saving. Retention policies must apply to persistent storage to the extent that it may be necessary to overwrite or destroy the media to ensure the destruction of the data.

Transient storage is used for storing data that has a short lifespan. Think of session cookies that are stored in a browser. As soon as the browser is closed, the session cookies, along with their contents, are purged from the system. Other types of transient storage include paging files in an operating system, temporary database tables created to perform transactions, the clipboard storage or the shopping cart on a website that sells goods or services. In the same manner that some websites save shopping cart data even after a user has left the website, organizations may want to protect transient storage in order to recover their data in case of a malfunction. There may also be cases where it would be prudent to delete transient storage to avoid access to the contents outside the user's control. Ways to protect transient data include storing online session data to preserve partial purchases that may have been abandoned, enabling auto-save for documents and enabling journal files for databases.

3.5 Destruction

"If no one has any other status updates for the privacy council, I would like to bring up one last issue," stated Amy. "We seem to have great retention policies in place, but we lack the follow-through when it comes to getting rid of data that has reached its expiration period. Most of our practices consist of manual procedures. With the workloads everyone has to deal with, it's not surprising that deleting old records gets pushed to the bottom of most people's priority lists. Does anyone have any suggestions on how we can tackle this?"

"I could ask some of our developers if they could create some scripts that would periodically look for expired records or files and delete them," offered David. "It may take a while to get the work scheduled, but I'm sure we could get it done."

"I could have our backup team rotate tapes back through the system on a regular schedule to help ensure that backup data is eventually purged," stated Euan.

"Great ideas," replied Amy. "Please look into those possibilities, and the rest of you, let me know if you come up with anything. We are done here for now. Enjoy the rest of your day."

At the end of its lifecycle, data should be destroyed. Destruction can be designated by a retention period applied to a data record's creation date, a request from a user or the completion of a transaction. Destruction can result in the deletion of files, clearing of records from a database or removal of data from a file such as a spreadsheet. A destruction plan should be applied to an organization's record management plan to ensure the proper removal of data. Simply stating that the data should be destroyed is not always sufficient. There should be clear guidelines on how to destroy the data based on its type.

To aid in the destruction of expired files, a custom attribute such as Retention Period can be added to the Properties dialog of the files, as shown in Figure 3-3 using Microsoft Windows 8.0. Once the custom attribute has been added, it is easier to retrieve the file to determine when it needs to be destroyed. It is also possible to create a program that runs periodically, reads the Retention Period value from the file and deletes it once the retention period has passed. One of the standard attributes under the Properties dialog Details tab can be used to flag files that need special operations performed on them.

Figure 3-3: Properties Dialog Box with Custom Attribute as Shown in Windows 8.0

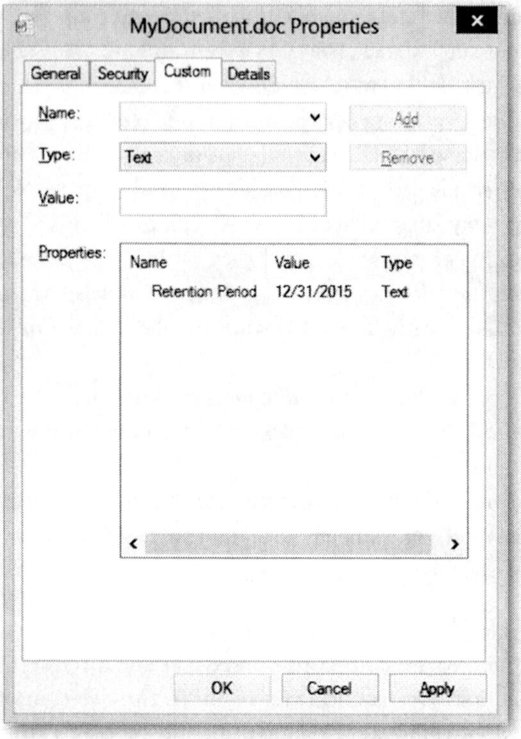

Used with permission from Microsoft.

3.5.1 Digital Content

The destruction of most digital content is simply a matter of deleting the data or the files containing the data. Care must be taken when deleting data from an entire disk or tape and handing it off to a third party. Using standard operating system commands to delete files typically deletes only the header information and leaves the contents of the files intact. Formatting the entire disk is the best way to ensure the data is removed from the disk. Proper formatting is important because using the standard formatting will clear only the headers from each file and once again leave the data intact on the disk.

The Format command exists within the Windows operating system. Using the Format command's /P:count flag will zero the entire disk and then write a random number to the disk "count" times. There are also several free applications that provide various levels of disk-clearing capabilities.[28] However, degaussing is the best way to remove data from hard drives, tapes and rewritable CDs and DVDs. IT departments can purchase their own equipment or rely on a company that specializes in the destruction of magnetic media.[29]

Digital rights management (DRM) is another method of removing access to digital content through programmatic means, by setting an expiration period in the content's DRM attributes. When the expiration period passes, the file will still exist, but it will be inaccessible due to encryption. Several companies provide DRM capabilities for digital content.[30]

3.5.2 Portable Media

When a portable medium, such as a flash drive, is used to store data, it is difficult to enforce deletion policies on it. When a device is not connected to the organization's network, running deletion routines against the data or performing a manual deletion is impossible. Proper training and reminders are the best way to keep employees aware of the need to delete expired data from portable media.

WORM (write once read many) media such as ROMs, CDs and DVDs require special treatment as the data on them cannot be erased.[31] Those types of storage media have to be destroyed to get rid of their data. Most organizations are not equipped to properly destroy WORM media. An industrial shredder or sander can be used to destroy this type of media.[32] However, it can be more efficient and less risky to personnel to leave the destruction of this type of media in the hands of professionals.[33]

3.5.3 Printers, Copiers and Fax Machines

Many printers, copiers and fax machines contain hard drives that are used to store a copy of the printed material that is presented to them. This can be a source of risks when the machines are returned after their rental period or otherwise disposed of. Before the machines are removed, the hard drives should be wiped clean or destroyed. Some manufacturers of these devices automatically scrub the hard drives after use, encrypt data while it is on the drive or provide features that permit the administrators of the machines to remove any data that may be stored on their drives.

3.5.4 Hard Copy

Destroying paper documents in an organization is an extremely difficult task, not because of the process, but because of the difficulty in determining which documents need to be destroyed. Paper documents rarely have a deletion date as they are typically printouts from files that do not have embedded deletion dates. Many documents are assigned a data classification that can help determine a destruction date as long as employees are properly trained in what the data classifications mean and how they apply to retention policies.

It is a best practice to place a destruction date on the paper. If the paper was printed from a file that does not have a destruction date, then the document should be destroyed once it is no longer needed and use the digital copy for future needs. For many companies it may be more efficient to hire a document destruction company to destroy expired documents.

3.5.5 Identify Appropriate Time to Avoid Early or Late Deletion

Prematurely deleting data can be just as damaging to an organization as keeping data too long. A needed contract, unfulfilled purchase orders or contact information for an important client could be inadvertently deleted when they are still necessary. An organization's lawyers may also place documents on legal hold, requiring that documents not be deleted until the legal requirement is dropped and the hold is lifted. There must be a way to comply with those requests. During retention planning, a risk analysis should be performed to determine the type of retention to apply to all data. Where practical, all organizational data should be assigned a minimum and maximum retention period.

3.5.6 Secure Transfer of Data for Deletion

Data to be deleted must be protected using standard security measures. Sensitive data should be encrypted during all transfers and during storage before deletion. Data being held by third parties and intermediaries that has reached its expiration date should be destroyed by them or returned for destruction. Copies of the content should not be retained. When data is being returned, it should be protected as well, depending on the sensitivity of the data.

3.5.7 Regulatory Requirements

Deletion of data is not just for minimizing organizational risk, it is also a regulatory requirement in several jurisdictions. The following regulations address the need for proper data destruction:

- Australia: Privacy Act of 1988

- European Union: EU Data Protection Directive

- India: The Information Technology Rules of 2011

- South Korea: 2011 Act on the Protection of Personal Data

- United States: Fair Credit Reporting Act

3.5.8 Secure Data Destruction Methods

When data is deleted, it should be done in a way that is assured of removing all the data from the media. There are several global data sanitation methods that can be used to delete data:

- Canada: CSEC ITSG-06[34]

- Australia: ISM 6.2.92[35]

- New Zealand: NZISM[36]

- Germany: VSITR[37]

- United States: DoD 5220.22-M[38]

3.6 Conclusion

> "It's been a few months since we completed the rollout of our information lifecycle program and I have to say, I'm pretty impressed," stated Amy. "We're not finished yet, but we have come a long way from where we were, and our scorecard has only a few yellow and one red indicator left on it. We just need to keep iterating through the teams to make sure they eventually become compliant. The biggest success here is that we now have a plan in place and we are executing it on all cylinders. The next big hurdle we need to get over is identity management and data protection. For now, let's celebrate our successes."

Developing and executing an information lifecycle program helps organizations ensure that they are collecting the right data, providing proper transparency for the collection, processing it properly and destroying the data once there are no longer business needs for it. Having an information lifecycle program in place is important for minimizing risk to organizations and the data subjects to which the data belongs.

Endnotes

1 Yahoo UK, https://uk.yahoo.com.

2 For guidance on creating layered notices see Travis Pinnick, "Layered Policy Design," TRUSTe Blog, May 20, 2011, www.truste.com/blog/2011/05/20/layered-policy-and-short-notice-design/; "Ten steps to develop a multilayered privacy notice," Center for Information Policy Leadership, Hunton & Williams LLP, March 2007, www.hunton.com/files/tbl_s47Details/FileUpload265/1405/Ten_Steps_whitepaper.pdf.

3 Patrick Gage Kelley, Lucian Cesca, Joanna Bresee and Lorrie Faith Cranor, "Standardizing Privacy Notices: An Online Study of the Nutrition Label Approach," Carnegie Mellon University, January 12, 2010, www.cylab.cmu.edu/files/pdfs/tech_reports/CMUCyLab09014.pdf.

4 Fred Cate, "Looking Beyond Notice and Choice," Privacy and Security Law Report, 9 PVLR 476 (March 29, 2010), www.hunton.com/files/Publication/f69663d7-4348-4dac-b448-3b6c4687345e/Presentation/PublicationAttachment/dfdad615-e631-49c6-9499-ead6c2ada0c5/Looking_Beyond_Notice_and_Choice_3.10.pdf.

5 "Complexity is the worst enemy of security," Gemalto (blog), April 5, 2013, http://blog.gemalto.com/enterprise/2013/04/05/complexity-is-the-worst-enemy-of-security/.

6 Alina Tugend, "Too Many Choices: A Problem That Can Paralyze," New York Times, February 26, 2010, www.nytimes.com/2010/02/27/your-money/27shortcuts.html?_r=0.

7 www.merriam-webster.com/dictionary/control.

8 As this content shows, consumers have the choice to enable Do Not Track, but no control over a website's collection of their data. Michelle De Mooey and Linda Sherry, "Consumers to online advertisers: No tracking for ANY reason," Consumer Action, June 18, 2013, www.consumer-action.org/press/articles/no_tracking_for_any_reason; Chris J. Hoofnagle, Jennifer M. Urban and Su Li, "Privacy and Modern Advertising: Most U.S. Internet Users Want 'Do Not Track' to Stop Collection of Data about their Online Activities," in Proceedings of the Amsterdam Privacy Conference (Amsterdam, October 8, 2012), http://ssrn.com/abstract=2152135.

9 Nicole Kobie, "Cookie Consent Banners Draw Complaints," *PC Pro*, December 18, 2012, www.pcpro.co.uk/news/378760/cookie-consent-banners-draw-complaints.

10 European Data Protection Supervisor, https://secure.edps.europa.eu/EDPSWEB/edps/site/mySite/pid/74.

11 For examples of the benefits that big data can bring, see David Kuketz, "7 Biggest Business Benefits from Big Data," *Utopia*, October 23, 2012, www.utopiainc.com/insights/blog/381-7-biggest-business-benefits-from-big-data; Celina Durgin, "Politicians Uncovering Big Benefits in 'Big Data,'" *Washington Times*, July 7, 2013, www.washingtontimes.com/news/2013/jul/7/politicians-uncovering-big-benefits-in-big-data/?page=all; Cas Purdy, "Infographic: Finding Big Benefits in Big Data," *Trusted News*, July 2, 2013, https://www.trustwave.com/trustednews/2013/07/infographic-finding-big-benefits-big-data/.

12 Harriet Swain, "Are universities collecting too much information on staff and students?," *The Guardian*, August 5, 2013, www.theguardian.com/education/2013/aug/05/electronic-data-trail-huddersfield-loughborough-university; "Their view: Is government collecting too much data?," *Las Cruces Sun-News*, July 30, 2013, www.scsun-news.com/silver_city-opinion/ci_23762828; Heather Clancy, "Does Your Business Collect Too Much Data?," *Business Brains* (blog), *Smart Planet*, February 20, 2012, www.smartplanet.com/blog/business-brains/does-your-business-collect-too-much-data/22109; Renee Boucher Ferguson, "How Much Data is Too Much Data To Mine?," *MIT Sloan Management Review*, June 8, 2012, http://sloanreview.mit.edu/article/how-much-data-is-too-much-data-to-mine/.

13 Martha C. White, "Big Data Knows What You're Doing Right Now," *Time*, Business and Money, July 31, 2012, http://business.time.com/2012/07/31/big-data-knows-what-youre-doing-right-now/; Pam Baker, "Security dangers in big data mining," Fierce Big Data, July 5, 2013, www.fiercebigdata.com/story/security-dangers-big-data-mining/2013-07-05; Andre Oboler, Kristopher Welsh and Lito Cruz, "The Danger of Big Data: Social Media as Computational Social Science," *First Monday* 17 no. 7 (July 2, 2012) http://firstmonday.org/ojs/index.php/fm/article/view/3993/3269; Margaret Heffernan, "Big Data, Big Risk," Money Watch, CBS News, July 18, 2013, www.cbsnews.com/8301-505125_162-57593647/big-data-big-risk/.

14 Samantha Murphy Kelly, "The World's Biggest Data Breaches in One Stunning Visualization," Mashable, July 22, 2013, http://mashable.com/2013/07/22/data-breach-visualization/.

15 "2013 Cost of Data Breach Study: Global Analysis," Ponemon Institute Research Report, May 2013, http://www.symantec.com/content/en/us/about/media/pdfs/b-cost-of-a-data-breach-global-report-2013.en-us.pdf?om_ext_cid=biz_socmed_twitter_facebook_marketwire_linkedin_2013Jun_worldwide_CostofaDataBreach.

16 "Plan cryptography and encryption settings for Office 2013," Microsoft, February 19, 2013, http://technet.microsoft.com/en-us/library/cc179125.aspx.

17 "MEO File Encryption Software," NCH Software, accessed September 17, 2013, www.nchsoftware.com/encrypt/index.html.

18 View a special on how many Americans have inaccurate credit reports, and the difficulty in fixing them. "40 Million Mistakes," *60 Minutes*, aired February 10, 2013, www.cbsnews.com/8301-18560_162-57599767/40-million-mistakes-is-your-credit-report-accurate/.

19 Article 6 of the Directive 95/46/EC of the European Parliament calls for a limitation in processing of data to those "specified, explicit and legitimate." Council Directive 95/46/EC, 1995 O.J. L 281 p. 31 art. 6, http://eur-lex.europa.eu/LexUriServ/LexUriServ.do?uri=CELEX:31995L0046:en:HTML. The Data Protection Act's second principle, on processing personal data for specified purposes, states, "Personal data shall be obtained only for one or more specified and lawful purposes, and shall not be further processed in any manner incompatible with that purpose or those purposes." "Processing personal data for specified purposes (Principle 2)," Information Commissioners Office of the United Kingdom, www.ico.org.uk/for_organisations/data_protection/the_guide/principle_2.

20 "Basel II: A global regulatory framework for more resilient banks and banking systems," Basel
    Committee on Banking Supervision, Bank for International Settlements, 2010, www.bis.org/publ/
    bcbs189.pdf; "Health Information Privacy," U.S. Department of Health & Human Services, accessed
    September 17, 2013, www.hhs.gov/ocr/privacy/index.html.

21 For examples of sites that can be used to generate test data, see www.generatedata.com and
    www.databasetestdata.com.

22 ISO 15489-1:2001 provides guidance on developing a records management system. "Information
    and documentation—Records management—Part 1: General," International Organization for
    Standardization, July 13, 2013, www.iso.org/iso/catalogue_detail?csnumber=31908.

23 Personal Information Protection and Electronic Documents Act (PIPEDA), S.C. 2000, c. 5, http://
    laws-lois.justice.gc.ca/eng/acts/P-8.6/index.html.

24 "Protecting Consumer Privacy in an Era of Rapid Change: A Proposed Framework for Business and
    Policymakers," Preliminary Staff Report of the Federal Trade Commission, December 2010, www
    .ftc.gov/os/2010/12/101201privacyreport.pdf.

25 "Proposal for a Regulation of the European Parliament and of the Council, on the Protection of
    Individuals with Regard to the Processing of Personal Data and on the Free Movement of Such
    Data," COM(2012) 11 final, January 25, 2012, http://ec.europa.eu/justice/data-protection/
    document/review2012/com_2012_11_en.pdf.

26 Alex Cocilova, "How to stretch the life of your SSD storage," *PCWorld*, July 17, 2013, www
    .pcworld.com/article/2043634/how-to-stretch-the-life-of-your-ssd-storage.html; Zsolt Kerekes,
    "SSD endurance—the forever war," StorageSearch.com, Applied Computer Science, Ltd., www
    .storagesearch.com/ssdmyths-endurance.html.

27 "Societal security -- Business continuity management systems -- Guidance," International
    Organization for Standardization, December 12, 2012, ISO 22313:2012, www.iso.org/iso/
    catalogue_detail?csnumber=50050.

28 For various types of disk-clearing utilities, see Tim Fisher, "30 Free Data Destruction Software
    Programs," About.com PC Support, updated February 2014, http://pcsupport.about.com/od/
    toolsofthetrade/tp/free-data-destruction-software.htm.

29 Security Engineered Machinery sells degaussers that are listed by the NSA. Security Engineered
    Machinery, www.semshred.com/magnetic_media_degaussers.

30 FileOpen Systems is a company that provides DRM solutions for multiple document formats and
    operating systems. www.fileopen.com/products/rightsmanager/.

31 Write Once Read Many (WORM) devices cannot be erased using normal delete or format
    commands. Definition: WORM, TechTarget, http://searchstorage.techtarget.com/definition/
    WORM-write-once-read-many.

32 Clary Business Machines makes NSA-approved industrial shredders. http://kobra-shredder.com/
    industrial-shredders/kobra-cyclone-shredder.html.

33 Iron Mountain is a well-known content retention and destruction company. http://www
    .ironmountain.com/Knowledge-Center/Reference-Library/View-by-Document-Type/Data-Sheets
    -Brochures/S/Secure-Media-Destruction.aspx.

34 "Clearing and Declassifying Electronic Data Storage Devices—ITSG-06," Government of Canada,
    Communications Security Establishment Canada, July 2006, www.cse-cst.gc.ca/its-sti/publications/
    itsg-csti/itsg06-eng.html.

35 "ISM—Information Security Manual," Australian Government, Department of Defense, accessed
    February 26, 2014, www.asd.gov.au/infosec/ism/index.htm.

36 "New Zealand Information Security Manual," Government Communications Security Bureau,
    December 2010, www.docstoc.com/docs/22660481/NZ-ICT-Security-Manual.

37 "Germany BSI Verschlussachen-IT Richtinien (VSITR) Standard," Secure Data Sanitization, http://securedatasanitization.com/news/?p=18.

38 "National Industrial Security Program Operating Manual," Department of Defense, February 28, 2006, www.dss.mil/documents/odaa/nispom2006-5220.pdf.

CHAPTER 4

Privacy in Systems and Applications

4.1 The Enterprise IT Environment

"Amy, we need to do a restart," Bill exclaimed. "Over the past couple of years, technology has been advancing at a rapid pace, and we've been responding to those changes piecemeal. That has been making my job to manage compliance a nightmare. The decision to let people use their personal devices at work before we even had policies in place to govern their use was a mistake. We should take a step back and look at how we re-architect our IT environment."

"Bill, you have a point," replied Amy. "I've been spending so much time dealing with privacy and security fires that I haven't had a chance to respond to your previous requests. Let's hire a consultant who is up on the latest technologies, IT architecture and compliance challenges. I want us to have a modernized IT department while minimizing any risks that may come from rapid changes. I'll let you lead the effort; just include the rest of the staff and department heads to ensure we are addressing everyone's needs."

Enterprises are thought of as large companies with many employees. The breadth of an enterprise can be vast, covering many geographical locations. Within an enterprise there can be many types of computer systems, personal devices, network devices, applications and access control systems, each with its own specific privacy challenges. Figure 4-1 gives an example of what an IT environment might look like.

What is missing from the diagram is the abundance of interfaces between the plethora of entities within an enterprise. BYOD (bring your own device) refers to the personal devices that an employee might bring to work and use to connect to the organizational network. IT professionals should be aware of each of the human, machine and software interfaces within their environment. Each of the interfaces represents an opportunity for sensitive data to escape or be accessed by the wrong person. Policies should be in place to cover the storage, access, processing and disposition of data on all systems within the enterprise. Asking a series of questions that encompass each of these phases can lead to the creation of meaningful policies. For each interface, ask the following questions:

Employees

- Do they still work at the company?

    ◦ If not, have their accounts been disabled?

    ◦ Has the deprovisioning process been run?

- Has the practice of least privilege been applied?

    ◦ This should be based on a user's need to know or access resources.

- Does their role in our role-based access control (RBAC) system match their current job role?

- Is their access to resources appropriate?

- Is their access to applications appropriate?

Remote employees

- Are they permitted access from outside the company?

    ◦ Does their level of access need to be restricted?

- Are they using an approved device to access company resources?

- Do their devices have the proper configuration?

- Are the hours of access appropriate for them?

- Should their data transfers be limited or monitored?

Remote sites

- Are there local laws that impact the organization's ability to access, transmit and share personal data stored there?

- Is there a need to customize our policies to adapt to local laws?

- Are we being consistent in our hardware and software choices and configurations?

Figure 4-1: Example IT Environment

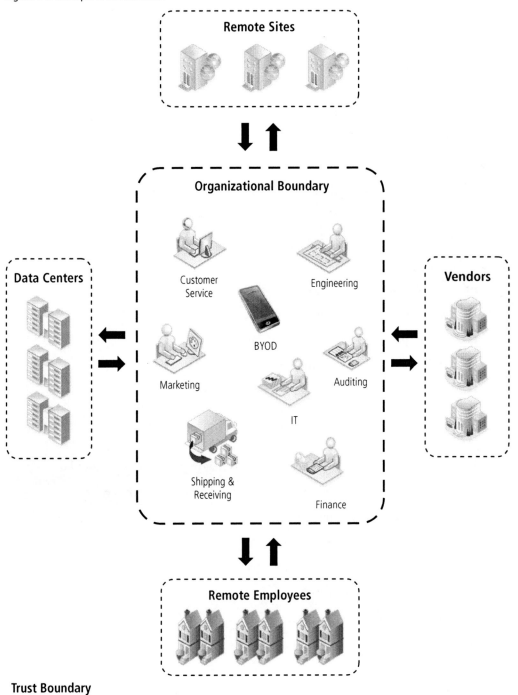

Vendors

- Is there a contract in place that covers their access to and processing of data?

- Is their access to resources limited based on the project(s) for which they were hired?

    ○ Is their processing of data limited to fulfillment of the contract?

- Are they clearly identified as vendors in the identity management system?

- Are they permitted remote access to company systems?

Network devices

- Are they performing the purposes for which they were deployed?

    ○ Do they block undesired traffic and permit desired traffic?

- Is access to the devices restricted?

Personal devices

- Are approved devices being used to access the network?

- Do the devices have the proper configuration?

- Is IT able to perform a remote lock or data wipe of the device?

- Should the data transfers be limited or monitored?

- Have employees read our BYOD policies and signed consent forms?

Printing devices

- Is the access control list for the devices appropriate?

- Are the devices shared outside of the department in which they are located?

- Are the devices discoverable for those who need access to them?

- Is sensitive data to be printed on the devices?

- Is local storage cleared of previously printed data?

Data centers

- Do they have physical security?

- Is physical and programmatic access to them limited?

- Are they storing data from different countries?

- Is the data being backed up?

- Are the systems redundant and geographically dispersed?

Backup systems

- Do they have physical security?

- Is physical and programmatic access to them limited?

- Is the data stored on them encrypted?

- Is there a retention policy governing the persistence of the backups?

The responses to these questions should lead to an action plan to address any deficiencies found. Having the right architecture, discussed in the next section, can help lessen the possibility that an investigation will yield undesirable results.

4.1.1 Architecture Considerations

Defining the right IT architecture can lead to a more effective privacy program.[1] The architecture determines how well systems work together, affects the ease with which data can be protected and can streamline the execution of policy. When deciding how to architect the IT infrastructure for an enterprise IT scheme, personnel should understand what type of data will be flowing through their systems, the global nature of their enterprise and the flexibility to deploy the desired software, hardware and policies. The IT department should include various stakeholders across the company when defining an architecture to help ensure that all viewpoints are included in the decision-making process. The following is a set of practices to consider when developing an IT architecture:

- **Technology standardization.** Deciding what technology to deploy in an organization involves many choices—the right hardware, operating system, client applications and server software. Standardizing each of these items simplifies training, application interaction, setting of policy, configuration management and sharing of information. Standardization also reduces the risk of a privacy incident. For example, when the type of database is known then the type of access control, encryption and backup capabilities can be understood and applied in a consistent fashion. This makes it easier for IT professionals to create one policy for applying privacy protection for sensitive data.

- **Policy consolidation.** Large enterprises often have many departments, each with its own data that it is responsible for. The enterprise can also have remote sites in different geographic locations that feel detached from the main office. Having a single global privacy policy that covers data-handling practices makes it easier for employees to follow policy, and for IT to ensure compliance with policies. It also streamlines the creation of privacy notices because they can be consistent across locales.

- **Data center distribution.** The location where data is collected and stored as well as the origin of the data subject may impact the laws and regulations that apply to the data. Every country has a different set of privacy laws and industry programs that apply to stored data. The transfer of data between countries and access to data by employees will be impacted by the origin and destination countries. A privacy review that includes the applicable laws and regulations should be performed to determine the restrictions on data access and transfers; the enterprise can then find the best placement for data to minimize the impact to business plans.

4.1.2 IT Involvement Through Mergers and Acquisitions

A merger or acquisition will likely involve the inclusion of new personal and organizational data as well as new computing infrastructure to the enterprise. The IT department along with a representative from the enterprise's privacy department should be closely involved in such a transition. A determination must be made about which data management policies will be applied to the data from both organizations. This is critical as mismanagement of the data could cause a lawsuit, regulatory scrutiny or a loss in revenue. A thorough review must be conducted to understand what inconsistencies may exist between the old and new policies. Consider the following when acquiring data via a merger or acquisition:

- **Service-provider processing of data.** Some companies may have contractual arrangements with vendors to process data for them. The purpose of the processing might be to manage online sales, order fulfillment or healthcare needs. In all cases, a review should be done to determine if the services should be continued. If not, care must be taken to ensure that all contractual agreements are upheld until the end of the contracts. If any data needs to be transferred to a new service provider or processed differently, the data subject must be made aware of the changes and given the opportunity to opt out of any changes in processing where permissible.

- **Vendor data.** Vendors sometimes provide companies with data. All contracts that govern the transfer of data from vendors must be reviewed to understand any restrictions that apply to the processing of the data that may conflict with how the receiving company may want to process the data. If the acquiring company's policies conflict with the contractual agreement with the vendor, then the company should work with the vendor to update the contract where possible. In the end the company may be required to return or destroy the vendor's data. The acquisition itself may trigger a contractual clause requiring the destruction or return of data to the vendor. There may also be additional restrictions on processing the data based on whether the data was collected from foreign nationals or another country.

- **Customer data.** Consumers will often give data directly to a company when creating an account, filling a subscription or making an online purchase. If the merger or acquisition causes a change in how the data will be processed, data subjects must be notified so that they are aware of the change in policy and have the ability to close their account and/or opt out of the use of their data based on the new policies.

- **Online data.** For data that was collected online, a review of the privacy notices that governed the data collection and processing should be made before the data is accessed or processed by the acquiring company.[2] Assurances must be made that the processing by the acquiring company will not go against the commitments made to the data subject. If the processing of the data needs to change, the data subject should be notified and given an opportunity to remove his or her data where required. If it is not possible to access the data subject, then the commitments made around how the data will be processed must be kept or the data must be deleted so that it is not improperly processed.

Data controller: *The natural or legal person, public authority, agency or any other body which alone or jointly with others determines the purposes and means of the processing of personal data.[3]*

Data processor: *A natural or legal person, public authority, agency or any other body which processes personal data on behalf of the controller. The processor must be a separate legal entity with respect to the controller.*

Data subject: *The person to which a set of personal data applies.*

4.1.3 Industry- and Function-Specific Systems

While governmental regulations apply to personal data, data collected from employees, customers or vendors is often covered by specific industry regulations or self-regulations. For example, EU financial data is covered by Basel III, credit card processing is covered by the Payment Card Industry Data Security Standard (PCI DSS), and the processing of data collected online for the purpose of targeted advertising is governed by the Interactive Advertising Bureau.

Because the collection, processing, sharing and retention needs of data will differ based on regulatory or legislative requirements, it may be necessary to store data based on the industry that governs it. This will at times require that the data be duplicated. Duplication should be avoided whenever possible due to integrity issues and increased risk from data breaches, but it may be necessary to avoid conflicts in how the data is treated. For example, medical and financial data often have similar fields; however, the access and processing requirements will differ based on the rules that apply to each data type. If a financial regulation requires that data be kept for nine years and a healthcare requirement mandates that data be deleted after five years, keeping the data in a single data store will cause a conflict with one of the regulations. A company also does not necessarily want medical personnel to have access to a client's financial data and vice versa.

4.2 Identity and Access Management

Amy was concerned that the company had become too lax regarding computer security. Computers were often left unlocked when no one was around, weak passwords were being used and administrators were sharing passwords. She sat down with Euan, the company's security officer, to discuss options. "Euan, we have got to improve our security practices. How can we expect the rest of the company to follow our security policies when we are doing such a bad job at it? And this is not just about security. Our computer systems contain a lot of personal data, and I don't want a visitor or curious employees inappropriately accessing sensitive data against our privacy policies."

"Amy, I understand the issue, and I have created an action plan based on the set of ISO/IEC 27001 standards," Euan replied. "Though it will probably be met with resistance, it's the right thing to do. First, we can modify the network policy to force all computers connected to the network to have a 15-minute timeout on keyboard usage which will password-lock the computer after the keyboard is idle for five minutes. We can modify the network policy to set passwords to expire after 90 days and force all new passwords to be unique and complex. For computers that are managed by administrators, we can force two-factor authentication via their smartphone so that even if they want to share a password, they won't be likely to share their smartphones."

"Euan, that sounds like a plan," Amy declared. "Let's implement that across the IT department over the next month, and if all goes well, we can push the policies across the rest of the company department by department. I don't want to be too disruptive, and I want to make sure our plan doesn't have any glitches. When this project is completed, I want to start training all of our security and compliance personnel on ISO/IEC 27001. One question before you get started, though. Why aren't we using the employee badges with the embedded chips for two-factor authentication?"

"Too many employees are leaving them in their card reader and locking themselves out of the building," Euan answered. "I know that sounds sort of lame, but it really got to be an issue, especially at night when the reception area is closed and there are fewer security guards around."

"You're right Euan, that does sound lame, but I understand. Let's move forward with your plan."

Identity management includes the processes involved in verifying the identity of an individual, group, process or device. Identification via most computer systems consists of a person typing her credentials (user ID and password) into an authentication screen. Most people are familiar with the login prompts for connecting to services such as Facebook, LinkedIn or Twitter. Many computers require that the user provide credentials to log in, which sometimes also authenticates the user for access to the organization's network. Single- or dual-factor authentication can be used to protect access to services, depending on the level of protection needed.

After an authentication occurs, authorization still has to take place to ensure that a user is permitted to access a resource or execute a command. Even if a user has access to a folder, it doesn't mean the person can access every file in a folder. And having access to a file doesn't mean that the user can modify the file or even print it. The access control list is typically used to determine which permissions a user has for a particular resource.

Authentication: The act of validating a person's identity with an identity management service before access to resources is permitted.

Types of authentication:

- **Something you know.** This type of authentication involves something the user knows, usually an ID and password.
- **Something you have.** This type of authentication involves something the user carries on her person, usually an RFID card, key fob or USB device.
- **Something you are.** This involves biometrics to authenticate, such as a fingerprint or retinal scan.
- **Where you are.** This type of authentication involves confirmation of the user's location.

Multifactor authentication: When more than one type of authentication is used to validate an individual.

Authorization: The act of confirming that an authenticated person has legitimate access to a resource or permission to execute a command.

Access control list (ACL): A set of identities associated with a resource that indicates the types of permission for which the identities are authorized. For example, Alice and Bob have write access to a file, but Carlos only has read access.

When the user is required to use only one method to access a system, it is called *single-factor authentication*. For example, entering an ID and password to log in to a computer, application or service is considered single-factor authentication, even though two values are being entered. Most phone devices provide a mechanism for the user to lock the phone unless a personal identification number (PIN) is entered. The PIN required to unlock a phone is usually a four-digit number. Even after the phone is unlocked, the user may be required to enter separate credentials to access an online service such as AOL or Yahoo. When a person uses an RFID card or key fob to gain access to an electronically locked door, selects predefined points on a picture or uses a fingerprint to unlock a device, those mechanisms are also considered single-factor authentication.

For higher levels of security, people are sometimes required to provide two types of authentication to access a device or service. *Multifactor authentication* is usually framed as consisting of two of four factors: something you have, something you know, something you are, or where you are. These factors refer to something the user holds, such as a smartcard or phone; a password or other secret the user knows; a biometric means, such as a fingerprint or retinal scan, or confirmation of the user's location. For example, users needing to access a computer may be required to have a smartcard as well as know its PIN to unlock and gain access to the computer. Similarly, ATMs require individuals to have an ATM card and enter a PIN to access their bank account. Some online banks offer two-factor authentication, where users are required to enter an ID and password as well as a code that is sent to their phone.

4.2.1 Limitations of Access Management as a Privacy Tool

Access management is an essential tool in enforcing privacy requirements regarding who gets to access data. ACLs can restrict the individuals, devices or services that get to access a resource or set of resources. Sophisticated access management techniques can restrict access to data based on the type of data being accessed, the role of the person accessing the data, the location of the user, the time of day or the type of device being used to access the data.

While strong access management can ensure that the right people access the right data in the right way, it can't ensure that people with legitimate access to the data do the right things with the data once it is in their possession. A user could always use data for the wrong purpose, share it with the wrong entity, place it on unprotected storage or sell it on the open market.

Where access management leaves off, proper policies, training and auditing can fill the gaps. Employees must understand their obligations before gaining access to data. There must also be accountability for the data that employees access. Enterprise policies must be in place so employees are clear about how they must handle data. Recurring training will keep employees informed of their obligations in regard to organizational privacy policies.

When overly complex, access management can also be an impediment to effective security and privacy. Overly complex identity management policies can lead to frustration and complacency. Employees may misconfigure the systems or be reluctant to follow complicated policies.

4.2.2 Principle of Least Privilege Required

The idea of least privilege focuses on granting individuals and services the lowest possible access rights to resources. This minimizes the ability of the user to access unnecessary resources or execute unneeded programs. For example, when placing a person in a role on a computer or the organization's identity system, choose the role with the fewest privileges necessary for the person to perform required duties. Likewise, when adding a person to ACLs for a resource, don't give the person write access if read access is sufficient. As an administrator, before assigning access privileges to someone, it is a good practice to ask yourself if the person could be given fewer privileges.

If rogue programs or hackers gain access to an employee's account, following a least-access regime can minimize what else they can access on the employee's computer or over the network. Also, even if the user sometimes needs to run as administrator to configure the computer or install applications, it is not necessary for the user to have administrator privileges all the time. The user can always have his or her privileges elevated as needed.

Care must be taken to not be too limited in the granting of privileges. Having to constantly ask for additional privileges can cause productivity problems and frustration for both employees and IT administrators.

4.2.3 User-Based Access Control

User-based access control relies on the identity of the person to determine the type of access to grant or deny to a desired resource such as a file, directory or website. The user's identity, as defined by the computer or network identity management system, is added to the resource's ACL along with the type of access being granted. For example, Carrie could be granted read access to a file by adding her account ID to the file's ACL and setting the access type as read. She will be able to read the contents of the file, but will not be able to modify or delete the file.

User-based access controls can be used to manage a set of individuals in the same way they can manage one person. For example, a security group named File Readers could be created. Individuals in the company could then be added to the group and the group added to a file with the access type set to read. This would permit everyone in the group to have read access to the file. Removing a person from the group would remove the person's access to any resources the group had been granted access to as long as the person did not have access directly or via another group.

User-based access control is a good way to protect the privacy of personal data by granting access rights only to individuals who need to access a resource based on organizational policy. The downside to this type of control is that administrators must remember to remove a user from all ACLs or groups when the user no longer needs access to a resource.

User-based access control can be implemented using discretionary access control (DAC) or mandatory access control (MAC). With DAC, users who own a resource can manage the ACLs of that resource, adding other individuals or groups to the resource's ACLs. While DAC makes managing security for resources easier, it provides leeway for employees to add users to a resource's ACLs against organizational policy.

With MAC, only the administrator is permitted to modify a resource's ACL. This mitigates the risk that employees will add users to a resource's ACL against policy. However, it places a greater burden on the IT department to manage the ACLs of all resources.

4.2.4 Role-Based Access Control (RBAC)

RBAC differs from user-based access control in that access to a resource is determined by a person's role in an organization rather than identity. Typically, an organization will have a fixed set of roles, such as shipping clerk, salesperson and privacy architect. Access to resources is allocated based on which roles should access a resource and how. Once the allocation has been completed, it rarely needs to change.

With RBAC it is more intuitive for an administrator to know when to move a person from one set of roles to another, versus trying to remember every ACL or group to which a person may have been assigned. It is also easier to adjust the resources an employee can access and the type of access to allow by adjusting a role's access privileges. The use of roles makes it easier to implement separation of duties and create an effective auditing program.

The downside to RBAC is that administrators must remember (or rather be told) to remove a given role from a user's definition when the user no longer has the role.

4.2.5 Context of Authority

The control over the access to resources over a network is based on the context in which the employee is connected to the network. The employee could have access to a single site, an entire enterprise or multiple enterprises. The broader the context of authority, the more challenging it will be to manage the privacy of resources. Not only will there be a lot more data to deal with as the scope broadens, but the number of privacy policies to deal with will also increase, as will the possible interactions between employees and data.

4.2.6 User to Site

In this context, a user is restricted to the resources within a single site. A site usually consists of a small number of people and departments in one geographic area governed by a simple set of privacy policies that cover the privacy practices for the data stored at the site. The user is typically a member of the site's identity management system and known by the small IT department that manages access control for all site employees. Understanding who can access data and at which level is not a difficult task. Auditing and compliance are not complicated and are easily managed by the IT department.

4.2.7 User to Enterprise

An enterprise is typically a large organization that can span multiple sites and geographies, and thus may be governed by a vast array of laws and regulations. Consequently, privacy policies for an enterprise will be more complex than those for a single site. For the most part, employees within an enterprise will use computers with the ability to access network resources across the enterprise. An employee's level of access will be based on the access privileges granted by the IT department, which may be geographically distributed. Knowing what an employee may access will not always be easy. It will vary depending on the location of the employee, the origin of the data and who the data owner is. Auditing and compliance will be much more difficult as they require coordinating efforts across the enterprise sites and knowing which policies apply to data, which may have been transferred several times over the course of its lifetime.

4.2.8 User to Multiple Enterprises

Cross-enterprise access control is a great way to share resources between enterprises. This permits employees in one organization to have access to resources that belong to another organization. One such multi-enterprise scenario is the outsourcing of major functions when they are outside the company's expertise or when using a service provider is just more cost effective, as in a software as a service (SaaS) model. For example, travel, purchasing, payroll and healthcare requirements could be provided by companies that specialize in those services. By developing a cross-enterprise capability, employees can access their records without entering new credentials even though the records are being hosted by a separate organization. Data access in these scenarios is typically one way, and access privileges are managed by contracts that are based on the privacy policies of the enterprise requesting the services. It is usually easy to manage data access in these types of scenarios as there is typically a one-to-one relationship between an employee and her record. Company administrators may need access to multiple records, but that is usually limited to a small set of people per outsourced function.

Another type of multi-enterprise scenario is when there is a joint venture between two enterprises requiring that they share resources for a joint project. Military contractors and movie studios often host a project with vendors on shared resources within one of the enterprises or a newly created enterprise for the joint project. Employees from both enterprises will need access to the resources. Unlike the outsourcing scenario, there will not be an obvious delineation between an employee and the data she might access. In multi-enterprise and outsourced scenarios, to simplify auditing and compliance of shared resources, the following guidelines should be followed:

- Have a single contract that covers where the project data is stored and expectations for the members of the project.

- A single privacy policy should cover the storage, access, sharing and disposition of the project data. Data that is transferred from the project computer to nonproject storage must be identified so the right policies will be applied to it.

- There must be no shared credentials. Each person on the project must have a separate set of credentials for accessing project resources.

- The administration of resources should be a shared responsibility such that a member from each enterprise has access to auditing records and shares in the accountability for compliance.

4.2.9 Cross-Site Authentication and Authorization Models

The ability to provide cross-site authentication and authorization is a powerful tool that can streamline access to resources. Also known as single sign-on (SSO), it means users have to remember only one ID and password that can be used across multiple sites. SSO can also be used across applications and services. Though a user can reuse the same ID and password to access each site, if the password is ever compromised the user has to go to each site to change it. With SSO, the user can go to the identity service and reset his or her password for all sites in one location. Single sign-on also poses the risk of permitting a user to be tracked across each site where the SSO credentials are used. For that reason, users should be requested to reauthenticate before being provided access to sensitive resources. Personal data may also be shared across SSO sites that the user visits. The following list describes some SSO technologies:

- **Open ID Federation.** The Open ID Federation is an organization that provides a mechanism that allows users to be authenticated to a relying party using a third-party authentication service. For example, Klout.com can be considered a relying party that uses Twitter.com or Facebook.com as an authentication service. This permits end users to use a single ID for multiple services and permits Klout.com, the relying party, to avoid having to develop its own authentication service. The privacy risk for the user is that the authentication service is aware of all the sites where the user relies on its service to authenticate and where there may be an exchange of personal data between the sites.[4]

- **Liberty Alliance.** The Liberty Alliance is a standards organization established to define open standards, guidelines and best practices for identity management. As of June 2009, the Liberty Alliance work was transitioned to the Kantara Initiative, which builds trust frameworks for verifying online identities.[5] The Kantara Initiative certifies identity providers via an assessment process, such that service providers can trust consumers who authenticate with them via credentials obtained from the identity provider. The Kantara Initiative provides four assurance levels, from minimal to stringent organization criteria, based on OMB M-04-04 and NIST SP 800-63.[6] This service is less susceptible to the OpenID privacy risk as it uses a federated approach to identity management and performs an assessment of identity providers.

- **Identity Metasystem Architecture.** The Identity Metasystem Architecture is a privacy-enhancing, security-enhancing identity solution for the Internet developed by Microsoft.[7] It was implemented as part of the Windows operating system as Windows CardSpace and later deprecated. It is based on Kim Cameron's Laws of Identity and is similar to Liberty Alliance and OpenID in that it permits users to log in to multiple sites with a single identity. However, it provides a more private solution as it does not permit the tracking of users by the relying party or identity provider.[8]

- **Social networks.** Facebook, Google+, and other social networks provide the ability to log in to other services with a single ID. This is a great feature, but users must take care to understand what data is exchanged between the services and how that data is used.

4.3 Credit Card Information and Processing

"Team, I just got off the phone with one of our customers," said Amy, pacing back and forth in her standard pensive fashion. "She was stuck in Paris with no credit card because her credit card number was stolen and maxed out. Why do I mention this, you might ask?" No one asked. Her staff members knew when she was like this it was best to stay out of her way. "I don't know for sure but it is quite possible that hers is one of over 300 credit cards that were hacked last night from our systems. During a preliminary investigation, it was discovered that one of our servers was writing transactions to the database unencrypted and the hackers used a cross-site scripting attack to dump the contents of our transaction table. Despite all our modern, technological advances, we have yet to solve the issue of stolen credit card numbers."

"So what happened to the customer?" asked Bill sheepishly.

"Since she used our system to pay for her vacation, I felt our organization was obligated to pay for her hotel and get her 100 euros so she could get her family to the airport and back home. I then found the problem, shut that server down and removed the unencrypted records from the database. Now I want all of you to help clean up this mess. Euan, find out why that server isn't encrypting the data and how those hackers got access to our database. Bill, notify the credit card companies and look at how this impacts our PCI compliance. Filo, prepare a PR statement and let the appropriate government agencies know what happened. Carrie, prepare a report on our legal obligations and David, find out how much this is going to cost us. I want to brief the executives in two hours, so make this your number one priority for the rest of the day." Amy ended with a serious tone. "I'm going to meet with our CIO and CSO and put together a plan to resolve this issue."

Credit cards are one of the major ways people pay for merchandise. They are an inextricable part of people's lives. It is difficult to rent a car, get a hotel room or purchase products online without one. But, with every purchase, a person is sharing credit card information, not only with the credit card vendor, but with the store and the clerk handling the card. Each of those points of contact represents an opportunity for someone to steal the credit card information or for a breach to happen.

4.3.1 Cardholder Data Types

Credit card data is some of the most sought-after personal information on the Internet. Part of the driving force behind identity theft is the ability to use the information to obtain a credit card. Credit cards are easy to use in person and online. Laws like California's Song-Beverly Credit Card Act can make it easier for credit card thieves to get away with illegal purchases as it limits the personal information a merchant may collect, thus curtailing the merchant's ability to verify the identity of the cardholder.[9]

Credit card data consists of the name, credit card number, expiration data and security code.[10] The credit card number itself is a formatted value that contains the major industry identifier, issuer identification number and account number and ends with a check digit.[11] Presenting these values to a cashier or a kiosk is typically all that is needed to make a purchase. Some gas stations and other retailers require the zip code for the billing address to be entered. Most online forms require that the full billing address be entered. These may seem like important safeguards, but an Internet search can easily pull up that information, permitting a thief to have the data needed to make a purchase with a stolen card.

Copying the magnetic stripe on a card provides the information needed to create a duplicate card. Illegally copying the magnetic stripe is called skimming.[12] A typical skimming device is small enough to fit in a person's pocket and basically consists of a magnetic stripe reader and memory to store the credit card information. A person stealing a small set of credit card numbers with a skimmer can make about $10 for each credit card number skimmed, while hackers who steal millions of credit card numbers can make about $3.50 per number.[13] Although they are paid less per card, they make up for it in volume.

Because of the ease of acquiring credit card data and using it to make purchases, it is the target of many thieves and online hackers. Some organizations that offer online purchases will capture the credit card information and store it in their database unencrypted. This leaves them vulnerable to viewing by employees or hackers or via a data breach. Several techniques can be used to mitigate this risk. First, credit card numbers can be encrypted right after processing. Once the processing has been completed, there should be no need to access the credit card number again. If an inquiry comes up from a cardholder, the credit card number can be provided at the time of the inquiry and can be hashed to perform a database lookup. The credit card number can even be stored in a separate database using a foreign key for an additional level of security.

Some credit card issuers offer a service that will issue a one-time credit card number for online transactions.[14] This prevents the reuse of a credit card number, thus mitigating the risk from data breach for organizations that use this capability.

Another method of protecting credit cards involves encrypted transactions, where the vendor gets only an encrypted version of the user's credit card number that can be decrypted only by the card issuer. The encrypted blob (binary large object) would also contain transaction data unique to the vendor. This method permits the vendor to keep the transaction information without fear of the repercussions that would come from a data breach.

4.3.2 Application of Payment Card Industry Data Security Standard (PCI DSS)

The PCI DSS is a global standard managed by the PCI Security Standards Council (SSC), which helps merchants and payment card processors apply information security best practices.[15] This section highlights PCI DSS as an example of one standard that can be used to protect credit card data. It was selected because it applies both privacy and security standards to a company. It should not be considered the only or best standard for protecting credit card data.

The standard consists of twelve requirements that apply to any organization that accepts payment cards and/or stores, processes and/or transmits cardholder data. It includes supporting materials such as a framework of specifications, tools, self-assessment questionnaires, measurements and support resources to help organizations ensure the safe handling of cardholder information. For the most part, PCI DSS is prescriptive in its guidance, making it easier to measure compliance than with regulations such as HIPAA and Basel III, which are more vague in regards to what is required to reach compliance.

These are the PCI DSS' twelve requirements:[16]

Build and Maintain a Secure Network
1. Install and maintain a firewall configuration to protect cardholder data
2. Do not use vender-supplied defaults for system passwords and other security parameters

Protect Cardholder Data
3. Protect stored cardholder data
4. Encrypt transmission of cardholder data across open, public networks

Maintain a Vulnerability Management Program
5. Use and regularly update anti-virus software or programs
6. Develop and maintain secure systems and applications

Implement Strong Access Control Measures
7. Restrict access to cardholder data by business need to know
8. Assign a unique ID to each person with computer access
9. Restrict physical access to cardholder data

Regularly Monitor and Test Networks
10. Track and monitor all access to network resources and cardholder data
11. Regularly test security systems and processes

Maintain an Information Security Policy
12. Maintain a policy that addresses information security for all personnel

These requirements are fulfilled by performing three steps:

1. **Assess.** Each organization covered by PCI DSS must perform an assessment and vulnerability scan based on the PCI DSS requirements, looking for technology and process vulnerabilities that may pose a risk to cardholder data. Organizations can perform a self-assessment using one of the self-assessment questionnaire validation tools provided by the PCI SSC or hire a qualified security assessor to perform the assessment.

2. **Remediate.** This process is for addressing any vulnerabilities found during the assessment process. Once the remediation process is completed, a reassessment and vulnerability scan is required to ensure that no vulnerabilities still exist.

3. **Report.** Regular assessment reports must be submitted to the organization's acquiring bank (the bank or financial institution that processes credit and/or debit card payments for products or services for a merchant) and global payment brands. The PCI SSC is not responsible for PCI compliance.

4.3.3 Implementation of Payment Application Data Security Standard (PA-DSS)

The PA-DSS is a set of requirements that applies to software vendors that are looking to develop payment card processing software. Vendors who create payment application software may not be required to be PA-DSS compliant if the software does not store, process or transmit cardholder data. Software vendors looking to create PA-DSS-approved payment application software must comply with requirements contained in the PA-DSS standard.[17] A synopsis of the requirements is as follows:

- Create the payment application

- Create a PA-DSS Implementation Guide for each application

- Educate customers, resellers, and integrators on how to install and configure the application

- Ensure that each application passes a PA-DSS review

- Provide customers with a copy of the validated application's PA-DSS Implementation Guide

4.4 Remote Access, Telecommuting and Bring Your Own Devices to Work

"Team, I have good news and bad news," Amy stated at the beginning of a weekly staff meeting. "Each of you is going to receive a company phone to use for business purposes. The bad news is you can no longer use your personal devices to access company resources. There is just too much liability associated with permitting personal devices to access our network. Last week an employee's husband took her phone while she was in the shower and copied the contact

data for several of our key clients. We didn't find out until his company started sending them e-mails. Luckily, the company has agreed to stop using the stolen e-mails, but there is no telling how much that hurt our relationship with our clients. Once again we are going to be the guinea pigs. I want everyone to stress test the new devices over the next week while I work with Euan and the privacy team on a set of policies for the new devices."

Permitting employees to work from home or use their own devices to access organizational resources can make them more productive and help to improve their work–life balance. Letting an employee attend his child's play in the middle of a workday can be disruptive. If the employee can access resources from his smartphone, it can lessen the disruption and keep the employee happy. Remote access and BYOD are a great benefit, but they do not come without risks.

4.4.1 Privacy Considerations

When using a personal device or computer to access enterprise resources, be it remotely or locally, employees run the risk of exposing their personal information. Data sent across the company's network can be viewed and captured by the company's scanning services. Data stored on the employee's device or computer could be scanned as well. The results of the scans could identify content that may go against organizational policies or even break the law. Interception of e-mail or other personal communications could be breaking laws in some jurisdictions. IT administrators should work with their legal and privacy departments to help avoid practices that may be viewed as illegal. Employees should limit personal communication or transfer of personal data over company networks or storing personal data on company resources.

4.4.2 Security Considerations

When personal devices are used to access organizational networks, IT departments often do not have an opportunity to validate the configurations of the devices. Devices could contain viruses, network scanners, key loggers or other types of malware that could be transferred to computers on the network. Devices could also be stolen, giving thieves access to organizational resources. Organizations looking to permit users to have remote access on their own devices to organizational resources should consider the following guidelines:

- **Use corporate devices.** Require employees to use organizational computers that the IT department has verified have the proper configuration, software and access controls. Policies should limit the personal use of corporate devices as this could significantly increase costs.

- **Use approved devices.** When organizational computers can't be mandated, ask employees to use devices that have specific features such as encryption, user login, antivirus software and remote wipe.

- **Limit data transfers.** Ask employees not to download content to their devices or upload content to the network. They can be asked to use their devices only to view content remotely.

- **Limit types of access.** Employees accessing the network remotely or with a personal device could be restricted to accessing a specific set of computers or networks or to using them during a certain time of day.

- **Mandate device controls.** Create policies that instruct employees to enable login, encryption and remote wipe. Have them install antivirus software.

- **Limit social access.** Do not permit employees to store company content on cloud services or social networks. Auto-upload features should be disabled to prevent accidentally sending content to a social site.

- **Provide notice and obtain consent.** Require employees using their own devices to read the policies governing the use of personal devices and sign a consent form outlining the employee's obligations and possibility of losing data from a remote wipe if the device is stolen.

4.4.3 Access to Computers

Within the organization it is normally easy to identify when a stranger is on the property and inappropriately accessing a computer. Individuals who access the network remotely cannot necessarily be verified as employees. Devices or computers can have the access credentials to a network preprogrammed so the user doesn't have to enter them each time. This causes the risk of a thief gaining access to network resources. IT departments can mitigate this risk in several ways:

- **Limit computer access.** Computers may contain so much sensitive data that employees accessing them must be physically verified. When this need arises, several means can be used to prevent employees from accessing the computer remotely.

- **Require manual authentication.** Employees can be required to manually log in or reauthenticate to sensitive services.

- **Use multifactor authentication.** Multifactor authentication can be used to help verify that the person accessing the computer is an employee.

4.4.4 Architecture Controls

When developing the IT architecture, IT professionals should consider the impact of remote employees and the use of personal devices within the company. By preparing for the possibility in advance, IT personnel can save time and mitigate risks to company resources. Several types of architectural controls can be considered:

- **Virtual private network.** By deploying a virtual private network, employees can access organizational resources over a secure network and not have to worry about their data being captured while working in public places (such as a local coffee shop or library).

- **Demilitarized zone (DMZ) networks.** Organizations will often have visiting customers, vendors and other non-employees who want to access the Internet. At times it may be difficult to say no to a valued visitor, and employees may be influenced to permit the visitor to use their computer or connect to the standard network using their device. Providing a separate network just for visitors to access the Internet that has limited or no access to the organization's network can mitigate the risk from visitors.

- **Multifactor authentication.** Multifactor authentication forces employees to provide two types of authentication to access network resources. This is a good way to lessen the risk that people who access the network and specific computers are evildoers.

4.5 Data Encryption

Encryption is an important means for protecting personal data and confidential organizational information. Access control, auditing and policies are important to the security of protected information. However, some scenarios need encryption to add an extra level of security. Hashing permits the encryption of passwords, credit card numbers and Social Security numbers while still permitting the verification of values by matching hashes. Encryption can help provide for the safe transmission of data between sites or storage of information.

While the decision to encrypt may be easy, the actual deployment can be full of uncertainty. There are various encryption algorithms, ways to apply the encryption, levels at which to apply the encryption and side effects to consider before deploying an encryption strategy.

4.5.1 Crypto Design and Implementation Considerations

Deploying encryption for an organization is not an easy task. Different types of encryption may be deployed depending on the scenario, contractual agreements or regulatory requirements. Also, some business needs can impact the type of encryption used. Below are some things to consider before deciding to deploy encryption within an organization:

- **Encryption size.** Encryption may increase the number of bytes needed for storing the data. When using block cyphers such as RSA or Advanced Encryption Standard (AES), the size of the ciphertext will be multiples of the block size. For example, if the text being encrypted has four bytes and the block size is 16 bytes, then the encrypted text will be 16 bytes, quadrupling the size. Application encryption can have an unexpected impact on the encrypted size of data and should be tested. For example, encrypting a Microsoft Word document with one four-letter word in it will change the file size from 10.9 kilobytes to 17.5 kilobytes.

- **Encryption performance.** The act of encrypting and decrypting data will add time to all other processing that will occur for data. The time it takes to encrypt a block of data will depend on the type of encryption being used, speed of the processor, size of the data and the size of the encryption key.

- **Complexity.** The degree of complexity encountered when encrypting data will depend on how the encryption is implemented. Using an application that performs the encryption with just a few settings will simplify deployment. When creating a line of business applications that use encryption, the implementation will be more complex. Encrypting data requires picking an algorithm, a key length and key value. Each encryption key must be securely stored and shared with all applications or services that use it. In the case of a data breach, new keys will have to be generated, and all data encrypted with the old keys will have to be re-encrypted.

- **Utility.** When a piece of data is encrypted, only a limited set of operations can be performed on the original value, and those operations require special computing functions. For example, performing searching, sorting, mathematics or modeling are all much more difficult on encrypted data. Applying operations on data before encryption is one way to maintain the data's utility. For example, a reverse IP lookup could be performed on an IP address to determine the city of origin for a client. Applying encryption-based operations on the data is another way to maintain its utility.

4.5.2 Application Encryption

Many applications provide built-in encryption, alleviating the need for developing encryption routines. Databases, word processors, e-mail programs and communication programs are examples of applications that provide encryption services as part of their list of features. This can be a huge benefit for organizations that do not have the resources to develop encryption features for their own applications. The drawback to using built-in encryption is there is often little choice in the type of encryption that can be applied to the data. When using an outdated application, the encryption algorithm being used by the application may provide weak protection for the data. When sharing data, each person involved in the sharing must have access to the same application or the data will have to be decrypted before exposing it to a data breach.

4.5.3 Record vs. Field Encryption

Record encryption encrypts one record at a time within an entire dataset. For databases, this would represent a row in a table. This type of encryption can provide better protection than disk, file or table encryption because the protection is more granular. If an assailant gains access to an encrypted disk, file or table, more data will be accessible to the assailant than if record-based encryption is used, where each record is encrypted with a different key or a salt, which is a value used to modify the results of an encryption. The downside to using record-based encryption is that it can cause performance issues because it takes time to encrypt and decrypt data as it is written to and read from the database, respectively. Record-level encryption can also make copying unencrypted versions of the data harder as it is done a record at a time and the person performing the copy must have access to all records if a special backup utility does not exist within the application.

Access to encrypted records can be based on an individual's role as defined by the application or company. This would make it easier for a person to retrieve database records to which she has access.

A user with access to an encrypted table might try to guess what data exists in the table by entering dummy data and looking for records with the same value. This attack can be mitigated by using a salted key, giving each record a slightly different encrypted value. For instance, the name "Smith" would be encrypted differently depending on the row in which it was placed in the table.

Field encryption provides the ability to encrypt only sensitive fields within a record while leaving other, less sensitive fields unencrypted. For example, a customer table might have the name, account ID, addresses and phone numbers in the clear, but encrypt the credit card and Social Security numbers. The last four digits of a credit card number or Social Security number may exist in the clear in a separate column to permit identifying records when there is a need to perform customer support functions while leaving the remaining value protected.

4.5.4 File Encryption

File encryption covers the encryption of the entire contents of a file. A file can be encrypted in several ways:

- **Password protection.** This method accepts a password from the user, which is typically applied to the creation of an encryption key used for encrypting a file. This is a simple method for encrypting a file as the user does not have to learn an encryption algorithm or deal with managing encryption keys. The user will have to share the password with anyone who needs to access the file. Care should be taken to prevent leakage of the password or to rotate the password on occasion to prevent previously stolen keys from working. IT professionals should ensure that password-protected files are indeed encrypted.

- **Third-party program.** This method requires that a third-party program be used to encrypt and decrypt the file.[18] The user can pick the type of encryption to be used based on the level of protection desired, understanding that the cryptographic performance and size of the file will be impacted by the type of encryption chosen. Each user must have the encryption program as well as the decryption key.

- **Digital rights management.** This mechanism can encrypt the file as well as restrict the operations that a receiver of the file is able to perform on the file. For example, a user may be able to read a file, but not print it out or share it with anyone via e-mail. Rights management requires that users have access to the rights management service in order to access documents. There may also be a requirement that the service hold a copy of the encryption keys, giving the service access to the file. No key or password sharing is necessary. This feature is often used to prevent organizational documents from being accessed outside the organization.

4.5.5 Disk Encryption

Disk encryption provides the ability to encrypt the entire hard drive on a computer.[19] This is one of the simplest ways to mitigate the risk of data being inappropriately accessed if a computer is stolen. Most people aren't aware that even though a person may not be able to log in to the computer, the hard drive can be removed and the data on it easily read if it is not encrypted. Encrypting the drive does not alleviate the need to protect computer login by using a strong password, since once a user is logged in and the disk drive is mounted, data on the drive is decrypted.

Another risk is the loss of the password used to encrypt the drive, which would cause loss of all the data on the disk. To mitigate that risk, important data should always be backed up, and that includes passwords. A trusted friend or family member should have a copy of your passwords in case your backup or memory fails. In enterprise scenarios, however, it is possible for the IT administrator to recover a disk if an employee has lost or forgotten the password for decrypting the disk, in the same way the password for the computer can be recovered.

4.5.6 LUKS Disk Encryption

Linux Unified Key Setup (LUKS) is a disk encryption specification that can be used to encrypt an entire disk. The key file for a LUKS-encrypted drive can be stored on a USB key.[20] This can provide protection if a computer is stolen or confiscated. As long as the owner of the computer being protected does not have the device on her person, she cannot be forced to unlock the device. A copy of the device could be kept at home or at work in a safe location so the computer would be safe in transit.

4.5.7 Encryption Regulation

There are several regulations that govern the encryption of data. Most national privacy laws suggest the use of encryption as a means for protecting personal information. Be aware that some countries have regulations against encryption in order to enforce censorship.[21] Below are some examples of industry-specific encryption regulations:

- **Basel III** requires mandatory encryption for financial reporting data and other related sensitive information at rest and in transit

- **HIPAA** suggests the use of encryption technologies to help ensure the confidentiality of patient health information

- **PCI DSS** requires encrypted transmission of cardholder data across open, public networks

- **Financial Instruments and Exchange Law of Japan** requires encryption of sensitive data related to financial reporting in public

4.5.8 Cryptographic Standards

Cryptographic standards fall into three categories: asymmetric, symmetric and hashes. Each has its own benefits and weaknesses. It is important to understand the scenarios where each category of cryptography is practical.

4.5.8.1 Asymmetric Encryption

Asymmetric, or public key, encryption uses a different key for encryption and decryption. An individual looking to share encrypted messages would generate two keys for himself or herself, one to encrypt messages and one to decrypt them. The encryption key is typically called the public key as it can be shared with the general public. People who wish to send this person protected messages would encrypt the message with the public key. He or she would use the other key, called the private key, to decrypt the message. This encryption method ensures that the only person who can read the message is the intended recipient. RSA and ElGamal are examples of asymmetric encryption algorithms.

4.5.8.2 Symmetric Encryption

Symmetric encryption uses the same key for encryption and decryption. This is a more practical means for encrypting large blocks of data and data to be shared with multiple people. Key distribution can be an issue as losing the key will expose encrypted data to anyone who has the key. Asymmetric encryption is a good means for sharing symmetric encryption keys. Data encryption standard (DES) and AES are examples of symmetric encryption algorithms. Symmetric encryption performs faster than asymmetric encryption and requires a smaller key for the same level of protection.

4.5.8.3 Hashing Functions

Hashing provides the ability to encrypt data so it can never be decrypted. This technique is valuable for encrypting sensitive data such as credit card or Social Security numbers that do not need to be decrypted. The beauty of hashes is that a lookup can be performed on a record that uses a hashed value as an index by getting the original value, hashing it and performing the lookup. The idea is that only the owner of the value ever knows the original value. For example, a user could enter a password of "bE;miNe4ever#" on the client and at the server it gets hashed to "47AA%snUx{{J;a9" where it is compared against the stored value for the user. Rivest Cypher 4 (RC4) and secure hashing algorithm 1 (SHA-1) are examples of hashing algorithms.

4.6 Other Privacy-Enhancing Technologies in the Enterprise Environment

Enterprises deploy several types of technologies to help protect the privacy of their customers, partners and employees. It is important to understand how these technologies work and when to use them.

4.6.1 Automated Data Retrieval

Users who have access to a database often have access to the entire database or table where records they need to retrieve are stored. This may give them access to records or fields within a record that are not needed for the employee's job. By using a form or application between the employee and the database, the user can be prevented from accessing data without authorization.

4.6.2 Automated System Audits

When employees have access to personal data, it is often difficult to determine if each time an employee views a personal data record it is a legitimate access. One way to mitigate the risk of improper data access is to limit the viewing of personal data to one record at a time and tie the record access to a work order or other task that validates the employee's need to access a record. For example, whenever a customer calls customer support, a tracking record is created for the call. The employee handling the call will be able to view a customer record as long as there is an associated tracking record for the access.

Automated system audits can be used to validate system logs to ensure that each access to a customer record has an associated customer call record. Audits can also help to ensure that data is being accessed during normal business hours and from appropriate terminals. Periodic verification of customer calls will help to mitigate collusion between an employee and a friend who calls in, impersonating a customer.

4.6.3 Data Masking and Data Obfuscation

Data masking is a means of permitting parts of a sensitive value to be visible while leaving the remainder of the value shielded from view. Masking a Social Security number or credit card number is a common example of this privacy technique. It is important to note that for the best protection, a value should be stored masked instead of just masking it when it is displayed. Consumer applications often expose the last four digits of a credit card number or Social Security number for identity verification, while leaving the remaining digits masked. The last octet of an IP address is often removed to reduce the risk of identifying the owner of the address while still allowing programs to discern other characteristics of the IP address. When entering a password, the password characters are masked by a character such as an asterisk so the user can see how many characters were entered, but not the characters themselves, preventing someone near the user from seeing the password.

Obfuscation is a means of hiding the contents of a value while maintaining its utility. Password masking, where the original value is obscured but something can still be known about the value, is also a means of obfuscation. Obfuscation can be performed by encrypting a value, performing simple math on the value or changing the value's precision. Hashing a password before storing it protects the original password but permits the hashed value to be used for password verification by hashing the password whenever it is presented by the user. Adding or subtracting statistically insignificant amounts from numbers hides the original value while permitting accurate statistics to be performed on a set of values. Removing the last four digits from a zipcode+4 value or rounding a GPS coordinate to one decimal place reduces the precision of the values without affecting their ability to be used by applications that do not need the greater precision.

Care must be taken when using obfuscation as a means of hiding the identity of an individual because re-identification can occur when obfuscated data is combined with other data. For example, a simple zip code combined with a person's birth date and gender provides a high probability of re-identifying a person.

4.6.4 Data Loss Prevention Implementation and Maintenance

Data loss prevention (DLP) helps to ensure that sensitive data is not inadvertently released to the wrong person or entity. Data loss can occur due to sensitive data being transmitted in the clear, a lost or stolen computer, a hacker breaking into an organization's network, improper ACLs protecting a resource or a rogue employee stealing data or via social engineering. With so many ways for data to leak out of an organization, a multipronged approach should be taken to minimize DLP that includes:

- **Policies and training.** Getting employees to do the right things begins with the creation of policies and practices that describe the desired expectations around DLP, followed by training in the policies and practices for avoiding DLP. Minimization in all aspects of data processing (i.e., collection, usage, storage, sharing) should be exercised.

- **Physical security.** Limiting physical access to sensitive areas and computers that contain sensitive data is an important policy.

- **Access security.** All data should have access controls to help prevent inappropriate access.

- **Hardware constraints.** Limit the movement of hardware. For instance, the attempted removal of a desktop computer should be scrutinized. The use of personal devices and USB drives should be limited.

- **Network monitoring.** Networks can be protected with encryption, firewalls, intelligent routers and data monitors that thwart attempts to send sensitive data outside the company.

- **Software tools.** On personal computers and devices, software such as antivirus protection, data encryption, data monitors and block protocols, close ports and rights management can help prevent data loss.

As technology advances, so will the number of possible exploits that can result in data loss from an organization. Current trends in DLP tools as well as new threats should be periodically examined to determine how they might impact an organization's DLP strategy. ACLs should be reviewed to ensure that they contain the right personnel and permissions. Cryptographic methods should be examined to help ensure that they provide adequate data protection. Hardware and software should be kept up-to-date with the latest versions.

4.7 Software Notifications and Agreements

Notifications provide users with concise, meaningful information about the privacy implications of an application, service or website. When provided at the right time and in the right way, notifications can put consumers at ease and assuage the fears of regulators who are fed up with the lack of transparency from companies. That represents context, which should not be taken lightly. While notifications are designed to be brief, agreements are more comprehensive, detailing the data collection and usage practices of software and an organization. Though software agreements are meant to be read by laypersons, they are more often written to be consumed by lawyers to avoid litigation due to incompleteness or miswording. Privacy practitioners must work to find the right balance between thoroughness and readability, and regulators must support this balancing act if the ultimate goal is to provide transparency to consumers in a form that is easily digestible.

4.7.1 Just-in-Time Notices

Today's wealth of Internet-enabled applications often have privacy implications over and above traditional desktop applications, though the details of the privacy practices are often buried in a privacy statement. A just-in-time notice alleviates the chasm between data collection and a privacy statement. It gives the users access to the information they need at the point where new data is being collected, letting them know what data is being collected and how it will be used. Presenting a just-in-time notice to the user during software installation, first run of an application or account creation is a good practice. For example, when creating a *New York Times* account, a link to a privacy policy and other information is provided in the form used to set up the account.[22] When entering a post on Facebook, members are presented with just-in-time privacy controls. This gives members an opportunity to indicate who can see their post before the post is submitted.

4.7.2 Website Sign-Up Screens

Websites often request demographic information or an e-mail address before permitting access to content. A good practice is to provide a link to the site's privacy statement at the time that the data is requested instead of forcing the site visitor to view the site's privacy statement. When the site shown in Figure 4-2 requests personal information, for example, it displays a short notice as well as a link to a privacy statement before the user has to enter the data.

Figure 4-2: Sign-Up Screen with Link to Privacy Statement

Image provided by MarketingProfs, www.marketingprofs.com.

Some sites request personal information without providing a link to a privacy statement. Which approach makes you feel more comfortable? Privacy professionals working with software developers should help ensure the right level of notice when personal information is requested.

4.7.3 Software Agreements

Software agreements represent the contract between the software vendor and the software user. They can manifest themselves as an end-user license agreement, terms of service or terms of use. Software agreements are traditionally presented to users for review and approval during the installation of the software. Software agreements normally contain sections on privacy and should be clear about the personal data the software collects and processes, as users aren't given an opportunity to modify the agreement; they can only accept it or not install or use the software.

For that reason organizations should strive to ensure that software agreements are complete without being overwhelming. A software agreement can be simplified by using a layered approach or providing a summary of the agreement at the top of the page. LinkedIn does a clever job of interspersing terse and verbose language alongside each other in its user agreement.[23] Having a readable agreement also avoids the scrutiny of regulators, who are always on the lookout for organizations that are burying language about sensitive data collection and usage practices in a long services agreement.

4.8 Conclusion

"Bill, I have to say that since you implemented our new IT architecture, our privacy incidents have decreased significantly along with our support engagements," said Amy. "Onboarding and discharging of employees has also become more efficient."

"It has certainly streamlined our compliance certification and reporting efforts," replied Bill. "Now it is much easier to centrally determine what a person has accessed without having to review a plethora of disparate systems."

"Our vendor and development costs have also gone down," stated David.

"I have to say that I'm delighted and a bit surprised that things have worked out as well as they have," said Amy. "No time to rest on our laurels, though. Having the right IT architecture is an ongoing effort that needs to be constantly monitored and improved."

Deploying the right IT architecture can help ensure that proper organizational practices are in place to provide consistent, end-to-end protection of resources, smoother compliance implementation and better interoperability between systems. Collectively, those things can lead to better protection of personal data.

Authenticating individuals before permitting them access to resources is an important step to protecting the privacy of personal data within an enterprise. Authorization of a user's privileges is another important practice that can be used to validate which action a person is permitted to perform on a resource, be it read, write, delete, share or print.

Remote access to organizational resources can make the protection of resources more challenging as it doesn't provide the ability to visually identify an individual. For that reason, extra care should be taken in limiting which resources a remote user can access and the operations that can be performed on them. Equally important is the deployment of encryption, auditing and DLP mechanisms to mitigate the risk of eavesdropping and data breaches.

Endnotes

1 The Institute for Enterprise Architecture Developments proposes the STREAM approach to enterprise architecture development. "Enterprise Architecture Standards Overview," Institute for Enterprise Architecture Standards, November 2010, www.enterprise-architecture.info/EA_Standards.htm.

2 Many of these concepts also apply to data collected offline, though it is not always a simple matter to provide notification to the data subject without a formal relationship.

3 Kevin Khurana, "EU Article 29 Working Party Clarifies Definitions of 'Data Controller' and 'Data Processor,'" Proskauer, *Privacy Law Blog*, March 29, 2010, http://privacylaw.proskauer.com/2010/03/articles/european-union/eu-article-29-working-party-clarifies-definitions-of-data-controller-and-data-processor/.

4 The OpenID Foundation, accessed October 25, 2013, http://openid.net/foundation/.

5 Kantara Initiative, http://kantarainitiative.org/.

6 Joshua B. Bolten, "E-Authentication Guidance for Federal Agencies: Memorandum to the Heads of All Departments and Agencies," Office of Management and Budget, December 16, 2003, www.idmanagement.gov/resource/omb-m-04-04-e-authentication-guidance-federal-agencies; William E. Burr et al., "Electronic Authentication Guideline," National Institute of Standards and Technology, U.S. Department of Commerce, August 2013, http://nvlpubs.nist.gov/nistpubs/SpecialPublications/NIST.SP.800-63-2.pdf.

7 "Microsoft's Vision for an Identity Metasystem," Microsoft, May 2005, http://msdn.microsoft.com/en-us/library/ms996422.aspx.

8 Kim Cameron, "Introduction to the Laws of Identity," *Kim Cameron's Identity Weblog*, January 8, 2006, www.identityblog.com/?p=354http://www.identityblog.com/?p=354.

9 The Song-Beverly Credit Card Act, Cal. Civ. Code § 1747.08 (October 9, 2011), essentially forbids the recording of personal information in connection with consumer credit card transactions unless the merchant is contractually obligated to do so or required to do so by law, the transaction is a sales transaction at a retail motor fuel dispenser and uses zip code information solely for prevention of fraud, or the collection of personal information is for a special purpose incidental to the transaction (such as a shipping address). The act does allow a merchant to require a positive form of identification in relation to the purchase; however, because the act prohibits recording the information, this is problematic in the instance of an online transaction. The Superior Court of Los Angeles found these prohibitions not to apply where the transaction is conducted electronically and the product is downloaded because the traditional safeguards against fraud (such as requesting a driver's license) do not apply. *Apple Inc. v. Superior Court* (2013) 151 Cal.Rptr.3d 841, 56 Cal.4th 128, 292 P.3d 883. Additionally, there are two bills that propose changes to this law: 2013 California Assembly Bill No. 844 (which would explicitly extend the protections of the bill to debit cards) and 2013 California Assembly Bill No. 383 (which would adopt the position of the Superior Court of Los Angeles and authorize merchants to require personal information as a condition to accepting a credit card in an online transaction).

10 Most credit cards have a security code. For a discussion of the types and purpose of these security codes, see Teresa Bitler, "How to find your credit card security code," Creditcards.com, April 8, 2013, www.creditcards.com/credit-card-news/credit-card-verification-numbers-security-code-1282.php#ixzz2hLP2nADe.

11 The format of the credit card number is well known as is the algorithm for producing the check digit. For an explanation of how to validate a credit card number using the mod 10 (Luhn) algorithm, see Tharaka Ragith Kumara, "Validate credit card number with Mod 10 algorithm," Code Project, January 15, 2013, www.codeproject.com/Tips/515367/Validate-credit-card-number-with-Mod-10-algorithm.

12 Kathy Lynn Gray, "Credit-card skimming becoming an epidemic," *Columbus Dispatch*, May 5, 2013, www.dispatch.com/content/stories/local/2013/05/05/credit-card-skimming-becoming-an-epidemic.html.

13 Credit card thieves routinely sell credit card numbers online like a regular business. Michael Riley, "Stolen Credit Cards Go for $3.50 at Amazon-Like Online Bazaar," Bloomberg, December 20, 2011, www.bloomberg.com/news/2011-12-20/stolen-credit-cards-go-for-3-50-each-at-online-bazaar-that-mimics-amazon.html.

14 Bank of America is one of the companies that provides a one-time credit card number feature. "What is ShopSafe® protection?" Bank of America, accessed October 25, 2013, https://www.bankofamerica.com/privacy/accounts-cards/shopsafe.go.

15 "PCI SSC Data Security Standards Overview," Payment Card Industry Security Standards Council, accessed October 25, 2013, www.pcisecuritystandards.org/security_standards/index.php.

16 "Payment Card Industry (PCI) Data Security Standards: Requirements and Security Assessment Procedures, Version 2.0," Payment Card Industry Security Standards Council, October 2010, www.pcisecuritystandards.org/documents/pci_dss_v2.pdf.

17 "Payment Card Industry (PCI) Payment Application Data Security Standard (PA-DSS): Program Guide, Version 2.0," Payment Card Industry Security Standards Council, January 2012, www.pcisecuritystandards.org/documents/pci_pa_dss_program_guide_v2.pdf.

18 "Best Free File Encryption Utility," Gizmo's Freeware, updated September 30, 2013, www.techsupportalert.com/best-free-file-encryption-utility.htm.

19 Disk encryption can be purchased from companies such as Symantec Corporation, http://www.symantec.com/drive-encryption, or it may come with the operating system, such as with Microsoft Windows 8, http://windows.microsoft.com/en-us/windows-8/bitlocker-drive-encryption.

20 "Unlocking LUKS with a USB key," Gaztronics, last updated February 17, 2014, http://www.gaztronics.net/howtos/luks.php.

21 Danny O'Brien, "High-tech censorship on the rise in East Africa," Committee to Protect Journalist, June 29, 2012, www.cpj.org/internet/2012/06/high-tech-censorship-on-the-rise-in-east-africa.php; Charles Arthur, "China tightens 'Great Firewall' internet control with new technology," *The Guardian*, December 12, 2012, www.theguardian.com/technology/2012/dec/14/china-tightens-great-firewall-internet-control.

22 The New York Times Company, https://myaccount.nytimes.com/mem/purchase/gateway/checkout.html?OC=1000010&adxc=240161&adxa=366291&page=homepage.nytimes.com/index.html&pos=Bar1&campaignId=44HQQ.

23 "User Agreement" LinkedIn Corporation, last revised September 12, 2013, www.linkedin.com/legal/user-agreement?trk=hb_ft_userag.

CHAPTER 5

Privacy Techniques

"Euan, I met with Filo this morning," stated Amy. "We've been receiving feedback that people don't feel safe sharing their personal information on our website. Though we have better security and privacy practices than the big guys, we don't have a well-known brand. I want that to change."

"Why don't we start an awareness program that informs people about how we protect personal information with a 'Learn More' link that leads people to our privacy controls?" suggested Euan. "We can also offer the privacy tools that we use internally to our website visitors. We can ask Filo to provide some PR around this as well."

"Good ideas," said Amy. "Let's look into providing an online privacy safety webinar as well that discusses the benefits of multifactor authentication and Privacy by Design. I don't want to spend a lot of time and money on these ideas until we have evidence that these approaches will bring real benefit to our website visitors."

"No problem," responded Euan. "I'll put together a project plan with some cost estimates and we can go over it with the privacy council if you like."

"Okay, let me know when you have something."

5.1 Authentication Techniques and Degrees of Strength

Authentication is a means for a system to identify an individual. ATMs, electronic doors, voicemail and computers are examples of systems that authenticate users. Authentication helps to ensure that the right person is accessing a system and the sensitive data it may hold. Different mechanisms can be used to protect access to sensitive data. The user name and password is the classic means for authenticating people for access to their online accounts. Fingerprint, radio frequency identification (RFID), magnetic stripe and picture passwords are other authentication mechanisms.[1] Some provide greater security, while others are just easier to use.

Multifactor authentication, as described in Chapter 4, provides a more secure mechanism by requiring an individual to provide two factors for authentication. These are usually two of the following: something the person knows, something the person has, something the person is, or where the person is. Be aware that increased security is typically accompanied by increased complexity, which tends to thwart the increased security. For example, multifactor authentication mechanisms will be harder to deploy, require more training of employees and require more support from the IT department to resolve access issues. Typical problems: I forgot my password, my card reader doesn't work, the fingerprint reader doesn't work, I forgot my key fob (or smartcard, or picture password).

5.1.1 User Name and Password

The user name or ID and password are still the most common form of authentication for computers, software and online services. For that reason, those two values are typically the only thing separating would-be thieves from personal data—data that reveals a person's interests, who their family and friends are, medical, financial and sexual information. The user name and password are also often used to protect access to other people's information and corporate secrets.

The importance of the user name and password should not be underestimated, and great efforts should be made to protect them. An enormous number of data breaches and identity thefts have been caused by the initial theft of a user name and password.[2] To mitigate threats to your password, start by creating a complex password having at least eight characters, mixed case, a number and a special character. For example, "My1sTrong,4password%" (PLEASE DON'T USE THAT EXAMPLE FOR ANY OF YOUR PASSWORDS!). A pass phrase is a set of words strung together to form a long, easy-to-remember password such as "MyLongPasswordPhrase." Using pass phrases can help you remember long passwords, but they shouldn't be something obvious like a common phrase or something you say often. They should also contain mixed case letters, numbers and punctuation.

Worst password ideas:[3]
1. Pet names
2. A notable date, such as a wedding anniversary
3. A family member's birthday
4. Your child's name
5. Another family member's name
6. Your birthplace
7. A favorite holiday
8. Something related to your favorite sports team
9. The name of a significant other
10. The word "password"

Worst passwords of 2012:[4]

#	Password	Change from 2011		#	Password	Change from 2011
1	password	Unchanged		13	1234567	Down 6
2	123456	Unchanged		14	sunshine	Up 1
3	12345678	Unchanged		15	master	Down 1
4	abc123	Up 1		16	123123	Up 4
5	qwerty	Down 1		17	welcome	New
6	monkey	Unchanged		18	shadow	Up 1
7	letmein	Up 1		19	ashley	Down 3
8	dragon	Up 2		20	football	Up 5
9	111111	Up 3		21	jesus	New
10	baseball	Up 1		22	michael	Up 2
11	iloveyou	Up 2		23	ninja	New
12	trustno1	Down 3		24	mustang	New
				25	password1	New

When it comes to the number of passwords we have to remember, many of us feel there are too many. According to a recent study, 30 percent of adults have at least 10 passwords and 8 percent have more than 20.[5] Since remembering a lot of passwords is difficult, we need to have a way to store them. It is astounding in this day and age how many people still store their passwords on a piece of paper or in an unencrypted file or secondary storage. If you are one of those people, put this book down right now and go encrypt your password file. If the file is called *passwords*, run and do it!

5.1.2 Simplifying the Use of Multiple Passwords

Products like Abine's MaskMe provide the ability to create random, unique values for e-mail addresses, telephone numbers and password fields.[6] The e-mail address that it creates can receive e-mails and can stay active as long as one likes. With this type of program, the user never needs to remember the password. The user simply clicks into the password field and the program automatically enters the value based on the current website domain.

The product LastPass permits the easy storage of multiple passwords as well as automatic login to the dozens of sites you might visit.[7]

5.1.3 Protecting Passwords in the Enterprise

While a lot of emphasis is put on entering credentials, there must be a focus on protecting the transfer and storage of passwords. The network over which this password is transmitted should be encrypted. Types of network encryption will be covered in the next chapter. Equally important, passwords should be encrypted during storage. It's disappointing to continue to hear about data breaches where passwords were stored in the clear. Encrypting also protects passwords from a rogue employee who might be looking to access a computer using someone else's credentials or to sell a set of them for monetary gain.

By hashing the password before storage, it is possible to protect the password such that the value cannot be decrypted and the hashed value can be used to validate the password during authentication attempts.

5.1.4 Single-Factor Authentication

Single-factor authentication provides protection to a resource using one type of authentication, which usually consists of an ID and password, which is *something you know*. An electronic key fob, magnetic stripe card (*something you have*) and biometrics (*something you are*) are other ways to initiate single-factor authentication. One recent form of single-factor authentication that has emerged is the picture password.[8] Selecting a picture and then using a series of gestures such as a circle, line or point provide a secure means to authenticate to a computer that can be easier to remember than a series of characters. With so many ways to protect access to resources, there is little excuse for not using authentication. IT administrators should insist on authentication for access to computers within the organization.

A fingerprint reader has been seen as a way to provide single-factor authentication. However, be wary of devices that have low sensitivity sensors or are susceptible to false positives. Some fingerprint devices can also be susceptible to the gummy bear attack, whereby latent fingerprints on glass are transferred to gelatin "fingers".[9]

5.1.5 Multifactor Authentication

Multifactor authentication has been used by consumers for years without their realizing what it was. For instance, some vendors require a driver's license when purchases are made with a credit card to confirm the identity of the cardholder. Those items represent something they have and something they are—their credit card and facial features, respectively. When ATMs were developed, consumers used the ATM card along with a PIN to obtain money. Those two items represent, respectively, something the person has and knows. (How amazing it was back then to walk up to a machine in the middle of the night and be able to get cash without a teller present. Now people can do that almost anywhere in the world.)

Many computer systems today allow for two-factor authentication using a password and chip card. Some more sophisticated systems send a verification code to a user via e-mail or text message to provide a secondary means of authentication. IT departments should consider implementing multifactor authentication for systems carrying sensitive data and for administrator terminals.

5.1.6 Biometrics

Biometrics enables users to authenticate themselves to a computer using a physical attribute as the authentication mechanism.[10] For example, a fingerprint, palm print, finger veins, iris scan, voice recognition and facial recognition are all types of biometric authentication. Biometrics can be one of the simplest types of authentication to use because there is nothing to remember or carry around. There is very little worry about losing your credentials or a person stealing them when you yourself are the credentials.

Biometric systems can suffer from false positives and false negatives. The extent to which these weaknesses will present themselves depends on how sensitive the biometric systems are. The more sensitive the system, the more false negatives will occur. The less sensitive it is, the more false positives will occur. Another weakness of biometric authentication is the inability to provide revocation capabilities. While it is simple to revoke a password or certificate, revoking a person's facial characteristics isn't an option. After all, a person has only one face to present to a facial recognition system.

Biometrics can have drawbacks such as being more expensive, requiring additional maintenance and support and having limited compatibility across systems. Biometric systems can also be a privacy risk as the system collecting the biometric information has a way to uniquely identify an individual. Even if users change their profile information, they cannot easily change their biometrics. The biometric template used by these systems could be passed around or stolen and used indefinitely to identify individuals. When deploying biometric systems within an organization, IT professionals should be careful to restrict access to biometric information and to encrypt the data during storage and for verification.

5.1.7 Portable Devices Supporting Authentication

Portable devices are things individuals can carry around with them for authentication purposes. A smartcard, USB drive and RFID tag are examples. These types of authentication devices can carry a simple code or consist of a sophisticated program. Authentication can occur by inserting the device into a reader or USB port or merely by placing it near the authentication device. They can help to strengthen authentication with computers when policies require that the device be connected to the computer in order to use it. The RSA SecurID, TAILS and LUKS devices are examples of the type of extreme security that can be provided by small portable devices.[11]

5.1.7.1 RSA SecurID

This small handheld device displays a one-time password to the user that is valid for only a short period of time. For the device to work, the user must enter her personal PIN along with the one-time password, thus providing two-factor authentication. The RSA device is also part of a risk-based authentication strategy started by EMC that looks at a range of factors before determining how and when to permit a user to authenticate to a computer system.[12]

5.1.7.2 TAILS Portable Operating System

The Amnesiac Incognito Live System (TAILS) device is basically a tiny computer contained on a USB drive. To use it, simply insert it into the USB port of a computer and boot it. It permits the user to run a self-contained computer from the USB device. All Internet traffic from the device goes through a Tor network.[13] The only storage space that it uses is the host computer's RAM, which is cleared when the computer is shut down. The device also comes with encryption tools for encrypting files, e-mail and other communications. This device lets a user turn any computer into his or her own personal computer with its own self-contained encryption mechanism.

5.2 Identifiability and Identifiers

Authentication and even authorization are mostly made possible by the ability to identify an individual, service or device by means of an identifier. An identifier can be a person's name, a user ID or code on a key fob. The choice of identifier will dictate the identity management systems that are used within an organization and the ease with which an employee can be identified.

The ability to identify individual owners of data is important to organizations that are looking to manage risk and validate access to resources. However, identifiability of individuals makes them susceptible to tracking, targeting and identity theft. Individuals can go through various levels of identifiability, from anonymous to well known. Anonymity can have its advantages, but it can be a liability when it is necessary to validate ownership of something or find a criminal.

Identifiers, for the purposes of this book, are codes or strings used to represent an individual, device or browser. For example, a globally unique identifier (GUID) could represent a user's login ID for a social network, the cookie identifier for a domain navigated to with an Internet browser or the identifier for a wireless router at a Starbucks (i.e., a public network).[14]

As we browse the Internet looking for content, we are often presented with requests to provide demographic information or even create a new account in order to access content. Not only can these requests be an annoyance, they can also invade your privacy by placing your e-mail address on a list to receive marketing e-mails when all you wanted to do was access content, not build a relationship with the website. Giving websites demographic information also increases a person's identifiability. Even giving a clerk your zip code after processing a credit card transaction makes it easier for the company to find your address in public records and send you marketing material.

5.2.1 Labels That Point to Individuals

Many labels can be used to point to individuals. Some labels are precise, but most are imprecise and even vague depending on context. We often state that a person's full name is PII, or personally identifiable information. However, can you say definitively who John Peter Smith is? You may know one, but is it the right one? It depends on context.

Understanding when or where the name is used can help to narrow a search to the specific person with that name.

A person's full name is considered PII even though we may not be able to determine to whom the name belongs. However, a single name is not considered PII, although many people who use a single name can be uniquely identified, such as Madonna, Cher and Arsenio.

We often use labels instead of names to identify people we don't know, such as the man with the cowboy hat, the lady with the red dress or the person with the balloon. Labeling people based on their attributes makes it easier to identify them in the context in which the description is used. For example, finding a specific person wearing a football jersey may be easy at a legal seminar, but not so easy at a football game. It is this ease of identification that we should be cognizant of when we use labels to identify people in our data processing systems. If it is desired to use labels to identify someone, care should be taken to understand the degree of identifiability that is needed. The specificity around the context will make the label more or less identifiable. Not understanding the distinction could inadvertently leak personal information.

5.2.2 Device Identifiers

Device identifiers are used to identify a device, which often can be linked to an individual. For this discussion I will exclude RFID tags associated with a smart ID or access badge that directly links to PII. The IP address is probably the most common type of device identifier. It is how traffic moves around on the Internet. A message with a destination IP address is sent, including a return IP address so the receiving device knows how to respond to the message. Using the ping or ipconfig command on Windows machines can be used to determine the IP address of the computer or the host name that the IP address represents.

Though the IP address does not point directly to an individual, the ISP can easily determine the person to whom an IP address belongs in the similar fashion that a mobile operator can determine the owner of a phone number or device ID. For that reason, IT personnel should understand when a device ID may point to an individual, which could expose the individual's identity.

Other than the IP address, devices may have a device ID, MAC (media access control) address or one of many other IDs assigned by the device manufacturer or operating system vendor. These IDs can be a source for user tracking as they often cannot be deleted, blocked or opted out of. For that reason IT personnel should understand when a device identifier may be used to track employees and work to mitigate the risk in their choice of device for use within the company. Product privacy professionals should work to persuade developers not to use persistent IDs that cannot be controlled by users.

5.2.3 Strong and Weak Identifiers

Identifiers can be strong or weak depending on how precise they are. Examples of strong identifiers are driver's license number, Social Security number and national ID number.

Examples of weak identifiers are a person's postal code, area code and shoe size. Some identifiers can be weak or strong depending on how uniquely they identify the person and the context in which they are used. In general, age is a weak identifier unless the person is 110 years old. Height is also a weak identifier unless the person is eight feet tall.

These distinctions are important to understand when building a database to categorize individuals. The strength of the identifier can make a database more or less susceptible to a data breach.

5.2.4 Pseudonymous and Anonymous Data

There has been a lot of confusion around the meaning of pseudonymous and anonymous. *Anonymous* means that there is truly no way to know who a person is. More importantly as it refers to privacy, there is no way to know to whom a set of data belongs. IT personnel often make the mistake of hashing a unique ID that identifies a record as being from a specific computer or person and declaring that the data is anonymous because there is no practical way to get back to the original value. An important distinction needs to be made between practicality and reality. First, if a law enforcement agent presents a unique ID and asks that it be hashed in order to find all associated records, it could probably be done. Second, a company typically creates and assigns only a finite number of unique IDs. That means that a lookup table could easily be created to match the list of unique IDs to their hashed values. In both cases the owner of the data becomes known, meaning the data is not anonymous.

> **IP Addresses**
>
> *An IP address, as defined by IPv4, is made up of four octets. (IPv6 consists of eight 16-bit values, but is still early in its deployment.)*[15] *Each octet consists of eight bits whose value can range from 0 to 255. An IP address is generally written out with a period between each octet. For example: 254.7.128.15.*

Some will state that an IP address is anonymous because it points to a computer, which could be shared, or because the last octet has been erased, which leaves it anonymous. Shared computers make up a small percentage of all computers, and the time stamp can help identify the person who was using the computer at the time that a log was captured based on a login event or other means. Even when a shared hub is used, the ISP can do some investigation to determine who was assigned to a specific session at a specific time.

Clearing the last octet of an IP address does obscure its original value, but is not very effective if only one person from the root IP address is accessing a website. An octet represents only 256 possible values, which is not many compared to the billions of possible IP addresses. So while there is a 1 in 255 chance that a different device would have the same root IP address, there is an extremely small chance that the same root IP address from a different person would be received by a server.

In general, if you are able to match two records as being from the same person or device, then the records are not anonymous. A good test of anonymity is to ask if there is any way to know whom a set of data came from or if a new dataset can be matched to a previous one. If so, then the data is not anonymous. Even when anonymity has been successfully achieved, IT professionals should be wary about the possibility of re-identification based on the fields within a record.

Pseudonymous means that the identity of a person isn't known, but one is able to tell when the same person appears or owns a dataset. Say, for example, that you run a local grocery store and a person walks up to your counter. If you cannot see the person's face whatsoever, then the person is anonymous. If you recognize the person but don't know his name, then the person is pseudonymous. Of course, if you know who the person is, then the person is identifiable.

With pseudonymity, an ID, rather than PII, is typically used to identify a data record as being from a specific person. IP address, GUID and ticket numbers are forms of pseudonymous values. People often use a claim check to retrieve their coats from a coat check room. The clerk may not know who the person is presenting the claim check, but she can reunite the person with the right coat. Pseudonymity hides the identity of a person. However, with enough effort the identity of the person represented by a pseudonymous ID can often be determined.

5.2.5 Imprecise Data

Making data less precise is another means of de-identifying data. Say you are collecting GPS data from someone's phone, but all you need is a person's zip code or current city. The GPS coordinates could be converted to a value less granular and then thrown away. The same could be said for other values:

- **Age or birth date:** Age range with a maximum age of 65
- **Location:** Convert to zip code, city or five-mile radius
- **URL:** Remove the subdomain data
- **IP address:** Remove the last octet or convert to a location
- **Search keyword:** Convert to nonsensitive category or delete

5.2.6 De-identification

When collecting logs based on a user's browsing experience, several pieces of extraneous data may be collected that could be used to identify someone. Performing de-identification on the data can mitigate the risk of retaining unneeded identifiable data.

In a server log, one typically finds an IP address, website address, time stamp, cookie values and possibly referer data. Now let's say you want to de-identify the data. The first thing you would do is get rid of unique IDs, so the IP address and cookie values would go.

If your database stores personal information about a user, to de-identify you would delete the name and birth date. Though the birth date by itself is not identifiable, when combined with gender and zip code, it could be used to identify a person using public records. Using Dr. Latanya Sweeney's research, you determine that the birth date is the safest thing to remove.[16] But now it is not possible to determine the uniqueness of records. Most research looks at patterns over time. Without the ability to collect data in a unique fashion, trends cannot be determined.

If the referer information is left in the logs, then it could contain clues to a person's identity. It could indicate that the user performed a vanity search. It could be the URL to a person's Facebook, LinkedIn, Twitter or blog site. It could contain map coordinates to the person's place of business, church, gym or friend's house. While this data may seem harmless to most people, a determined adversary could take the data and use it to find the person's identity. The AOL and Netflix exploits taught us that.[17]

Before setting up an analytics or research program, determine how many days of data you will need. Move the data to a separate database. Remove unique IDs, convert precise locations to something less precise (less than 10 miles), remove URLs or, if needed, use only the URLs to common sites and truncate everything other than the main domain value. Each unique record can be given a unique ID, but it should not be based on any previous record values or it will introduce the possibility for re-identification. Even hashing values is not sufficient as the hashed values could all be calculated and placed in a table where they could be looked up. If data under one ID contains patterns of public behavior, it can be used to re-identify the person. For example, a series of places visited, movies watched or books read can be indicators of who a person is.

The U.S. Health Insurance Portability and Accountability Act (HIPAA) provides a standard for de-identification. To assist with the de-identification of health information, the Department of Health and Human Services created the paper "Guidance Regarding Methods for De-identification of Protected Health Information."[18] Companies claiming HIPAA compliance must validate that they are de-identifying data as the HIPAA standard requires. Even companies not subject to HIPAA compliance can benefit from the de-identification guidelines.

The HIPAA Privacy Rule proposes the use of the safe-harbor method for de-identification described in section 164.514(b)(2) of the Privacy Rule,[19] which dictates that the following identifiers of the individual, or of relatives, employers, or household members of the individual, are removed (this is an abridged version):

A. Names

B. All geographic subdivisions smaller than a state, including street address, city, county, precinct, zip code, and their equivalent geocodes

C. *All elements of dates (except year) that are directly related to an individual*

D. *Telephone numbers*

E. *Fax numbers*

F. *E-mail addresses*

G. *Social Security numbers*

H. *Medical record numbers*

I. *Health plan beneficiary numbers*

J. *Account numbers*

K. *Certificate/license numbers*

L. *Vehicle identifiers and serial numbers, including license plate numbers*

M. *Device identifiers and serial numbers*

N. *Web universal resource locators (URLs)*

O. *Internet protocol (IP) addresses*

P. *Biometric identifiers, including finger and voice prints*

Q. *Full-face photographs and any comparable images*

R. *Any other unique identifying number, characteristic or code*

5.2.7 Re-identification

Re-identification is the act of identifying someone who was previously not identified or was de-identified. When a record has a pseudonymous identifier or has gone through de-identification, it is still possible for the owner of the data to be re-identified. Often, the process of re-identification is difficult, but not impossible. Re-identifying a person associated with an IP address often requires making a visit to the owner's Internet service provider. When the birth date, zip code and gender of a person are known, finding the person's identity requires looking through a public record. In the Netflix debacle, the IMDb database was used to identify the owner of movie records. Individuals can often be re-identified by combining data from multiple databases. One database could have a list of items purchased, medical prescriptions or spa visits based on an ID number. Another database might list account information indexed by the same ID number. Hashes can be indexed, encrypted values can be decrypted and patterns can be used to re-identify an individual.

5.2.8 Degrees of Identifiability

"Euan, I sort of understand degrees of identifiability, socially speaking. Tell me how it applies to privacy," requested Amy.

"Think about how you are familiar with someone from your high school, but you can't remember the person's name," suggested Euan. "Or you recognize a person and remember that they like the symphony, but nothing else. That is similar to online identities where you may know the person's e-mail address, but you don't know their real identity. Or you can identify a website visitor by their cookie value, know the kinds of things they like, but don't know if the cookie represents an individual or a family."

"So how do we apply that at work?" asked Amy.

"We should always strive to use the lowest level of identifiability necessary when processing data to minimize any possible privacy risks," replied Euan.

"Won't that require that we keep multiple databases? Is that really necessary when we are all one company?" wondered Amy.

"Even though we are one company, we engage in many different practices," explained Euan. "Just because a person provided their data for a product that applies to one practice doesn't mean that they want to provide it for all of our practices."

Amy sighed. "Privacy is a tricky thing to get your head around. I'm glad we have a team of experts working together on this."

"In general that's what it takes," agreed Euan. "It's difficult for one person to understand all aspects of privacy."

5.2.9 Identifiability and Linkability

Identifiability is the extent to which a person can be identified. The ability to which a person can be identified depends on the amount of data available and the context in which it is given. The more information that is provided about a person or the more context that is given, the easier it is to identify the person. For example, a single name is typically not enough to identify someone. However, given the name Madonna, most people would say it referred to the famous entertainer. Inside a Catholic church, someone would likely say it refers to Mary, mother of Jesus. Giving the full name Madonna Louise Veronica Ciccone would clarify that "Madonna" refers to the singer.

When measuring identifiability, linkability needs to be taken into consideration. Though looking at a person's age, gender or zip code may not lead to any obvious conclusions about the individual's identity, we know that when linked with public information there is a good possibility of identifying the person. Records are often de-identified of obvious identifiable fields such as name, address, phone number or e-mail address. However, other data or forms of ID, though by themselves harmless, can sometimes be linked with other records and lead to re-identification. Sometimes it may take the combination of multiple records. Information about a person's background, interests, arrest record or friends can lead to re-identification. Anonymity is difficult to achieve while keeping the utility of a data record. The word "blue" is certainly anonymous, but it is equally meaningless. As we add context around a word, where and when it was collected, the type of people who liked it or other seemingly meaningless traits, re-identification all of a sudden becomes a possibility.

5.2.10 Identifiability and Regulations

To help govern organizational practices for managing identities, government agencies often produce a set of regulations and guidelines. Organizations should take these to heart as they can help avoid inquiries and risks to reputation.

5.2.10.1 FTC Staff Report

Section IV.A.4 of the FTC's Final Staff Report, *Protecting Consumer Privacy in an Era of Rapid Change: A Proposed Framework for Businesses and Policymakers*, makes this statement: "There is significant evidence demonstrating that technological advances and the ability to combine disparate pieces of data can lead to identification of a consumer, computer, or device even if the individual pieces of data do not constitute PII. Moreover, not only is it possible to re-identify non-PII data through various means, businesses have strong incentives to actually do so."[20] Later in the section, in reference to de-identification, the report states, "This means that the company must achieve a reasonable level of justified confidence that the data cannot reasonably be used to infer information about, or otherwise be linked to, a particular consumer, computer, or other device."

Those recommendations reflect a high bar to reach and in many cases one difficult to ascertain. However, it shows the degree to which the FTC seeks to protect the privacy of individuals. Organizations should understand what can make data linkable and work to de-identify the data to reduce the risk of linkability.

5.2.10.2 OECD Paper on Identity Management

In June 2009, the Working Party on Information Security and Privacy of the Organisation for Economic Co-operation and Development (OECD) created the paper "The Role of Digital Identity Management in the Internet Economy: A Primer for Policy Makers."[21] In this paper the OECD describes the differences between the siloed, centralized and federated approaches to identity management. In the end it is felt that the user-centric approach keeps users in control of their identity, with personal information in the hands of the user. In this scenario the user gets to choose an identity service to use to connect to a desired service provider. The type of identity service used can affect the linkability between services. While sharing identities across services can provide a lot of value, one has to determine if it is worth making transactions across the services linkable.

5.2.11 Article 29 Working Party Opinion

In the EU Data Protection Directive EC/95/46, personal data is defined as follows:

> *Personal data shall mean any information relating to an identified or identifiable natural person ("data subject"); an identifiable person is one who can be identified, directly or indirectly, in particular by reference to an identification number or to one or more factors specific to his physical, physiological, mental, economic, cultural or social identity.*[22]

The Article 29 Working Party issued Opinion 4/2007, which provides guidance on the concept of personal data.[23] This opinion clarifies that "a natural person can be considered as 'identified' when, within a group of persons, he or she is 'distinguished' from all other members of the group," while "a natural person is 'identifiable' when, although the person has not been identified yet, it is possible to do it." For that reason, when performing privacy reviews, privacy professionals should get validation that someone who has been de-identified is subsequently not identifiable.

5.2.12 Data Aggregation

Data aggregation is a great way to glean understanding from data via statistical analysis while protecting the privacy of the users to whom the data applies. Aggregation as it applies here is the process of combining data from multiple records into a single record around a common index. For example, a thousand website visitors could be monitored to see which articles they read, searches they make or advertisements they click on. The analysis could group the visitors by the region from which they access the site, the selected browser language, the type of device being used or the originating website. If the website visitors have filled out a profile with the website, more personal information could be used to classify the visitors. The downside to using personal information is that it could be used to re-identify an individual. Grouping individuals via aggregation mitigates this risk. So instead of stating that John Smith, age 47 from Seattle, Washington, likes Justin Bieber's music, aggregated statistics could state that 120 males between the ages of 40 and 50 from Seattle, Washington, like Justin Bieber's music.

An online company can use aggregated data to determine interest categories from its visitors, such as the books they like to read, games they like to play, where they like to vacation and how often they get allergies. There should be a large enough sample in each category such that the individuals in the category aren't known. For example, if the category is people over the age of 100 from Lansing, Michigan, or all the people in an age group that you are studying, then it will be easy to identify the participants who are members of the category. Some rules to follow:

- There should be a large enough group population of people involved in any set of data

- Categorizations should include a broad set of participants without including them all

- No data captured in a dataset should make it easy to identify a participant, such as one brown eye and one green eye

Regulators view aggregation as a reasonable way to achieve de-identification and unlinkability. The FTC Privacy Report and EU Data Protection Directive both refer to aggregation of data. Organizations should work with a statistician and privacy professional on any aggregation plans to ensure the right amount of privacy protections are being applied to the data gathering and analysis without compromising the ability to learn valuable information from the data.

5.3 Privacy by Design

The term *Privacy by Design* (PbD) has been used for many years by many people in the privacy community. While Information and Privacy Commissioner of Ontario, Ann Cavoukian brought the term into prominence and gave it structure.[24]

The resistance to embedding privacy into products stemmed from the reluctance of developers to take privacy into account when building applications. Early on there was a natural trust of employees to do the right thing and no Internet to provide external intruders with an easy way to access organizational systems. Data breaches were rarely heard of. They usually presented themselves as a lost tape or disk. Most thieves back then weren't savvy enough to know how to read tapes, and what would they do with the data anyway?

Software practices contributed to the onslaught of cyber attacks in the 1990s before they were even called cyber attacks. Default passwords were used to streamline the install process. Encryption was avoided, as it added complexity to applications and impacted performance. Applications frequently connected to online services to gather the most current information, leaking user data in the process. Very little was done to protect against malware, hackers or even spam. In those days an "I Love You" e-mail could bring an enterprise to its knees.[25]

As for sharing online data, it was the Wild Wild West. Online companies could share data willy-nilly with anyone they chose with impunity. There were very few privacy statements, privacy officers or privacy protections for consumers. As you could imagine, the situation turned into a train wreck, with consumers being the victims. A long string of data breaches occurred, with ChoicePoint being the poster child for what can happen to a company when proper privacy practices are not in place.[26]

The number of hacking incidents grew exponentially as the thirst for data and the price for hacking exploits grew. Buffer overflow became a common vernacular of the day. A realization came over regulators that something had to be done to stem the tide of privacy breaches. California led the states with privacy laws, demanding privacy statements for all online companies and the first data breach notification law.[27]

Article 23 of the recently proposed EU General Data Protection Regulation is devoted to data protection by design and default.[28] Likewise, Privacy by Design is the FTC's number one principle in its December 2010 Staff Report.[29]

Commissioner Cavoukian often speaks on PbD at conferences internationally. The demand for PbD has come from regulators, advocates and practitioners for some time now. The continued need for it is self-evident in light of ongoing data breaches. The willful collection and sharing of personal data continues to happen without consent. The simple tenets of notice and choice are often pushed aside while greater focus is placed on squeezing utility out of consumer data.

This doesn't mean that all organizations are bad actors. Here are some things that organizations can do to institute good PbD:

1. **Commit to a PbD program.** Just letting employees know that PbD is a priority to executives will help shift the mindset of employees toward greater awareness of its importance. The commitment to the PbD program should be included in employee training.

2. **Create a privacy standard.** The importance of privacy standards is widely known.[30] All organizations should have a privacy standard that applies to all new projects, applications and services. The standard should describe expectations around the PbD program, provide guidelines and practices for adhering to the standard and help to ensure that commitments made in the privacy policy are met.

3. **Perform privacy reviews.** A privacy review should be performed on all new projects, applications and services. It should confirm that the guidelines in the privacy standard are being followed or validate any exceptions to the guidelines. Privacy reviews should be performed early in the design phase for new projects to help minimize the impact on the project, and be repeated as often as necessary to validate any remediation that occurred or review any changes to the design.

4. **Perform a data flow analysis.** An evaluation should be made of all data that is collected, stored, processed and transmitted. An inventory of the data should be made that describes the categorization of the data along with the origin of the data and custodian, if known. The data category should be matched against how the data is handled at each step along the data flow to ensure it is being handled properly.

5. **Transparency.** All data that is being collected and processed by an organization should be described in the organization's privacy notice. For data that falls into sensitive categories like financial, medical or location, provide a prominent notice at installation time, first run of an application or service or at the time the data is being collected.

6. **Control.** Settings should be made available that permit users to manage how their data is processed or shared by an organization. Organizations should consider providing users with granular control over their data so they are not forced into an all-or-nothing approach to its management. Privacy settings should be easy to find, use and understand. Prior consent should be obtained before collecting sensitive data. The default value for privacy settings should not place users or their data at risk.

7. **Access.** There should be a means for users to view data that is collected from them, whether it was observed, declared or inferred. There will be cases where the owner of the data is not certain, in which case prudence should be observed to avoid leaking potentially sensitive information to the wrong party. Users should also be able to modify and delete their data and export it in a usable format.

8. **Retention.** A retention policy should be applied to all data being collected. A de-identification or deletion plan should be associated with the retention period so the proper disposition can be applied to the data. The retention policy should be recorded so that all employees accessing the data are aware of their obligations. Data belonging to users should be deleted once they close their account or securely stored until the end of the applicable retention period.

9. **Security.** The proper level of security should be applied to data to keep it secure during transmission and storage. Access to data should be limited to those who have a legitimate business reason to access it.

5.4 Privacy by Redesign

Privacy by Design is a great concept for new projects, but what about projects that have already been completed and deployed? The concept of Privacy by Redesign (PbRD) was developed by Commissioner Cavoukian to address that scenario.[31]

Over time, an organization's privacy policies can change; regulations, laws and self-regulatory regimes can be updated; technology can evolve; and threats to data can intensify. Those factors can place an organization's data-handling practices out of compliance, security protections may need to be updated or user consent may need to be obtained.

A company cannot rest on its laurels and assume that once it has ensured privacy compliance for all its systems, a later review is unnecessary. In large organizations where data collection and processing can be done by many teams, new ways of extracting value from data will be found that are not covered by current privacy notices and policies. In cases where the new functionality is desired, the privacy notices will need to be updated to reflect the new practices. Website visitors and users of the organization's applications and services will need to be informed of the changes. In some cases, additional consent will need to be obtained.

Each time a privacy event occurs that may impact the way your organization handles data, an evaluation should be made of the systems that may have been impacted. The next steps are to estimate the new work to be done then prioritize and schedule it. To be a world-class privacy organization, it is not enough to say that new products meet high standards of privacy. An organization must strive to ensure that all products, new and old, meet high standards.

5.5 Conclusion

"Filo, I saw your PR report and I'm pleased to see that our de-identification techniques have been well received," said Amy.

"Amy, much of the credit goes to Euan, who implemented a lot of the work," replied Filo. "He even followed the HIPAA guidelines and contracted a de-identification expert to help define some of our policies. David has had those practices integrated into our deployment process as part of our Privacy by Design program."

"We should get the word out on that work as well," said Amy. "The more organizations that are aware of these practices we are implementing here, the faster we will mitigate the risks to privacy everywhere."

There are several ways to implement authentication within an enterprise via something a person knows, has or is. Care must be taken to choose a mechanism that provides the right amount of protection without causing too much complexity. Complexity can cause people to seek shortcuts, which can diminish the protective qualities of an authentication regime. In the same manner, the right level of identifiability can permit the safe use of personal data without exposing the original owners of the data to privacy risks.

The ability to reliably de-identify and unlink data is an important technique for an organization to learn. It permits a company to obtain utility from data while protecting personal privacy. Using the HIPAA Privacy Rule safe-harbor de-identification guidelines and aggregation are good ways to perform de-identification.

For organizations developing applications and services, a Privacy by Design program will help to mitigate privacy risk early on in a project and help organizations avoid the mistakes of the early days of the Internet. For applications and services that are already in use, it's not too late to deploy Privacy by Redesign.

Endnotes

1 RFID is s a generic term for technologies that use radio waves to automatically identify people or objects. "Frequently Asked Questions," *RFID Journal*, www.rfidjournal.com/site/faqs.

2 According to a recent study, stolen passwords played a role in 48 percent of the data breaches that involved hacking. Sam Curry, "Transforming Identity Assurance through Risk-Based Authentication," *EMC Pulse* (Product & Technology Blog), February 26, 2013, http://pulseblog .emc.com/2013/02/26/transforming-identity-assurance-through-risk-based-authentication-2/. About 90 percent of all attacks happening to larger corporations and government in 2012 had weak or stolen credentials. Robert Lemos, "Targeted Attacks, Weak Passwords Top IT Risks in 2013," *eWeek*, January 1, 2012, www.eweek.com/security/targeted-attacks-weak-passwords-top-it-security-risks-in-2013/.

3 Fox Van Allen, "Google Reveals the 10 Worst Password Ideas," *Time*, Tech, August 8, 2013, http://techland.time.com/2013/08/08/google-reveals-the-10-worst-password-ideas/.

4 "Worst Passwords of 2012—and How to Fix Them," Splashdata, http://splashdata.com/press/pr121023.htm.

5 Sam Laird, "38% of Us Would Rather Clean a Toilet Than Think of New Password," Mashable, August 23, 2013, http://mashable.com/2012/08/23/password-overload/.

6 "How Does Mask Me Work," Abine, accessed December 5, 2013, www.abine.com/maskme/.

7 LastPass, https://lastpass.com.

8 Picture Password Classic is an example of a program that uses a picture as an authentication mechanism. David Lane, "Picture Password Classic—Unique Lock to Secure your Media and Files," Red Mouse Media Version 1.2, Apple, iTunes Preview, July 16, 2013, https://itunes.apple.com/us/app/picture-password-classic-unique/id505944899?mt=8.

9 John Leyden, "Gummi Bears Defeat Fingerprint Sensors: Sticky Problem for Biometric Firms," *The Register*, May 16, 2002, www.theregister.co.uk/2002/05/16/gummi_bears_defeat_fingerprint_sensors/.

10 "Introduction to Biometrics," Biometrics Consortium, accessed December 5, 2013, www .biometrics.org/introduction.php; "Definition of Biometrics," International Biometric Society, accessed December 5, 2013, www.biometricsociety.org/about/definition-of-biometrics/.

11 "RSA SecurID: Software Authenticators, Flexible Software Tokens for a Mobile Workforce," EMC2, accessed December 5, 2013, www.emc.com/security/rsa-securid/rsa-securid-software-authenticators.htm; "Tails: Privacy for anyone anywhere," Tails, last edited October 29, 2013, https://tails.boum.org; "3.2.4. LUKS Disk Encryption," Red Hat, accessed December 5, 2013, https://access.redhat.com/site/documentation/en-US/Red_Hat_Enterprise_Linux/6/html/Security_Guide/sect-Security_Guide-LUKS_Disk_Encryption.html.

12 Curry, "Transforming Identity Assurance through Risk-Based Authentication."

13 "Tor: Anonymity Online," Tor Project, accessed December 5, 2013, www.torproject.org.

14 P. Leach, M. Mealling and R. Salz, "A Universally Unique IDentifier (UUID) URN Namespace," Memo on Proposed Standard, Network Working Group, Internet Society, Internet Engineering Task Force (IETF), July 2005, http://tools.ietf.org/html/rfc4122.html.

15 Phil Roberts, "IPv6 Deployment Hits 2%, Keeps Growing," Internet Society, *Tech Matters* (blog), September 24, 2013, www.internetsociety.org/blog/2013/09/ipv6-deployment-hits-2-keeps-growing/.

16 Latanya Sweeney, Akua Abu and Julie Winn, "Identifying Participants in the Personal Genome Project by Name," Harvard University, Data Privacy Lab, White Paper 102-1, April 24, 2013, http://dataprivacylab.org/projects/pgp/index.html.

17 Chris Soghoian, "AOL, Netflix and the end of open access to research data," CNET, November 30, 2007, http://news.cnet.com/8301-13739_3-9826608-46.html.

18 "Guidance Regarding Methods for De-Identification of Protected Health Information in Accordance with the Health Insurance Portability and Accountability Act (HIPAA) Privacy Rule," U.S. Department of Health & Human Services, November 26, 2012, www.hhs.gov/ocr/privacy/hipaa/ understanding/coveredentities/De-identification/hhs_deid_guidance.pdf .

19 HIPAA, 45 CFR 164.514(b)(2).

20 *Protecting Consumer Privacy in an Era of Rapid Change: Recommendations for Businesses and Policymakers*, FTC Report, Federal Trade Commission, March 2012, www.ftc.gov/sites/default/ files/documents/reports/federal-trade-commission-report-protecting-consumer-privacy-era-rapid-change-recommendations/120326privacyreport.pdf.

21 "The Role of Digital Identity Management in the Internet Economy: A Primer for Policy Makers," Organisation for Economic Co-operation and Development, June 11, 2009, www.oecd.org/ internet/ieconomy/43091476.pdf.

22 Council Directive 1995/46/EC, 1995 O.J. L 281 p. 31, http://eur-lex.europa.eu/LexUriServ/ LexUriServ.do?uri=CELEX:31995L0046:EN:HTML.

23 Article 29 Data Protection Working Party, "Opinion 4/2007 on the Concept of Personal Data," Directorate C (Civil Justice, Rights and Citizenship) of the European Commission, B-1049 Brussels, Belgium, Office No LX-46 01/43, Tech. Rep. 01248/07/EN WP 136, June 20, 2007, http:// ec.europa.eu/justice/policies/privacy/docs/wpdocs/2007/wp136_en.pdf.

24 Commissioner Cavoukian also runs a website by the same name where she describes the "7 Foundational Principles" of Privacy by Design:

> Proactive not Reactive; Preventative not Remedial
>
> Privacy as the Default Setting
>
> Privacy Embedded Directly into Design
>
> Full Functionality—Positive-Sum, not Zero-Sum
>
> End-to-End Security—Full Lifecycle Protection
>
> Visibility and Transparency—Keep it Open
>
> Respect for User Privacy—Keep it User-Centric

Ann Cavoukian, "7 Foundational Principles," Privacy by Design, www.privacybydesign.ca/index. php/about-pbd/7-foundational-principles/.

25 Definition: I LOVEYOU virus, Search Security, last updated February 2006, http://searchsecurity .techtarget.com/definition/ILOVEYOU-virus.

26 "Consumer Data Broker ChoicePoint Failed to Protect Consumers' Personal Data, Left Key Electronic Monitoring Tool Turned Off for Four Months," Federal Trade Commission, October 19, 2009, www.ftc.gov/news-events/press-releases/2009/10/consumer-data-broker-choicepoint-failed-protect-consumers.

27 Beth Givens, "California Security Breach Notification Law Goes into Effect July 1, 2003," Privacy Rights Clearinghouse, June 23, 2003, www.privacyrights.org/ar/SecurityBreach.htm.

28 "Proposal for a Regulation of the European Parliament and of the Council, on the Protection of Individuals with Regard to the Processing of Personal Data and on the Free Movement of Such Data," COM(2012) 11 final, January 25, 2012, http://ec.europa.eu/justice/data-protection/ document/review2012/com_2012_11_en.pdf.

29 "Protecting Consumer Privacy in an Era of Rapid Change: A Proposed Framework for Businesses and Policymakers," Preliminary Staff Report of the Federal Trade Commission, December 2010, www.ftc.gov/os/2010/12/101201privacyreport.pdf.

30 The continued importance of privacy standards is evidenced by the IETF Network Working Group's Privacy Considerations for Internet Protocols specification to make people aware of privacy-related design choices. A. Cooper et al., "Privacy Considerations for Internet Protocols: draft-iab-privacy-considerations-09.txt," Internet Engineering Task Force, November 23, 2013, http://tools.ietf .org/html/draft-iab-privacy-considerations-09. The NTIA and California both recently released recommendations for mobile privacy. "Privacy Multistakeholder Process: Mobile Application Transparency," National Telecommunications & Information Administration, November 12, 2013, www.ntia.doc.gov/other-publication/2013/privacy-multistakeholder-process-mobile-application-transparency; Kamala D. Harris, "Privacy on the Go: Recommendations for the Mobile Ecosystem," Office of the Attorney General, California Department of Justice, January 2013, http://oag.ca.gov/ sites/all/files/pdfs/privacy/privacy_on_the_go.pdf.

31 The approach of PbRD is for organizations to rethink, redesign and revive legacy systems. Ann Cavoukian and Marilyn Prosch, "Privacy by Design: Building a Better Legacy," Privacy by Design, May 2011, http://www.ipc.on.ca/images/Resources/PbRD-legacy.pdf.

## CHAPTER 6

Online Privacy Issues

"Good morning, everyone," said Amy, greeting her team. "I would like to start today's privacy council with a discussion on social networks. It has come to my attention that a couple of our colleagues got carried away over the weekend chatting on Facebook about an upcoming conference. They were having a conversation on what they should wear when meeting with a company with whom we are in acquisition talks. While nothing about the acquisition was mentioned, the company name was used several times. These discussions fueled rumors already floating around on the Internet, producing a flurry of conversations and messages, and creating further unwanted interest in the acquisition. We need to ensure that our employees and partners understand that posts seen by friends may also be seen by friends of friends, unless you change your privacy settings. Even with the privacy settings properly set, we need to ensure they also understand our company policy on Internet use and the public release and discussion of business transactions. As an example, there was the incident of a developer responding to a tweet correcting a journalist about a tweet he made about our new product launch. The journalist was merely fishing and caught a live one."

"Amy, should I start blocking access to social sites from our corporate network?" asked Euan.

"No, the best approach is to update our training and awareness program," responded Amy. "We can complete it over the next few months and announce the updated program during Data Privacy Day at the beginning of next year."

"I'll brief executives about the incidents during the next senior leadership team meeting and our plan to address them through awareness and training," stated David.

"Thank you both for your assistance. There is also another matter about online sharing. Some customers have complained about us leaking data to advertisers even after users have opted out of behavioral advertising on our site. Bill, could you take a look into that issue?"

"Sure, Amy, I'll get right on that after this meeting."

"Thanks, Bill. Finally, for any of you who have sent me a friend request on Facebook, don't hold your breath waiting on a response. If you want to connect with me after hours, you're going to have to do so the old-fashioned way, with encrypted e-mail," said Amy with a smile.

6.1 Specific Requirements for the Online Environment

The power of the Internet can be seen in everything individuals do at work, play, home and school. Services like Lockbox permit the sharing of multi-megabyte documents with people across the globe in an instant. People can participate in multiperson video conversations, check the status of servers across multiple sites and track the movements of company vehicles, all while sitting behind a desk or using a mobile smart device/phone.[1] Our ability to reach out and connect with people also provides the ability for sensitive data to intentionally or unintentionally be shared with the wrong people or organizations. External parties, unbeknownst to us, can also connect with us and gather information surreptitiously. IT professionals need to permit their organizations to benefit from the power of online interactions without becoming susceptible to its trappings or denying critical functions with too much security.

6.1.1 Organizational Privacy Strategy for Social Media

When it comes to the online space, organizations can't be too careful. Employees often use social networks, where there are many opportunities for leaks to occur from inappropriate sharing with people outside the organization or for viruses to spread within the organization due to premature trusting of content received from a supposed friend, a colleague, or application. But some social interaction is good for organizations as it helps them to connect with current and potential customers. Many employees will have friends and past employees who look them up on the professional social network LinkedIn to see where they currently work, providing familiarity with the company name and its products and services. Posts on these pages can also help the company learn what people like and dislike about the company's products, advertising methods and branding.[2]

How and when to engage social networks is not an easy decision to make. There are many risks involved, but the possible benefits are huge as well. Here are some guidelines to follow when developing an organizational privacy strategy for social media:

- **Determine your audience.** Knowing your audience will help you determine the data you want to collect, how you want to use it and with whom you plan to share it. Limiting the amount of data collected and your organization's data processing practices will help to mitigate privacy risks regarding the use of online data.

- **Determine your message.** Once an audience or set of audiences is defined, organizations should determine the message they would like presented to each audience. Random tweets or blog posts are not good for projecting a consistent, authoritative image for an organization. Organizational positioning may change weekly by audience. Therefore, updates should be disseminated in an organized fashion to all key stakeholders.

- **Assign owners.** The number of people tweeting for a company can be problematic as the messaging can become disjointed, overexposed or muddled. For each area of the company or each messaging strategy, there should be one owner who controls the messaging and is responsible for relaying it to the appropriate people. Employees should still be able to show their own individuality, but not to the extent that they veer off message.

- **Create content guidelines.** Employees who are on social media may want to use it to distribute information about public events, product launches, support issues, management changes or policy changes. Content guidelines need to be developed around the use of social media to prevent leakage of sensitive information, improper statements or premature releases of information. Organizations should consider having employees use separate accounts for personal and business content. Each employee should take training and sign an agreement before being permitted to post content on social media for the organization.

- **Use corporate IDs.** When deciding to use social media to engage an audience, organizations should insist that employees using social media include an organizational designator in the ID and follow organizational content policies. By controlling the ownership of the account, organizations can control the messaging and prevent former employees from using the account to redirect followers to competitors or to post negative messages after leaving the company.

- **Limit what can be shared.** Social media jockeys often get loose and free online and cross the line when it comes to sharing content with their followers. Even when policies are in place against sharing, some employees may feel that some content is okay to share with trusted journalists or under a nondisclosure agreement. Policies often cannot cover every specific scenario, so limits should be set and disseminated for each new project to avoid misunderstandings. Organizational content should also be tagged with an appropriate classification that will let employees know whether it is safe to share outside the organization. If necessary, the organization can segregate the most important company data by creating a "need to know" policy that would be assigned to data that should never be shared with the public.

6.1.2 Regulatory Requirements Specific to the Online Environment

The following is a summary of regulatory requirements that apply to the online environment.

- The **Children's Online Privacy Protection Act** (COPPA) restricts websites' ability to collect or use data from children under 13 without verifiable parental consent.[3] Targeted advertising may not be served to children. These requirements also apply to websites that are targeted at children.

- The **e-Privacy Directive** as amended by the EU Cookie Directive covers the processing of personal data and protection of online privacy.[4] It requires that websites that use cookies for tracking purposes provide enhanced notice to website visitors. Websites should also provide users with the ability to see, modify and delete their data.

- The **California Online Privacy Protection Act** (CalOPPA) requires that websites provide a privacy statement to visitors and an easy-to-find link on their web pages.[5] Websites that carry personal data on children under 18 years of age must permit them to delete their data. Websites must inform visitors of the type of Do Not Track mechanisms they support or if they do not support any at all.

6.1.3 Consumer Expectations

Many consumers view the online world much as they view the physical world. They may walk through a mall that has many shops in it, stop at a shop to view items in its window and then move on to the next shop. If they like what they see in the shop, they may go inside and wander through the shop to see what is inside. They may make a purchase with cash or a credit card. If they frequent the shop, they may build a relationship with the shop's salespeople, who may make recommendations to them on subsequent visits.

Consumers manage which stores they go to as well as the type and depth of relationship they wish to have with each shop and its salesclerks. They can pay cash and be anonymous, use a credit card and/or form a relationship with salespeople. There is an assumption that the clerks or shops' accounting systems won't share their information with others, even the consumers' friends if they are known. Some consumers use loyalty cards in order to receive discounts on merchandise, understanding that the store and the corporation behind it will get access to their purchasing history.

The bricks-and-mortar model of engaging customers is thousands of years old. People are not only familiar with that model, but have become comfortable with it. In the transition to the Internet, people have become disillusioned that their experience with websites does not mimic what they have experienced in physical stores. Some may feel that a website "knows" them even before they have spent any time on the site.

While surfing the Internet, many consumers overlay their experiences in physical stores onto the sites that they visit. That is why, when visiting a website for the first time, many are surprised to see an ad featuring a product they were viewing on an unaffiliated site. Amazon's method of engaging its customers with recommendations and wish lists from friends and family is welcomed by many of its visitors because they feel they have a relationship with Amazon through the people they know. Amazon helps you find the products you want and makes sure that you get them in a timely fashion. Your purchases and browsing on the Amazon site help Amazon to make meaningful recommendations. Accordingly, users can easily control Amazon's ability to provide recommendations or share data through wish lists.

Understanding how websites and advertisers track people is not as intuitive or easy as you would think. Most people do not fully understand the "opt-in" and "opt-out" choices when they are presented or how to configure their user account to deny data sharing. One method to do this is via the AdChoices icon that advertisers may place on or near their ads or a publisher may place in the footer of its web pages.

The AdChoices program is run by the Digital Advertising Alliance (DAA), which consists of over 100 members from the advertising industry.[6] It is denoted on web pages by the AdChoices icon on or near ads or in the footer of a web page. By clicking on the icon the user is presented with information on how targeted ads are being served, who may be serving the ad and how to opt out of behavioral advertising from advertisers on the site or from all advertisers who are members of the DAA. It may also pop up a small window giving users inline information and a choice of links that provide additional information or access to an opt-out mechanism. Unfortunately, not all advertisers are members of the AdChoices program, so they may continue to track consumers across the Internet even though they have opted out of targeted advertising.

By going to the program's opt-out website, a user can opt out of behavioral advertising from any of the individual program members or all of them collectively by clicking a single checkbox. The site will also show the opt-out status for each of the member sites. Using the DAA site is the same as going to each of the member sites individually to opt out.

As an IT or privacy professional in the online advertising business, you should consider following a regime like the self-regulatory principles of programs such as the DAA's Self-Regulatory Principles for Online Behavioral Advertising, IAB's Self-Regulatory Program for Online Behavioral Advertising or other industry standards that promote privacy.[7] These programs help to ensure that user profiles created for advertising purposes are based on industry best practices and user preferences. Antiquated data gathering, usage and sharing practices that were previously part of a retailer's DNA have been replaced globally by different laws, regulations and standards. Given the increased use of the Internet to shop, communicate and purchase, websites should provide clear information to users about the organization's privacy practices. These should be easy to understand and allow the consumer to opt out of tracking without the fear that they will continue to be profiled afterwards.

6.1.4 Children's Online Privacy

In most countries children online are a specially protected group, as they should be. A 2010 survey showed that 73 percent of sexual solicitation occurs online and 40 percent of all teen abductions involved Internet activity.[8] Many countries across the globe provide special privacy protections for children, though they vary in how they classify children and the extent to which the laws protect them. In the United States, the personal information of children under 13 is protected. In Australia and Spain, privacy laws protect children under the age of 18.[9] A website from Harvard University lists laws for protecting children from almost 60 countries.[10]

Cyberbullying has received a lot of attention in recent years due to its impact on children. It not only affects a child's ability to focus on education, but has caused several teen suicides.[11] Laws against cyberbullying are now being enacted to protect children and to help lower the risk of teen suicide. Canada recently introduced bill C-13, Protecting Canadians from Online Crime Act.[12] In Australia, cyberbullies can face jail time.[13] In the United States, since 2010 more than 35 states have produced laws against cyberbullying and online luring of children.[14] Most states view children as people under 16 years of age.

A new book by danah boyd, *It's Complicated: The Social Lives of Networked Teens*, focuses on teen privacy.[15] It has been often said that children and teens don't care about privacy, but boyd, a researcher at Microsoft, argues otherwise: "I think that the big message of my book is to recognize that kids do care about privacy and they're doing all sorts of things to achieve it in spite of parental surveillance."

IT professionals and online organizations should examine the services they provide to their website visitors and how they might be used in negative ways against children. Social networks such as Twitter and Facebook are great places for children to build communities where they can communicate with their peers. However, they can also be dangerous places for children. Advice for online companies that cater to teens and children:

- Provide rules of conduct and enforce them

- Monitor open forums for those breaking the rules

- Provide features to permit users to block unwanted contact

- Provide the ability to report bad behavior and inappropriate posts

- Validate that your site's services are not being used to house criminal activity

- Involve the authorities when it appears laws have been broken

- Provide guidance to members on how to get help if they feel threatened online

- Study the international laws and initiatives designed to protect children[16]

6.2 Social Media and Websites That Present a Higher Level of Privacy Challenges

Humans have always had an enormous desire to connect with each other. Before the advent of electronic communications, there were smoke signals, drums, yodeling, letters and other means to communicate across distances. Within large organizations, people had to depend on a fellow employee's memory or paper-based organizational directories to be able to contact someone. When Alexander Graham Bell invented the telephone, he didn't expect many people to use it, but it soon became an expected fixture in most homes. The phone itself was not as instrumental as the phone book, which provided the information to connect with people. The telephone system can be viewed as the first rudimentary social network. Imagine for the first time being able to pick up a book and find the address and phone number of anyone in town and call or go to that person's address—even the mayor or the chief of police. To find people in other cities, you called directory assistance to learn a person's address and phone number and didn't have to explain why or who you were. Today, the phone book has not changed much, but it is rarely used since online search engines are typically used to look up a person's phone number or address.

In 1978, the French invented the Minitel system, which was a monitor that came with the phone system and replaced the phone book.[17] Households could search for the address or phone number of any person or business in the country by entering a search query. People could create bulletin boards or engage in online chats. The French Minitel network could be viewed as having established the first online social community.

When the Internet came into prominence in the late 1980s, it provided a global means for people to connect with each other. Online social networks began as simple text-based bulletin board systems (BBS).[18] Areas were categorized by interest such as music.rock .heavymetal or art.painters.impressionists.french. It was an easy, albeit crude, means to find people with similar interests.

Chat evolved from text chat to comic chat, virtual reality chat and back to text chat with emoticons. Organized social networks emerged with Friendster taking the lead, followed by Myspace; for now, Facebook is the clear winner, with Google+ quietly closing in on it.

The point of this walk down memory lane is to show how humans have always sought more efficient and innovative ways to communicate. In many cases, those technologies far exceeded our expectations. As we continue to expand our horizons, we must be sure to expand privacy safeguards in equal measure.

6.2.1 Social Networks and Their Benefits

As with the BBS systems of old, social networks permit people to communicate with each other in many different ways. As the communication needs of people evolve, including the need for privacy, new social networks arise to address the need. For example, consider this short list of social networks that have come along in recent years:

- About.me: An online identity page that serves as an online identity card
- Chatroulette.com: A chat website that permits users to connect with random strangers over video
- Facebook.com: A social network that lets people create online communities
- FamilyCrossings.com: A social network dedicated to families and privacy
- FamilyHQ.com: A social network dedicated to families and privacy
- FamilyLeaf.com: A social network dedicated to families and privacy
- FamilyLobby.com: A social network dedicated to families
- Foursquare.com: A website for sharing one's location with friends
- Friendster.com: A social network that lets people connect with friends
- Instagram.com: A social site for sharing pictures
- LinkedIn.com: A social network dedicated to a person's professional career
- Kidmondo.com: A social site for sharing a journal of a child's first years
- Myspace.com: A social network that lets people create online communities
- Plus.google.com: A social network that lets people create online communities
- Sgrouples.com: A social network dedicated to families and privacy
- Snapchat: A social network that lets people share chats that delete themselves
- Twitter: A social network that lets people share 140-character messages with followers
- Whisper.sh: A place to anonymously leave secrets
- Yammer.com: A social network designed for commercial use

The fascinating thing about social networks is that they permit people to connect with other people all over the world, almost instantly, in many different ways. People can blog, chat, e-mail, text or tweet; post text, pictures, songs or videos; communicate with voice or video; check in at different places; and form relationships in different ways. The compelling nature of social networks entices people to let their guard down and to post more and more personal data online. The more information a person volunteers about themselves, the more likely a past friend, family member or colleague will be able to find them. Social networks also permit people to connect with online communities with similar interests such as skydiving, biking or mountain climbing. Most social networks don't charge money; instead they use the information members provide to target advertisements at them. People can also use this same data to cause harm to individuals, to commit identify theft or to carry out other malicious acts.

IT professionals should be wary of the impact that social networks can have on their organizations. First, they can reduce productivity as hours can easily go by while catching up with an old friend or family member, or just by posting daily updates. Employees may also forget that while they are sharing information with an old friend, many other people may be listening in on the conversation or viewing posted content—even the social network company itself. The eavesdropping may not be malicious, but it can present a risk to organizations. Sensitive release dates, new features, acquisition plans or important contacts could inadvertently be released, causing harm to the company. In other cases, posts considered offensive or outside the social norm could get an employee fired or put the company in a negative public light. A recent example is Jofi Joseph of the National Security Council, who was fired by the White House for posting highly offensive tweets about officials in Washington under the Twitter handle @NatSecWonk.[19]

6.2.2 Personal Information Collected

The beginning of a relationship with a social network starts with the sign-up process. It is expected that new members will provide a user ID, name, e-mail address and birth date. You may also be asked for a home address, phone number and business affiliation. This type of information is considered demographic; it enables social networks to cross-reference member information against several public databases to learn more about its members, and they do! When a zip code is given to a salesperson during a credit card purchase, that additional information along with the data on the card makes it easier to find customers' addresses and send them flyers in the mail.

When using a social network, members will be asked for other information such as their interests, where they work, where they went to school, the branch of service they were in and any affiliation with local groups. Members may be provided with a means to enter contacts or connections and even categorize them. This information can be used to target people as a group on the assumption that people who are connected have similar interests. Advertisements or recommendations can be sent to the entire group instead of a single person. If a person in the group clicks on one of those targeted ads, it reinforces the assumption that the content of the ad is relevant to the group. People in the group may even be informed that one of them has shown interest in the ad or content that was presented.

A person's demographic information, interests and associations are considered "declared data," or data that a member gives to the social network. This declared data can be used to build an online profile. Collectively, user profiles can be used to improve the service, address security and fraud issues, provide better content and serve more relevant advertisements. Individuals often create multiple accounts using different declared data in order to distinguish between different online personas and their relationships with people and organizations. Each of those personas will cause a different profile to be created in order to serve personalized content relevant to that persona.

Over time, all interactions with and within a social network add to a person's profile. Every time a member of a social network posts text, pictures, videos or links or interacts with connections using chat, games, invites, tags or check-ins, the service may take note of them. Whenever a member visits a website where the social network has a presence, the visit may be recorded along with any interactions with its social widgets. While a person may be interested in tracking her online browsing habits or even sharing them with friends, she may not care to share them with the social network and have them used to serve personalized content. Most services provide a means to opt out of the use of their data for personalization and sometimes even to delete their history. IT professionals should be cognizant of the different social networks and their possible risk to organizational data and provide guidelines for engaging them. Yammer is a type of social network that is focused on business use and thus might be more appropriate for sharing data between employees. Organizations that provide social networks should ensure they are giving its members the right level of transparency over their data as well as control over its use.

6.2.3 Personal Information Shared

Sharing of personal information across social networks has become the norm in many cases, and users have come to expect it. At some level people see it as a convenience; being able to log in to sites using a Twitter, Google or Facebook account seems practical. Being able to post on Twitter and LinkedIn at the same time is more efficient. The ability to let my friends know which articles and products I like as I browse the web is a great convenience. However, in each case personal data is being shared across social networks and other sites.

When using Facebook to connect to a site, Facebook becomes aware of that connection and the new site probably gets some of your Facebook data in return. This is not necessarily a bad thing, but people should be aware of the data exchange that goes on when connecting sites together or clicking on social widgets that are provided on a web page. During the sign-up or connection process between sites, options are sometimes provided for controlling what is shared between the sites. Online services also have privacy settings that permit the control of what data is being shared. When performing a search for shoes on Bing while connected to Facebook, I can see posts from my friends that mention shoes. While it may be useful for me to see those posts, I have to remember that Bing gets to see them as well.

Websites and services that share personal data with other sites and services should follow these guidelines:

- Have a policy that limits what organizations can do with data you share with them

- Inform users of the data sharing that may occur

- Permit users to control the sharing of their data

- Permit users to remove any previously shared data

- Share only the data needed to provide the service or feature

- Ensure users benefit from the sharing of their data

- Apply a retention policy to collected data

6.2.4 No Clear Owner of Content Published or Data Collected

When data is entered into a social network via posts, uploads or clicks from third-party sites, such as when using Google's +1 button, it is difficult to determine who owns the data that was captured by the service. Social networks typically have terms of use that members agree to when they sign up for the service. However, the terms of use do not trump laws or public outrage. Facebook found that out when its terms of use declared that it could keep content from users forever. There was such a backlash that Facebook changed its policy.

Ownership is important, and concerns over how data is used and shared continue to surface in the news. Social networks often wish to use content shared by its members to earn revenue to run the service. Considering that the use of the service is typically free, it would seem reasonable for the service to monetize some of the content it receives. To what extent should that be allowed, though, and what control should be given to the user? A general rule of privacy is that a person should not be surprised by the use of his or her data.

Let's say that Brandon takes a picture of Coley and Dee and sends it to Erica, who posts it on her Facebook page. Coley is unhappy with the picture and requests that Facebook take it down. Does Facebook have the right to take the picture down? Does Erica or Brandon own the picture, or both? What if Coley likes having the picture displayed? When do First Amendment rights come into play? What happens if people start copying the picture around the Internet? Who can request that copies be taken down? When does fair use come into play?

These are the issues that owners of websites that permit posting of content have to deal with quite often. Unfortunately, there are no clear answers. When in public there is little expectation of privacy. Restrictions may be applied to the placement of content, depending on the subject matter and how it is used. Often, a lawyer must get involved when standard requests for content removal do not yield the desired results.

6.3 Online Threats

While online, individuals can be exposed to many threats that can steal data, take over accounts or delete files. These exploits can also be of threat to organizations in the way of decreased productivity, theft of corporate or customer data, deletion of content, modification of device configurations or legal liability. Understanding the type of threats that exist can assist IT professionals with mitigating those threats and training employees in how to avoid them. This section will discuss some of those threats and provide examples.

6.3.1 Phishing Exploits

Phishing (pronounced fishing), a data-gathering exploit, was initially launched via instant messaging but is now accomplished mostly via e-mail. The spelling comes from hackers' custom of using the letters "ph" in place of "f." With most phishing exploits, a fake e-mail is disguised to look like it is from a legitimate organization or person to lure an unsuspecting consumer to click on a link embedded in the e-mail. Once the link is clicked, the user is either sent to a fake website designed to look like a legitimate company's website, such as a banking or shopping website, or prompted to download software onto the computer. Phishing exploits can occur in the following ways:

- **Fake websites.** Most phishing exploits occur through illicit content being sent to an individual pretending to be from a legitimate user or business. The content can be sent within an e-mail or instant message or during a chat session. The content usually consists of text intended to encourage an unwary user to click on a link that connects to a fake site, which may look like a legitimate website, in order to get the user to fill out a form with their personal information or provide a login to a website such as a banking site. The fake site could redirect the user to the real banking site after capturing the user's credentials.

- **Malware execution.** Some phishing exploits involve sending fake content to encourage a user to download malicious software or open a document that contains malicious software or macros. A malware download request can be disguised as a game or account tool. Once downloaded, the malicious software could capture files, data or keystrokes, copy communications that are sent from the computer to the Internet or the company network and send any captured data to the perpetrator over the Internet. Downloaded malware could also delete files from the user's computer or encrypt the files and ask for a ransom before they are unencrypted.

- **Faulty search results and ads.** After performing a legitimate keyword search, a search engine could return results or advertisements that send the user to a fake site where the user's data could be collected. Fake advertisements could also show as display ads or video ads. These types of exploits are usually caught rather quickly by the search engine service or advertising network. Be sure to report any specious advertisements or websites to known authorities. Most websites and search engines will have a feedback link at the bottom of the page where security or privacy issues can be reported.

- **System modification.** Malware previously downloaded to a user's computer could modify the user's *Hosts* file or browser configuration, causing the user to be sent to the wrong website. Once at the website, the user could be fooled into believing that she is at her banking, healthcare or software download site. This could lead to takeover of an account, identity theft or loss of money. In any case, users should validate from the address bar that they are at the expected location. IT professionals should ensure that systems within their enterprise are using up-to-date browsers and the latest anti-malware software to help mitigate this risk. The following box is an example of a *Hosts* file from a Microsoft Windows computer:

```
# Copyright (c) 1993-2009 Microsoft Corp.
#
# This is a sample HOSTS file used by Microsoft TCP/IP for Windows.
#
# This file contains the mappings of IP addresses to host names. Each
# entry should be kept on an individual line. The IP address should
# be placed in the first column followed by the corresponding host name.
# The IP address and the host name should be separated by at least one
# space.
#
# Additionally, comments (such as these) may be inserted on individual
# lines or following the machine name denoted by a '#' symbol.
#
# For example:
#
#      102.54.94.97    rhino.acme.com        # source server
#      38.25.63.10     x.acme.com            # x client host

# localhost name resolution is handled within DNS itself.
#      127.0.0.1       localhost
#      ::1             localhost
```

6.3.2 Spear Phishing

Spear phishing is used to send phishing e-mails to a group of people from a known organization. For example, e-mails could be sent to alleged Facebook users about a post to their News Feed or to employees at a company known to use Fidelity to manage their 401K, asking them to verify their yearly bonus.

6.3.3 Whaling

Whaling is a type of phishing exploit that goes after people who are known to have lots of money. Senior executives at many companies have public e-mail addresses, which can be used to contact them. The return address of an e-mail can be easily faked to represent a known acquaintance or well-known business. The e-mail could contain enough valid information to persuade the recipient to give up personal information.

6.3.4 Pharming

Pharming is similar to the forms of phishing that send a user to a malicious website, though the tactic for achieving the goal is somewhat different. Pharming redirects a valid Internet request to a malicious site by modifying a *Hosts* file or corrupting the contents of a network router domain name system (DNS) server. There is not much individuals can do to protect themselves from pharming exploits except using up-to-date browsers with features that can identify phishing sites.

6.3.5 Mitigating Phishing Exploits

First, using up-to-date software and anti-malware protection is the best way to mitigate most computer exploits. Current operating systems, browsers, e-mail clients and anti-malware software can detect many of the known phishing exploits that exist today. Avoiding many phishing exploits can be as simple as deleting suspicious e-mails without clicking on links or opening attachments. The sender of an e-mail, if known, can always be contacted to verify the content.

When going to a known website, it is a good practice to always type the URL for the website into the address bar of the browser instead of clicking on a link in an e-mail. Users can also save common links in their browser favorites or address book to make it easier to navigate to websites with long URLs. Erroneous links hidden in e-mail text can sometimes be identified by hovering over the link with a mouse or in Windows, right-clicking on the link and selecting Edit Link from the mouse menu to view it.

Most e-mail applications are able to detect phishing schemes or suspicious attachments and redirect questionable e-mails to the spam or junk e-mail folder. Users should be very careful about clicking on links from any e-mail that has been flagged as junk or spam. Most browsers are also able to identify fake websites. Users should heed the warnings that appear in browsers and avoid websites that are identified as suspicious.

Some websites that have accounts with the user have implemented configurable images or other indicators that the user can choose. When the user logs in, the indicator will be displayed. If the indicator is not seen, then the user can assume that she is at a phishing site.

A site can use a code verification system where the site sends the user a code via a known e-mail address or phone number. If the code is not sent, then the user can assume that the site is a phishing site.

6.3.6 Browser Phishing Protection

The Chrome, Firefox and Internet Explorer browsers provide features that mitigate the risk from phishing and malware. IT professionals should be familiar with these features and ensure that employees are trained on them. The following figures show screenshots of the browsers' antiphishing and anti-malware settings.

Figure 6-1: Internet Explorer SmartScreen Filter

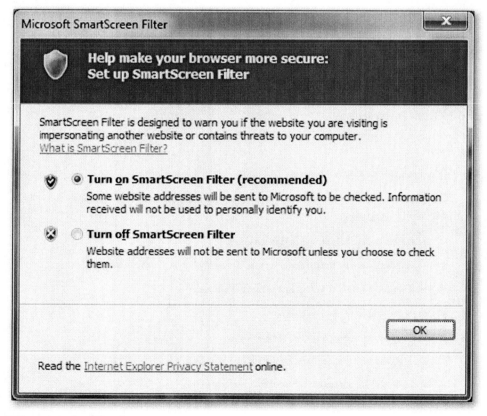

Used with permission from Microsoft.

Figure 6-2: Firefox Security Settings

Figure 6-3: Chrome Privacy Settings

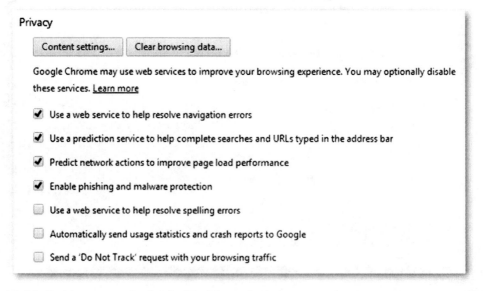

Google and the Google logo are registered trademarks of Google Inc.; used with permission.

6.3.7 SQL Injection

Structured Query Language (SQL) is the software language used for most online databases today. When a person visits a website and fills out a form, it is typically a SQL script that captures the data from the form and places it into a database for processing. Since the script combines whatever is in the form with SQL commands, anything in the form that represents a SQL command could get executed as such. SQL injection occurs when a person intentionally inserts SQL commands in places where data may be captured and sent to a database for processing. SQL injection could expose personal data, insert inappropriate data into a database, delete data from a database or shut a database down.

SQL injection is one of the oldest and most well-known threats used on the Internet today. IT professionals should ensure that databases are properly configured and that the database code on their websites is written to minimize the risks that can come from SQL injection.

Example of SQL Injection

The command "DELETE FROM MyTable" is meant to delete all data from the table MyTable. Let's say a person knows that a Customer table exists in a database and entered the following string into a name field of a web form:

"My Name'); DELETE FROM Customer; --"

If the code processing the form is not written properly, it could cause all data to be deleted from the Customer table.

The book *Writing Secure Code* provides a lot of great guidelines for creating secure code that avoids online threats.[20] Of course, the more secure the code, the more likely that it can help to mitigate privacy risks. Below is one of the book's several checklists, organized by the various roles in a company:

Designers

- Someone on team signed up to monitor BugTraq computer security mailing list

- Competitor's vulnerabilities analyzed to determine if the issues exist in our product

- If creating new user accounts, they are low privilege and have strong passwords

- Sample code reviewed for security issues. You must treat sample code as production code.

- Privacy implications understood and documented

Developers

- Check all untrusted input is verified prior to being used or stored

- All buffer management functions are safe from buffer overruns

- Review the latest update of dangerous or outlawed functions

- All DACLs well-formed and "good"—not NULL or Everyone (Full Control)

- Error messages do not give too much info to an attacker

Web and Database

- No web page issues output based on unfiltered output

- No string concatenation for SQL statements

- No connections to database as administrator

- No use of *eval* function with untrusted input in server pages

- No reliance on REFERER header

Testers

- List of attack points derived from threat model decomposition process

- Comprehensive data mutation, SQL and XSS tests in place

- Past vulnerabilities in previous versions of product analyzed for root cause

- If the application is an administrative tool, test that it fails gracefully and early if the user is not an administrator

- Application attack surface is as small as possible

6.3.8 Cross-Site Scripting

Cross-site scripting (XSS) is also an older exploit where an attacker embeds client-side script into a page that gets executed when a user visits a site. This can happen when a person enters data in a form, fills out a comment at the end of an article or posts something to a friend's social site. Most scripting exploits begin with the HTML tag <script>. For example, <script> alert('Error'); </script> could be placed in a form box to display an alert on the screen. There are several online sources that can help reduce XSS threats.[21]

6.3.9 Spam and Common Tactics for Dealing with Spam

The term "spam" originated from the Monty Python skit in which one of the characters repeats the word "spam" over and over again, referring to Spam, the canned precooked meat product. It was first used as a form of undesired communication in a chat relay room when a person annoyed by a conversation during the communication ended it by sending the word "spam" to the recipient repeatedly. Thus was born the term "spamming someone."

Today most e-mail clients have a built-in spam filter that blocks and eventually deletes fraudulent-looking e-mails. A lot of spam is legitimate e-mail in the form of unwanted solicitations. Some of it may consist of some type of phishing or malware exploit. Unfortunately, even when a spam filter is working properly, users still have to validate that e-mail sent to the spam folder is indeed undesired, as new correspondence from a reputable person or organization can often be mistaken as spam. Organizations can also protect their users by using an e-mail server that blocks known spam before it gets forwarded to employees' inboxes.

6.4 E-commerce Personalization

E-commerce sites such as Amazon and eBay track what users purchase in order to better understand what users want, how to improve recommendations and what they should stock. E-commerce sites differ from most websites and even social networks in that they know the products their customers purchase and often what led up to the purchase. The path from browsing to research to selection to purchase is often called the purchasing pipeline. Advertisers and product manufacturers are often looking to determine where consumers are along the pipeline in order to understand which type of advertisement to present to them. They also want to know which actions led to the purchase, including interactions with friends and family.

6.4.1 End-User Benefits

E-commerce sites have been careful to deploy features that not only provide information about their visitors' intent but also offer value in a way that will lead to a closer relationship. They offer memberships to their site to permit users to store the credit card and shipping information, which in turn streamlines the shopping experience and permits customers to view their shopping history. When customers return to the site, it is able to display their customers' purchasing history and not only recommend products similar to ones previously purchased, but also recommend products that others bought along with the same item.

A key differentiator here is the fact that e-commerce companies are providing recommendations based on hard facts versus targeted advertising, which makes assumptions about the advertisements to serve website visitors based on their browsing habits. Another differentiator is that users who see recommendations within an e-commerce site can make an immediate decision to purchase instead of going to an advertising site, where they may need to log in or sign up to join the site.

E-commerce sites typically have a wish list program that makes it easier to let friends and family not only know what you want, but easily purchase it using a link to the product within the e-commerce site.

6.4.2 End-User Privacy Concerns

Just as recommendations are more powerful than behavioral advertising because they are based on direct purchasing knowledge, so too is the risk to privacy greater since there will be greater insights into what a person likes based on the purchases made. The e-commerce site will also have the purchaser's true identity, address and credit card numbers. These sites may also have collected the purchaser's phone number and social connections via wish list and friend recommendation programs. E-commerce sites should be diligent in protecting consumer data, ensuring consumers gain value from the data and giving them control over their data's use that is not part of the purchasing transaction. Amazon does a good job of providing users with recommendations based on the data it collects from users, which they may disable if they wish.

6.5 Online Advertising

Online advertising consists of the common image-based ads that are seen when people browse the Internet. They are typically displayed as a banner spread across the top of a web page, and are often scattered throughout the page as well. Ads come in different sizes and formats and appear in various locations. While ads aren't necessary for all sites to survive, many do rely on ad revenue, and a lot of money is spent on online advertising. In the first half of 2013 Internet ad revenues reached a record $20.1 billion.

For some companies, their sole business is serving ads on websites. The advertising ecosystem is very complex and is ripe with opportunities for privacy breaches due to the large amounts of data that flow during ad serving. The websites with the most traffic can charge the highest ad premiums. Likewise, the more that is known about the person visiting a website, the more a website can charge to serve an ad to the person. Below is a list of different ad types and their relative value:

- **Remnant.** This is the cheapest type of ad to serve. It is used when there is no campaign to run, no data about the user or web page is available or no ad could be found that matches the criteria for the user or web page.

- **Premium.** This is the most expensive type of ad to buy. It is associated with an advertising campaign and is typically run to improve the brand of a company. Premium ads are typically found on the homepage of a website and are usually for big-name products and companies.

- **Contextual.** This is the most common type of targeted ad served. The content of the ad is typically based on the topic of the web page, website or data entered by the user. For example, if a web page has an article about travel or the website is about travel, then the advertisements served on the site will probably be about travel as well. When users enter search terms using a search service such as Bing or Google, the ads that are included with the search results will be related to the search terms that are entered.

- **Demographic.** This type of ad is based on an individual's demographic data, such as the person's age, weight, zip code, occupation, height, gender or shoe size. For example, if a user performs a search about shoes or is reading an article about shoes, then an ad featuring male or female shoes may be displayed based on whether the person reading the article is known or believed to be a male or female. If the user is signed into an account where gender is collected, then the gender will be known. Otherwise, the advertising network may make an assumption about the person's gender based on the types of articles that are read or searches that are made.

- **Psychographic.** This type of ad is based on a person's interests, such as sports, travel, shopping, hobbies, entertainment or food. For example, if a person reads golfing and travel articles, she might receive ads about golfing in Hawaii even if she is not currently on a golf or travel site.

- **Behavioral.** This type of ad is based on users' browsing habits, which can include sites they visit, articles they read, searches they make and ads they click on. For example, if a person visits travel sites and reads travel articles, he is likely to get travel ads even when not on a travel site. Behavioral ads may also be based on aggregated data from groups of people. For example, if it is determined that lots of people who read articles about extreme sports and winter travel tend to click on ads depicting snowboards, then a person reading an article about extreme sports after visiting a winter travel site is likely to see ads featuring snowboards.

6.5.1 Understanding the Common Models of Online Advertising

The following list is a simple overview of how advertising works and privacy risks.

- **Search ads.** Search ads are displayed alongside the results from a search performed with a search engine. They are typically based on the keywords the user entered for the search. Demographic or behavioral data may be used to select the type of ad to display. The specific ad to display is also based on how much an advertiser spends on a keyword to be used in a search. The amount that an advertiser bids on a keyword will impact whether an ad is shown and in which order.

- **Display ads.** Display ads are the image ads that are commonly viewed on a web page. They usually appear as banners at the top of the page, skyscrapers on the side of pages or square images placed throughout a page. The specific sizes are defined by the Interactive Advertising Bureau.[22]

- **Publisher ads.** Owners of websites are often called publishers. Publishers can display ads on their website using their own ad network. Under this model the publisher would form an agreement with an advertiser to display a specific ad.

- **Third-party ads.** Most ads seen on a website are displayed by third-party ad networks. In the simplest form, an ad network makes an agreement with a set of advertisers to display ads on various publisher sites with whom it has made agreements to serve an ad. Publishers run a script on their site that creates an iframe that permits the ad network to display an ad.[23]

6.5.2 The Serving of an Ad

When a user visits a website, also known as a publisher, a lot of decisions are made before an ad is served on the site. The content of the website, the user's general location, time of day and the user's browsing habits may be taken into account. Figure 6-4 shows a simple sequence that often occurs when an ad is served on a website. Exchanges between the publisher site and the various servers happen via a series of redirects. There could also be a series of cookies deployed and an exchange of data between the publisher site and other servers involved in the serving of an ad.

Figure 6-4: Ad Serving Diagram (at right, key below)

1. A user visits a website (the publisher) and an ad is to be served

   a. The website makes a call to the publisher's ad server

   b. The call includes the ad size and category within the URL

   c. The server checks its set of advertisers to determine which one gets to serve an ad next

2. The URL to the selected advertiser is returned

3. The advertiser's ad server is called

   a. The call includes data about the ad size and may include info about the user

   b. The ad sever may have info on the user or obtain some from a data aggregator

   c. The ad server checks for an ad matching the specified attributes and selects one

4. The URL to the ad is returned to the website

5. A call is made to the content delivery network (CDN) to display the ad

   a. The call will contain the ID of the ad to be served

6. The CDN displays the ad on the web page

   a. The ad may contain beacons from other sites looking to gather info on the user

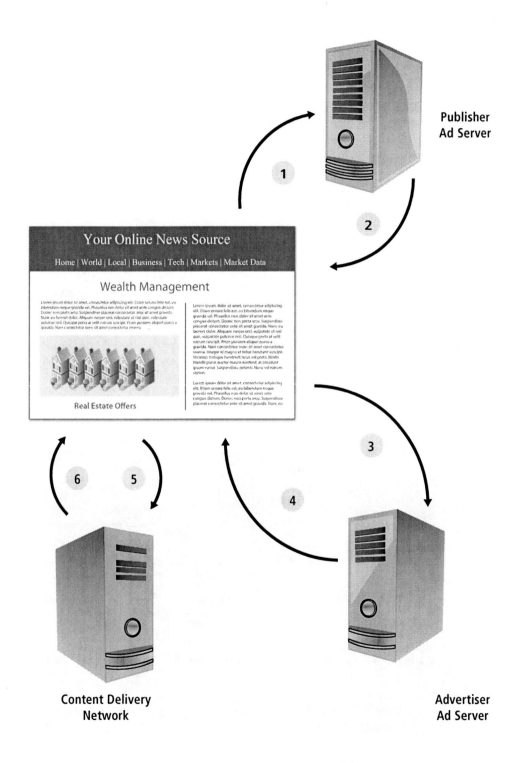

6.5.3 Key Considerations When Working with Third Parties to Post Ads on Your Company's Website

Owners of websites will find it quite simple to make money by displaying third-party advertisements. They can simply contact one of several advertising networks, fill out the paperwork necessary to form a relationship, add the code needed to create the ad on their website and they are in business. This can be an easy way to raise revenue, though site owners should be aware of certain privacy risks.

When an advertising network is given the ability to place an ad on a first-party site, it also has the ability to place a cookie on the site, which can contain a unique identifier used to identify the visitor to the ad network. This cookie will permit the ad network to create a profile on the user about the websites the user visits anywhere the ad network serves ads. In addition, the ad network could have a relationship with analytics or data aggregation companies to place beacons on the ad such that they are able to create profiles of the user as well.

For example, an ad network could have a relationship with publishing sites abc.com, def.com and ghi.com. This would permit the ad network to determine if the same user visits any of those sites. An analytics company may have a relationship with several ad networks and be able to determine which sites a person visits across all sites served by the ad networks. These companies have the ability to know more about the person visiting a site than the site the individual is browsing. Mozilla's Lightbeam (previously called Collusion) program shows the proliferation of connections that can occur as a person browses from site to site.[24] Figure 6-5 shows the 21 third-party sites that existed during the visit on cnn.com.

Figure 6-5: Lightbeam for Firefox Screenshot Showing Active Third-Party Websites

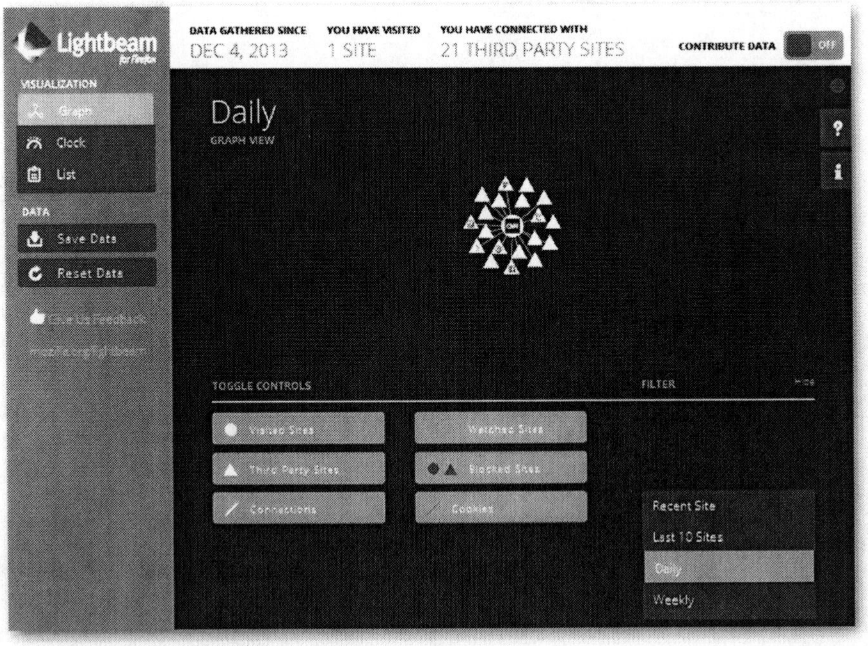

After going to Fox.com, a total of 57 third-party sites were detected, eight of them shared between the two sites. Lightbeam allows the data to be shown in a graph, clock or list format. The tool can help users see which sites are more privacy friendly by the number of third parties on their site. IT professionals can use the tool to see how their sites may be perceived by website visitors and to check on how third parties interact with other parties and deploy cookies.

Most visitors to a website realize that the site keeps a record of the fact that they are there and the pages they visit on the site. The visitors are probably less aware that the third parties on the site are also recording their visits across the current site and multiple sites.

When placing third-party ads on your site, consider taking the following precautions:

- Have a contract in place that describes the obligations of the ad network and places limitations on how the data collected is used, including sharing with others

- Limit the ability for ad networks to have other entities place cookies on your site

- Provide a behavioral advertising opt-out mechanism for visitors to your site

- Insist that ad networks on your site provide an opt-out mechanism and be members of the DAA's self-regulatory program

6.6 Understanding Cookies, Beacons and Other Tracking Technologies

A browser has various mechanisms that websites can use to identify users and possibly store data about them. This section looks at those mechanisms and how to manage them.

6.6.1 Cookies

Cookies are text files that are used to store information for a website. Websites store configuration, demographic and identity information. Only the website that creates a cookie is able to access it. Cookies simplify the user's experience by maintaining the look and feel of a website, assisting with login and making shopping easier. Cookies can also be used to track users, unbeknownst to the user. Cookies can be read with a text file, but it is safer to manage cookies with the right tools. Cookies are stored in the following locations in Windows for the following browsers:

- **Chrome:** C:\Users\<userID>\AppData\Local\Google\Chrome\User Data\ Default\Cookies

- **Firefox:** C:\Users\<userID>\AppData\Roaming\Mozilla\Firefox\Profiles\ zq8dgekq.default\cookies.sqlite

- **Internet Explorer:** C:\Users\<userID>\AppData\Local\Microsoft\Windows\ Temporary Internet Files\cookie:*

6.6.2 Web Beacons

Web beacons, web bugs, pixel tags and clear GIFs are several names for a resource that exists on a page, but is not visible to naked eye. These items may also exist within the ads that are displayed on a website. Even though a publisher may have an agreement with an ad network to display an ad on its website, the ad network may have an agreement with other companies to perform services for it such as analytics, audience intelligence or conversion tracking. These types of resources are able to place cookies in an individual's browser.

6.6.3 Local Shared Objects (LSOs)

LSOs represent memory within a browser component that can be used to store data similar to the way it is stored in a cookie. Also similar to a cookie, only the website that stored the data in an LSO can access the data. LSO storage is available with Adobe's Flash and Microsoft's Silverlight component (see Figures 6-6 and 6-7).[25] Adobe provides settings for whether a website can store data and how much it can store (see Figure 6-8).

Figure 6-6: Adobe Flash Player Settings Manager: Website Storage Settings

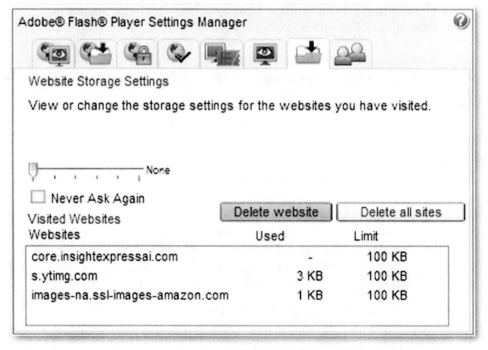

Figure 6-7: Silverlight Configuration Settings: Application Storage

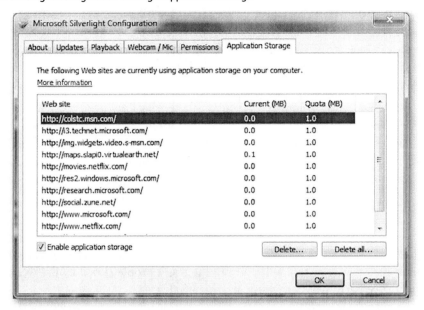

Figure 6-8: Adobe Flash Player Settings Manager: Local Storage Settings

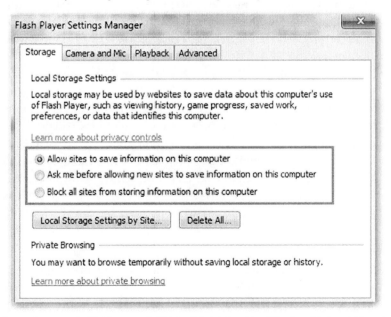

6.6.3.1 HTML5 Storage

Version 5.0 of the HTML specification provides a new feature that permits applications to store data within the browser in the same manner that data is stored in cookies.[26] The current versions of the Chrome, Firefox and Internet Explorer browsers provide the ability to clear HTML5 storage. Access to HTML5 storage is blocked for a website when cookies for a website are blocked.

6.6.3.2 Browser Fingerprinting

Browser fingerprinting consists of using the IP address sent during a browsing session to a website and the browser's user agent string to uniquely identify the browser. According to the Electronic Frontier Foundation's Panopticlick site, this can be 85 percent accurate in identifying a return visitor using the same browser on the same machine.[27]

6.6.3.3 Super Cookie

Super cookie is the term given to a mechanism for ensuring the value of a cookie persists even after it is deleted. This is usually done by using a combination of browser fingerprinting, LSO storage, HTML5 storage and other techniques. The value is usually an identifier for the user as this will point to the user's profile stored by the website or advertisers that wish to personalize the user's experience.

6.6.4 Privacy Considerations

Tracking technologies can be used to re-identify users when they revisit one website and as they browse across several websites. Once users are identified, profiles can be created or updated that indicate the sites they visit, articles they read, words they search for, people they know or products they purchase. These profiles can also infer users' interests, location, age or gender.

Blocking and deleting cookies is the simplest way to avoid being re-identified when revisiting a website. Deleting cookies may also clear LSO and HTML5 storage. Be aware that some sites may use methods to track users that cannot be blocked or cleared. Using a browser's private browsing mode will force the creating of new cookies when visiting a website and automatically delete all cookies when the browser is closed. Be careful not to sign in to any sites or services while using private browsing mode as it will create an identifiable cookie. Using a tool such as Ghostery, DoNotTrackMe or Internet Explorer's Tracking Protection can block sites entirely, but be aware of side effects such as social widgets not working or videos from third-party sites not appearing.[28]

6.6.5 Responsible Practices

Users should always familiarize themselves with a browser's security and privacy settings.[29] After all, the browser is the critical barrier between them and every website they visit as well as the third parties that occupy those sites. There are a lot of conflicting messages around which browser settings are the right ones to use. The proper level of privacy is a personal matter that each individual should decide for himself. It is not easy to determine which site or third party may have a data management practice that places one at an inappropriate level of risk. And likewise, bad actors have forced the need for a more conservative stance around browser settings. Within organizations, IT professionals should set the appropriate guidelines for browser settings. It is even possible to enforce settings for browsers such as Chrome and Internet Explorer, thus simplifying the task for employees.[30]

6.7 Machine-Readable Policy Languages

Over the years many machine-readable privacy and security policy languages have come into existence. Most floundered for a while before fading into obscurity. While the developers of each language had good intentions, the languages failed, like many ideas that were more trouble to deploy and maintain than the problem they were trying to solve. A language can also die from lack of adoption by developers or consumers.

Microsoft's Clippy turned out to be more of an annoyance than an aid to users of Microsoft Office who were looking to create content. The cost to create, deploy and maintain chip-based credit cards would have far exceeded the loss that credit card companies were losing via credit card fraud.

Not only must a technology serve a purpose, it has to be something people want to use. In general, people won't change their default settings or switch to a new program or service unless they expect to receive a tangible increase in benefits for doing so.

IT professionals looking to deploy a privacy policy language should consider the following issues:

- Does the language solve the problem it is intended to address?

- What is the adoption rate for the language by companies, applications and consumers?

- How well does it interoperate with identity, database, content management and other systems?

- What is the deployment criteria for the language?

- What is the training requirement for the language?

- What does it take to maintain the language as systems, roles and data categories change?

6.7.1 Platform for Privacy Preferences Project (P3P)

P3P was a project run by the World Wide Web Consortium (W3C) to develop a specification to provide websites with a standardized way to express their privacy practices.[31] It enabled websites to express their privacy notices in XML format. The P3P spec also provided a series of codes to create an abbreviated form of a privacy notice, called a compact policy, that could be consumed programmatically by browsers. By consuming the compact policy, browsers could inform the user of a site's privacy practices as well as programmatically determine whether cookies should be blocked or deleted at the end of a browsing session. In the end, very few websites implemented P3P. At its height only 10 percent of websites had ever fully implemented P3P. In addition, only three browsers ever implemented P3P: Internet Explorer (IE), Mozilla and Netscape. Today, IE is the only browser that continues to support P3P. Not only is that support continued in IE10, but IE has extended it by adding the Strict P3P Validation feature.[32]

6.7.2 Application Preference Exchange Language (APPEL)

APPEL is a complementary specification to P3P that permits users to express their privacy preferences in a browser. Those preferences can be formatted into an XML document. The browser would be able to compare the user's preferences to a website's stated policies expressed in P3P. Based on the comparison and how users set up their privacy settings, cookies could be blocked or relegated to session cookies. Unfortunately, APPEL has never received wide adoption.

6.7.3 Enterprise Privacy Authorization Language (EPAL)

EPAL was a privacy language that was proposed by IBM based on the Privacy Rights Markup Language work done by Zero Knowledge Systems. (That company has changed its direction, and now does business under the name Radialpoint.)[33] EPAL was built into IBM's Tivoli Privacy Manager. EPAL was a full-featured privacy language that expressed the access rights an entity would have to a resource for a specific set of purposes along with accompanying obligations. For example, shipping clerks could read a customer's address for the purpose of shipping an order and the system would be obligated to write an audit log recording who accessed the address and against which sales order. EPAL was deployed by IBM, but IBM no longer supports it or Tivoli Privacy Manager.

6.7.4 Security Assertion Markup Language (SAML)

SAML is an XML-based security language created as a standard by the OASIS consortium.[34] SAML allows organizations to make assertions about the identity, attributes and entitlements of an individual to entities, such as a resource, company, application or service.

The benefits of SAML include:[35]

- **Platform neutrality.** *SAML abstracts the security framework away from platform architectures and particular vendor implementations. Making security more independent of application logic is an important tenet of Service-Oriented Architecture.*

- **Loose coupling of directories.** *SAML does not require user information to be maintained and synchronized between directories.*

- **Improved online experience for end users.** SAML enables single sign-on by allowing users to authenticate at an identity provider and then access service providers without additional authentication. In addition, identity federation (linking of multiple identities) with SAML allows for a better-customized user experience at each service while promoting privacy.

- **Reduced administrative costs for service providers.** Using SAML to "reuse" a single act of authentication (such as logging in with a username and password) multiple times across multiple services can reduce the cost of maintaining account information. This burden is transferred to the identity provider.

- **Risk transference.** SAML can act to push responsibility for proper management of identities to the identity provider, which is more often compatible with its business model than that of a service provider.

6.7.5 eXtensible Access Control Markup Language (XACML)

XACML is an XML-based security language created as a standard by OASIS.[36] XACML applies a set of tokens to a resource that describe the type of access permitted by a set of predefined roles. XACML takes up where SAML leaves off. Like SAML, it provides a mechanism for protecting access to data, but it goes further by providing a request/ response language that permits the development of an access request such as "Does this person have the rights to print this document?" A response will then indicate whether the request is granted or more data is needed.

XACML has several points in its favor:[37]

- **It's standard.** By using a standard language, you're using something that has been reviewed by a large community of experts and users, you don't need to roll your own system each time, and you don't need to think about all the tricky issues involved in designing a new language. Plus, as XACML becomes more widely deployed, it will be easier to interoperate with other applications using the same standard language.

- **It's generic.** This means that rather than trying to provide access control for a particular environment or a specific kind of resource, it can be used in any environment. One policy can be written which can then be used by many different kinds of applications, and when one common language is used, policy management becomes much easier.

- **It's distributed.** This means that a policy can be written which in turn refers to other policies kept in arbitrary locations. The result is that rather than having to manage a single monolithic policy, different people or groups can manage sub-pieces of policies as appropriate, and XACML knows how to correctly combine the results from these different policies into one decision.

- **It's powerful.** *While there are many ways the base language can be extended, many environments will not need to do so. The standard language already supports a wide variety of data types, functions and rules about combining the results of different policies. In addition to this, there are already standards groups working on extensions and profiles that will hook XACML into other standards like SAML and LDAP, which will increase the number of ways that XACML can be used.*

6.8 Web Browser Privacy and Security Features

Understanding browser privacy and security features helps mitigate risk to employees and their data, not only at work but also while they are at home using their personal computers and devices. Organizational privacy training should include a description of how to use a browser's security and privacy features.

6.8.1 Private Browsing

Most online browsers have a private browsing mode. Internet Explorer calls it InPrivate Browsing, Chrome calls it Incognito Mode and Mozilla calls it Private Browsing. When a browser session ends, all cookies, storage, browsing history and content created during the session will be removed. Do not log in to an online service while using the private browsing feature as the service will be able to track you using your membership identity.

It is important to note that private browsing features provide privacy only to users on the client side of a browsing session. Websites can use browser fingerprinting to track users and create profiles. However, a person using a shared computer will not be able to view the browsing activity of others if they used private browse mode on that computer.

6.8.2 Tracking Protection

Tracking protection refers to features that decrease the ability of websites to track users across multiple sites or at the same site during recurring visits. By minimizing a site's ability to track a person, the site will be less likely to create profiles on individuals or serve personalized content such as ads, articles or search results. While some may view personalization as a benefit, others may see it as an intrusion.

- **Cookie blocking.** Cookie blocking prevents a website from being able to store a cookie in the browser that could contain a unique ID for identifying a website visitor. Most users can block first-party or third-party cookies. Most tracking concerns come from third-party websites that are responsible for serving most ads on the Internet and have a vested interest in creating profiles on users. First-party sites may create profiles on users as well, but they also provide services to users that may be inhibited by cookie blocking, such as logging in to the site and storing configuration information.

- **Cookie deletion.** Cookie deletion is similar to cookie blocking except it permits websites to use cookies while the browser session is active, which avoids any possible anomalies while visiting a site. Most browsers permit users to delete cookies whenever they wish or have them deleted when the browser is closed. While a website may be able to create a profile during the active browsing session, once the browser is closed or the user manually deletes cookies, the profile will no longer be associated with the user. The following figures show screenshots of cookie controls from various browsers.

Figure 6-9: Chrome Cookie Management

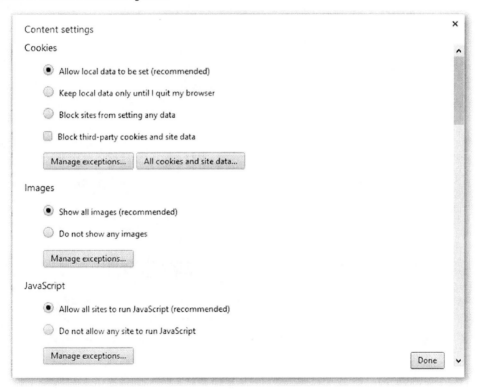

Google and the Google logo are registered trademarks of Google Inc.; used with permission.

Figure 6-10: Firefox Cookie Management

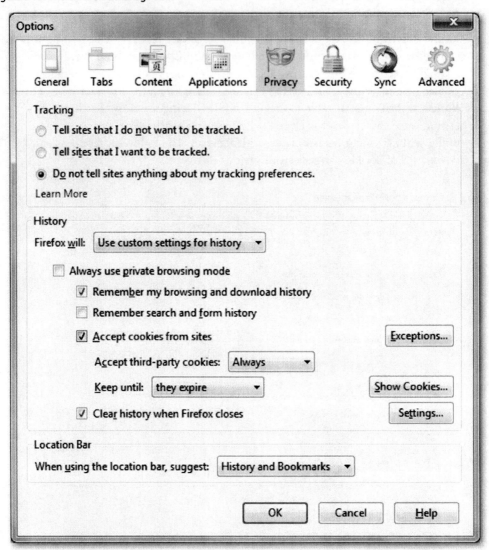

Figure 6-11: Internet Explorer Cookie Management

Used with permission from Microsoft.

Cookies are the standard way that websites re-identify users who return to a website. This gives the user the ability to control this type of tracking by blocking or deleting cookies. Some websites identify users through browser fingerprinting, which is not easy to detect and almost impossible to protect oneself against. Browser fingerprinting uses the IP address and attributes of the browser and the user's computer system to create a near-unique profile of the user in a way that the user cannot easily control.

- **Tracking Protection.** Tracking Protection is a feature in Microsoft's Internet Explorer browser. The feature permits blocking of third-party websites based on their entry on a tracking protection list (TPL). This feature blocks not only cookies from the site, but all communications. Users can have a TPL created dynamically as they browse the web or download a TPL from a site that has created one, or from Microsoft's Internet Explorer Gallery.[38] Figure 6-12 is a screenshot of IE's Tracking Protection screen.

Figure 6-12: Tracking Protection in Internet Explorer

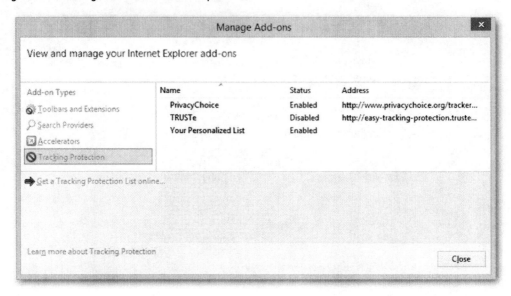

Used with permission from Microsoft.

6.8.3 Do Not Track

The Do Not Track (DNT) header is an idea initiated by privacy advocate Chris Sogohian in conjunction with privacy developer Sid Stamm in 2009.[39] The idea was expanded with the creation of a website dedicated to DNT[40] run by Arvind Narayanan and Jonathan Mayer.[41] Unfortunately, their work never gained traction until a meeting of supporters was held at MIT in the fall of 2010.[42] A group of academics, privacy advocates and industry representatives submitted proposals that kicked off the World Wide Web Consortium (W3C) Tracking Protection Working Group (TPWG) to create a set of documents for how DNT should work and be complied with—the Tracking Protection Expression, Tracking Compliance and Tracking Protection List documents. Once completed, these would become nonbinding recommendations for industry to follow.

The idea around DNT is that the user can cause a special header to be sent to a website from the browser with a value of DNT:1 or DNT:0. Upon receiving the header, the website would either not track the user or be able to track the user, respectively. The full meaning of the DNT header is still under debate and varies from not collecting data from a user across multiple nonaffiliated sites to no creation of user profiles and/or no personalization of content for the user. For now, it is up to websites to decide whether they wish to honor the DNT header and how.

At the time of this writing, the W3C work is still ongoing. The expectation for the work was that when third-party websites received a DNT:1 header from a user agent, websites receiving the header would not collect data on the user except for permitted uses such as security, fraud prevention and troubleshooting. The California state legislature passed a law requiring all websites collecting PII from California residents to describe their level of DNT support in their privacy notices.

The W3C TPWG ended up with over 90 academics, privacy advocates, practitioners, regulators and industry representatives working on the project. The group has also gone through several leadership changes since its inception. The group started with Aleecia McDonald and Matthias Schunter as co-chairs. After one year Peter Swire took over for McDonald and later, Justin Brookman and Carl Cargill took over for Swire when he joined the National Security Agency (NSA) privacy oversight board. The group has been mired in continual disputes since its early beginnings. Each change in leadership brought new hope of a quick resolution, which was quickly dashed. A vote by TPWG members on how to continue after the last leadership change resulted in a decision to complete the creation of the Tracking Protection Expression, followed soon after by completion of the compliance spec. The work was slated to be completed in June 2012 and it now appears it will go beyond June 2014.

Firefox was the first browser to incorporate the DNT feature, followed soon after by Internet Explorer, Safari and Chrome. To date barely more than 20 companies acknowledge the DNT header.[43] The main reason is a lack of understanding of what DNT should mean. Companies could certainly make assumptions about it, but that could lead to wasted work that would have to be redone at a later date, including a modification of their privacy notice, which could require additional consent from users if a change in data usage is required. In addition, some companies would be placing themselves at an economic disadvantage by throwing away data that is valuable to their advertising business when their competitors don't.

6.9 Web Security Protocols

"Euan, I want you to see what it will take to support secure communications on all of our sites. I want this to include our server-to-server communications, such as from our e-mail servers to external e-mail servers," requested Amy.

"Okay, Amy, but you do understand that it means adding extra servers in our data center, new coding across all of our servers and possible performance hits for some of our applications."

"I understand that," Amy replied, "but let's perform the research so we have solid facts to present to the affected business teams. I want us to provide our website visitors with complete end-to-end protection of their data. To the fullest extent possible, I want to be able to publicly state that we are not susceptible to the communications snooping that has been prevalent in the press. That will be beneficial not only to our customers, but to our business as well."

> *"That makes perfect sense, Amy. I'll see what I can find out and get back to you."*

In a post-Snowden era, it is important to understand the security protocols that exist to make it more difficult for individuals and organizations to capture the content of communications. This section looks at how communications can be protected between client and server or between servers.

6.9.1 Secure Sockets Layer and Transport Layer Security

Secure sockets layer (SSL) is an Internet security protocol developed by Netscape to protect data transmitted between a user's browser and a web server. Transport layer security (TLS) was developed by the Internet Engineering Taskforce based on SSL 3.0 and defined in RFC 2246.[44] Though TLS is a derivative of SSL, they are not interoperable. Most browsers support SSL and TLS, though the term SSL is typically used to refer to the encryption that occurs between the browser and the server. TLS is often used to encrypt server-to-server communications such as between e-mail servers. IT professionals should look at implementing TLS encryption to help mitigate man-in-the-middle attacks, which have been popularized by the NSA revelations.

Websites desiring to support SSL can obtain an SSL certificate from a certification authority such as VeriSign.[45] When an individual accesses a site supporting SSL, the browser will obtain the site's SSL certificate, ensure it has not expired and validate that it was issued by a trusted certificate authority. If the certificate is not valid, the user will be warned of that fact. Otherwise, the client and server will exchange encryption keys to be used to encrypt the session. Figure 6-13 shows the message displayed when Chrome discovers that the certificate for a website has expired.

Figure 6-13: Expired Certificate as Shown in Chrome

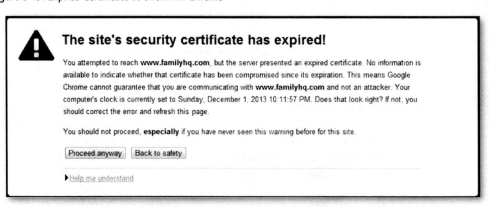

Google and the Google logo are registered trademarks of Google Inc.; used with permission.

6.9.2 HTTP Strict Transport Security (HSTS)

HSTS is a new protocol that helps to ensure that websites that support secure communications are connected over a secure link by browsers that support HSTS.[46] To date only Firefox, Opera and Chrome support HSTS. Websites that support SSL should implement HSTS.

6.9.3 Hypertext Transfer Protocol Secure (HTTPS)

HTTPS is the secure version of the HTTP protocol that operates on top of SSL. It is used to create an encrypted session with a website. By default most websites transmit data between the browser and web server unencrypted. For example, if a person types yahoo .com into the address bar of a browser, the browser will connect to http://www.yahoo .com. However, an individual can enter https://yahoo.com to force an encrypted session with the Yahoo website. Some websites, such as Twitter.com, default to an encrypted session all the time.

> *Websites should support HTTPS wherever possible. Even though the user may not be transmitting personal information over the Internet, items they search for, articles they read and products they shop for can provide insights into website visitors' interests that could be used to embarrass or discriminate against them.*
>
> *Forward secrecy provides an additional level of protection by rotating the keys used for encryption and ensuring that they are not derived from a single master key. This prevents multiple messages from being decrypted if one encryption key is compromised.*

To determine if a website session is being encrypted, look for the https:// in the address bar next to the domain name for the site. A lock should also be visible in the browser's address bar. Clicking on the lock should provide the identity for the site and permit viewing of the site's SSL certificate used to perform the encryption.

6.9.4 Limiting or Preventing Automated Data Capture

Automated data capture covers the many means by which systems and tools may record information from individuals, typically without their knowledge. Whether individuals are merely walking around in public or using systems for a specific purpose, personal data may be taken from an individual in ways that can't be detected. This data collection is typically connected to online systems that can combine the data with previously collected information to expand one's profile.

- **Facial features.** Cameras are prevalent in today's society. They can not only record video and audio, but may be able to identify people using facial recognition. Hats and glasses can mitigate the risk of being identified. Companies deploying these technologies should warn people with signs and other means.

- **Magnetic stripe.** ATMs have been known to have magnetic stripe readers surreptitiously attached in front of their own readers to steal data from cards. Cashiers in stores and servers in restaurants have been known to use credit card skimmers to steal data from unsuspecting clients. Using ATMs from reputable institutions, looking out for ATM modifications and keeping your credit card in sight or using cash can reduce these risks.

- **RFID tags.** Data from an RFID tag such as an access card or digital identity card can be easily read by any RFID reader within range of the tag. Tags can contain a simple ID or a string of data about a user. Using an RFID tag that encrypts its data or placing an RFID-enabled device in a foil holder can prevent a rogue reader from capturing the tag's data when it is not in use.

- **USB drive.** Data from a USB drive can be quickly copied by being plugged into a smart device that can copy its contents. Using a password-protected device or encrypting its contents can minimize this risk.

6.9.5 Anonymity Tools and Privacy-Preserving Data Mining

Protecting one's identity on the Internet can be done from the perspective of the client, the web server or the database that may be storing the data. To date much more research has been done on privacy-preserving databases than on practical applications. Books such as *Privacy-Preserving Data Mining, Privacy in Statistical Databases, Protecting Data Through "Perturbation" Techniques: The Impact on Knowledge Discovery in Databases* and *Translucent Databases* describe a lot of the research.[47] Unfortunately, there is more work to be done to make a lot of this research mainstream.

- **Site blockers.** Blocking cookies or using private browsing modes does little to prevent third-party websites from identifying visitors to first-party sites, as data will still flow to them. Tools such as Adblock Plus, DoNoTrackMe and Internet Explorer's tracking protection feature not only block cookies but also block the connection between third-party sites and the browser, preventing them from using browser fingerprinting or other techniques to track users visiting a website.[48] Be aware that blocking third-party sites can cause shopping carts, videos, stock feeds or comment blocks managed by third parties to fail to work properly.

- **Tor.**[49] Tor was started back in 2002 as a project for the U.S. Navy to provide secure communications and anonymity to individuals on the Internet. Normally, when a person visits a website, communication happens directly between the person's browser and the website. The IP address received by the website can typically be traced directly back to the origin computer. Tor works by directing traffic between two endpoints through multiple intermediate nodes. In that way, someone observing a website or other client computer would not be able to determine the origin of the connection. Tor not only disguises the originator of a communication, but encrypts the communication to minimize man-in-the-middle attacks.

- **The Free Network.**[50] Freenet is similar to Tor in that it provides encrypted communications over the Internet, incorporating multiple nodes in the process. It differs in that it can provide point-to-point communications and restrict connections to only those using the Freenet software.

- **E-mail anonymity.** MaskMe and Lockify provide e-mail anonymity in different ways. MaskMe permits the creation of a dynamic e-mail address that can be used in filling out forms and signing up for accounts.[51] E-mails sent to the address go to a temporary storage managed by MaskMe. The e-mails can be viewed and responded to and the account can be deactivated at any time. MaskMe will also create IDs, passwords, phone numbers, credit card numbers and zip codes on the fly, masking the user's true information and automating data input. Lockify permits the sending of encrypted e-mails to specific recipients such that only the sender and receiver can view the e-mails.[52] The e-mails can also be automatically deleted after being read or after a certain period of time.

- **Differential privacy.**[53] This database technique permits the analysis of user data stored within the database without revealing any information about individuals that is unavailable to those without access to the database.

- **Homomorphic encryption.** Homomorphic encryption provides the ability to encrypt data while still being able to perform mathematical functions on the data. Initially, this mechanism was plagued by limitations on the types of functions that could be performed and slow performance. However, Fujitsu has come up with a way to perform advanced functions on encrypted data.[54] This is an area that organizations should look to cultivate because it reduces the risk of data exposure while maintaining its utility.

6.10 Conclusion

"Team, this has been an amazing quarter," Amy stated, standing in front of the privacy council members seated around the table. "Not only have we solidified our position within the online community to protect customer privacy, but we've done it in a way that we can hold our heads up high. Plus, I have to let you in on a little secret. The training that we gave to employees on online privacy, I gave to my two teenage kids, and they loved it. Do we have any other updates?"

"Amy, my tweet on our support for TLS and HSTS got over 300 retweets, including one from Jeff Chester," said Filo.

"We must be doing something right if we are getting the attention of the Executive Director of the Center for Digital Democracy," responded Amy.

"Our developers have already started a project using XACML," said Euan. "If it goes well, they are going to standardize all new projects handling personal data on the protocol. I feel that the work we've done around online privacy has been our most important work to date. We should certainly write a paper on our effort."

"Why stop there?" chimed in Bill. "Let's write a book. This is not just about tooting our own horn, but making the Internet safer for all companies, and our families as well."

"I hate to pile on here, but after Filo's blog about our privacy enhancements, we closed a couple of new contracts from EU customers," said David. "Embracing privacy does pay, and sometimes in a big way."

Endnotes

1 Lock Box, Inc., www.lock-box.com/.

2 LinkedIn, www.linkedin.com/.

3 Children's Online Privacy Protection Act of 1998, 15 U.S.C. §§ 6501-6505, www.ftc.gov/ enforcement/rules/rulemaking-regulatory-reform-proceedings/childrens-online-privacy- protection-rule.

4 Directive 2002/58/EC of the European Parliament and of the Council of 12 July 2002 Concerning the Processing of Personal Data and the Protection of Privacy in the Electronic Communications Sector (Directive on Privacy and Electronic Communications); Directive 2009/136/EC, of the European Parliament and of the Council of 25 November 2009.

5 Cal. Bus. & Prof. Code §§22575-22579.

6 "The Self-Regulatory Program for Online Behavioral Advertising," Digital Advertising Alliance, accessed February 20, 2014, www.aboutads.info/.

7 Digital Advertising Alliance, "The DAA Self-Regulatory Principles," accessed April 1, 2014, www.aboutads.info/principles/; Interactive Advertising Bureau, "Self-Regulatory Program for Online Behavioral Advertising," accessed February 20, 2014, www.iab.net/public_policy/self-reg.

8 Rebecca Hagelin, "HAGELIN: Shutting out cyberstalkers," *Washington Times,* March 1, 2010, www.washingtontimes.com/news/2010/mar/01/hagelin-shutting-out-cyberstalkers/.

9 "Decision Making by and for Individuals Under the Age of 18," Australian Law Reform Commission, last modified August 31, 2012, www.alrc.gov.au/publications/68.%20Decision%20 Making%20by%20and%20for%20Individuals%20Under%20the%20Age%20of%2018/existing -australian-laws; Legal Protection of Minors Act (Organic Law 1/1996).

10 "Laws of the World on Children and Adolescents," Harvard School of Public Health, accessed February 20, 2014, www.hsph.harvard.edu/population/children/childrenlaws.htm.

11 About 4,400 young people commit suicide in the United States every year and over 40,000 more attempt it. A study in Britain found that at least half of suicides among young people are related to bullying. "Bullying and Suicide," Bullying Statistics, accessed February 20, 2014, www.bullyingstatistics.org/content/bullying-and-suicide.html.

12 "An Act to Amend the Criminal Code, the Canada Evidence Act, the Competition Act and the Mutual Legal Assistance in Criminal Matters Act," Parliament of Canada, accessed February 20, 2014, www.parl.gc.ca/LegisInfo/BillDetails.aspx?Language=E&Mode=1&billId=6301394.

13 Renee Viellaris, "Internet trolls and cyber-bullies face jail under amended Commonwealth law," *News.com.au,* November 30, 2013, www.news.com.au/national/queensland/internet-trolls-and -cyberbullies-face-jail-under-amended-commonwealth-law/story-fnii5v6w-1226771735572.

14 "Cyberbullying Enacted Legislation: 2006–2010," National Conference of State Legislatures, accessed February 20, 2014, www.ncsl.org/research/education/cyberbullying.aspx; "State Laws: Electronic Solicitation or Luring of Children," National Conference of State Legislatures, last updated March 13, 2012, www.ncsl.org/research/telecommunications-and-information -technology/electronic-solicitation-or-luring-of-children-sta.aspx.

15 boyd's research examines social media, youth practices, tensions between public and private, social network sites, and other intersections between technology and society. It focuses on how young people use social media as part of their everyday practices. danah boyd, *It's Complicated: The Social Lives of Networked Teens* (New Haven: Yale University Press, 2014). Her first public talk about her book occurred at the Family Online Safety Institute Conference in 2013. danah boyd, "It's Complicated: Teen Privacy in a Networked Age," in *Proceedings of the FOSI's 7th Annual Conference* (Washington, DC, November 6–7, 2013), www.youtube.com/watch?v=5t9ck8K1Ddc.

16 "Convention on the Rights of the Child," Unicef, updated April 4, 2013, www.unicef.org/crc/; African Member States of the Organization of African Unity, "African Charter on the Rights and Welfare of the Child," entered into force November 29, 1999, www.africa-union.org/official_ documents/Treaties_%20Conventions_%20Protocols/A.%20C.%20ON%20THE%20RIGHT%20 AND%20WELF%20OF%20CHILD.pdf; "European Convention on the Exercise of Children's Rights," Council of Europe, entered into force January 7, 2000, http://conventions.coe.int/Treaty/ Commun/QueVoulezVous.asp?NT=160&CL=ENG; Federal Trade Commission, "Children's Online Privacy Protection Act," 1998, www.coppa.org/coppa.htm; Federal Communications Commission, "Children's Internet Protection Act," updated 2011, www.fcc.gov/guides/childrens-internet- protection-act.

17 Angelique Chrisafis, "France says farewell to the Minitel—the little box that connected a country," The Guardian, June 28, 2012, www.theguardian.com/technology/2012/jun/28/minitel-france- says-farewell.

18 "A Brief History of BBS Systems!" BBS Corner, last updated November 29, 2009, www.bbscorner .com/usersinfo/bbshistory.htm.

19 Jennifer Steinhauer and Jackie Calmes, "White House Official's Career Twitters Out," New York Times, October 24, 2013, www.nytimes.com/2013/10/25/us/politics/white-house-officials-rising -career-twitters-out.html.

20 Michael Howard and David LeBlanc, Writing Secure Code: Practical Strategies and Proven Techniques for Building Secure Applications in a Networked World, 2nd edition (Redmond, WA: Microsoft Press, 2004).

21 "Anti–Cross Site Scripting Library," Microsoft, http://msdn.microsoft.com/en-us/security/ aa973814.aspx; "Cross-site Scripting (XSS)," Open Web Application Security Project, last revised February 3, 2014, https://www.owasp.org/index.php/XSS; "A Java library for filtering XSS attacks from user input fields," xssprotect, accessed on February 20, 2014, https://code.google.com/p/ xssprotect/.

22 "Ad Unit Guidelines," Interactive Advertising Bureau, accessed February 20, 2014, www.iab.net/ iab_products_and_industry_services/1421/1443/1452.

23 The iframe element allows one HTML page to be embedded inside another. "HTML/Elements/ iframe," World Wide Web Consortium, www.w3.org/wiki/HTML/Elements/iframe.

24 Lightbeam for Firefox, Mozilla, accessed February 28, 2014, www.mozilla.org/en-US/lightbeam/.

25 "Website Storage Settings Panel," Adobe Systems Inc., accessed February 20, 2014, www.macromedia.com/support/documentation/en/flashplayer/help/settings_manager07.html; "Application Storage: Using Application Storage," Microsoft, accessed February 20, 2014, www.microsoft.com/getsilverlight/resources/documentation/AppStorage.aspx.

26 "HTML5," World Wide Web Consortium, accessed February 20, 2014, www.w3.org/TR/html5/.

27 "Panopticlick: How Unique—and Trackable—Is Your Browser?" Electronic Frontier Foundation, accessed February 20, 2014, https://panopticlick.eff.org/.

28 Ghostery, www.ghostery.com/; DoNotTrackMe, https://addons.mozilla.org/en-US/firefox/addon/ donottrackplus/.

29 "Firefox Privacy and Security Settings," Mozilla, http://support.mozilla.org/en-US/products/ firefox/privacy-and-security; "Chrome's Privacy Settings," Google, https://support.google.com/ chrome/answer/114836?hl=en; "Windows: Change Security and Privacy Settings for Internet Explorer," Microsoft, http://windows.microsoft.com/en-us/internet-explorer/ie-security-privacy -settings#ie=ie-11.

30 Scott Matteson, "Set up the Chrome for Business browser in your organization using Group Policies" *Tech Republic*, July 17, 2014, www.techrepublic.com/blog/google-in-the-enterprise/set -up-the-chrome-for-business-browser-in-your-organization-using-group-policies/; "Group Policy Objects and Internet Explorer 11 (IE11)" Microsoft, http://technet.microsoft.com/en-us/library/ dn338142.aspx.

31 "Platform for Privacy Preferences (P3P) Project," World Wide Web Consortium, last updated November 20, 2007, www.w3.org/P3P/.

32 "Internet Explorer 10 Privacy Statement for Windows 7," Microsoft, last updated December 2012, http://windows.microsoft.com/en-US/internet-explorer/ie10-win7-privacy-statement.

33 "Zero-Knowledge Systems Inc. Files Motions on IP Rights in PRML, EPML, and EPAL," Cover Pages, June 7, 2004, http://xml.coverpages.org/ZKSMotions.html.

34 OASIS is the Organization for the Advancement of Structured Information Standards, which drives the development, convergence and adoption of open standards for the global information society. OASIS, www.oasis-open.org; "OASIS Security Services (SAML) TC," OASIS, https://www.oasis -open.org/committees/tc_home.php?wg_abbrev=security.

35 "SAML V2.0 Executive Overview," OASIS, April 12, 2005, https://www.oasis-open.org/ committees/download.php/13525/sstc-saml-exec-overview-2.0-cd-01-2col.pdf.

36 "OASIS eXtensible Access Control Markup Language (XACML) TC," OASIS, (2014), accessed March 26, 2014, https://www.oasis-open.org/committees/tc_home.php?wg_abbrev=xacml.

37 "A Brief Introduction to XACML," OASIS, last updated March 14, 2003, https://www.oasis-open .org/committees/download.php/2713/Brief_Introduction_to_XACML.html.

38 "Internet Explorer Gallery," Microsoft, www.iegallery.com/en-us/trackingprotectionlists.

39 Christopher Soghoian Biography, www.dubfire.net; Sid Stamm, *Extreme Geekboy* (blog), http://blog .sidstamm.com; Christopher Soghoian, "The History of the Do Not Track Header," *Slight Paranoia* (blog), January 21, 2011, http://paranoia.dubfire.net/2011/01/history-of-do-not-track-header.html.

40 "Universal Web Tracking Opt Out," Do Not Track, accessed February 25, 2014, http://donottrack.us/.

41 Arvind Narayanan, http://randomwalker.info; Jonathan Mayer, http://stanford.edu/~jmayer.

42 "Tracking Protection Working Group," World Wide Web Consortium, September 21–22, 2011, www.w3.org/2011/tracking-protection/f2f1-logistics.

43 "Implementations," Do Not Track, accessed February 25, 2014, http://donottrack.us/ implementations.

44 Christopher Allen and Tim Dierks, "The TLS Protocol Version 1.0," Internet Society, January 1999, www.ietf.org/rfc/rfc2246.txt.

45 VeriSign, now owned by Symantec, is a certification authority that provides SSL certificates to companies. "SSL Certificates," Symantec Corporation, www.symantec.com/verisign/ssl -certificates?inid=vrsn_symc_ssl_index.

46 J. Hodges, C. Jackson and A. Barth, "HTTP Strict Transport Security (HSTS)," November 2012, https://ietf.org/doc/rfc6797/.

47 Charu C. Aggarwal and Philip S. Yu, eds., *Privacy-Preserving Data Mining* (New York: Springer, 2008); Josep Domingo-Ferrer and Ilenia Tinnirello, eds., *Privacy in Statistical Databases*, (Heidelberg: Springer, 2012); Rick L. Wilson and Peter A. Rosen, "Protecting Data Through 'Perturbation' Techniques: The Impact of Knowledge Discovery in Databases, in *Information Security and Ethics*, ed. Hamid Nemati (Hershey, PA: IGI Global, 2008), www.igi-global.com/ chapter/protecting-data-through-perturbation-techniques/23176; Peter Wayner, *Translucent Databases*, 2nd edition (Baltimore, MD: Flyzone Press, 2009).

48 Adblock Plus, https://adblockplus.org/; "Add-ons: DoNotTrackMe," Mozilla, December 23, 2013, https://addons.mozilla.org/en-US/firefox/addon/donottrackplus/; "Use Tracking Protection in Internet Explorer," Microsoft, http://windows.microsoft.com/en-us/internet-explorer/use-tracking-protection#ie=ie-11.

49 The Tor Project, Inc., https://www.torproject.org/. Similar services include Guardster, http://www.guardster.com/; Anonymizer, https://www.anonymizer.com/; and Megaproxy, www.megaproxy.com/.

50 Freenet, https://freenetproject.org/index.html.

51 Abine, Inc., https://www.abine.com/maskme/.

52 Lockify, Inc., https://lockify.com/.

53 Cynthia Dwork, "Differential Privacy," *Microsoft Research*, July 2006, http://research.microsoft.com/apps/pubs/default.aspx?id=64346.

54 "Fujitsu Develops World's First Homomorphic Encryption Technology that Enables Statistical Calculations and Biometric Authentication," Fujitsu Laboratories Ltd., August 28, 2013, www.fujitsu.com/global/news/pr/archives/month/2013/20130828-01.html.

## CHAPTER 7

Technologies With Privacy Considerations

"Euan, as we look at ways to expand our services to the cloud, I want to make sure that we take what we have learned from developing end-to-end encryption and apply it to our cloud services. I would like us to differentiate ourselves from other cloud service providers in the way we treat customer data," said Amy.

"Well, Amy, the end-to-end encryption we developed only helps protect the data in transmission," replied Euan. "We need to look for ways to protect customer data in a way that can't be tampered with or accessed except by the customer."

"I've been communicating with some researchers from Microsoft and Carnegie Mellon University on some ideas that may address that," noted Amy. "I'll have Bill look into setting up an intimate workshop where they can come in and present their work to us. In addition, I would like to understand the threat that our employees may be under from wireless and location-based services. I don't want them tracked or hacked when they are out in public."

"I'll look into our enterprise policy for mobile settings and make sure the defaults are protecting our employees," offered Euan. "We should also warn our employees about the threat from smart technologies they may be wearing or using."

"I'll also update our training," added Bill, "to make sure employees understand the risks and how to protect themselves. I think we should also cover the various surveillance technologies that exist with a focus on how we should limit what we are collecting and the importance of restricting access to the data."

"Thanks, Bill, I like your thinking!"

7.1 Cloud Computing

In IT terms, the cloud is the Internet and cloud computing refers to performing computing on servers over the Internet. The term was first used by Professor Ramnath K. Chellappa in his 1997 presentation "Intermediaries in Cloud-Computing."[1] Cloud computing as a service was first developed by Amazon and offered as Amazon Web Services (AWS) in 2002.[2] AWS provides for storage, database and application services for enterprises. Cloud service platforms were later developed by Google, IBM, and Microsoft.[3] Enterprises can decide to store their data on premise or store it in the cloud in a cloud provider's data center. Sometimes, cloud storage is simply for storing files while the applications remain within the organization's data center. This provides the added benefit of still being able to run applications when the connection to the cloud is lost. However, some organizations may wish to outsource certain applications as well, giving rise to the need for companies to provide cloud computing programs.

Cloud computing is a great idea for organizations with limited resources as it can help address issues with scalability, cost containment, maintenance, accessibility, efficiency, specialized talent and performance. Public- as well as private-sector organizations can benefit from the cost savings of moving to cloud computing. The financial crisis that swept over countries has pushed governments to move to cloud services to cut government IT costs. The UK government has adopted a "Cloud First" policy to address its IT costs.[4]

While cloud systems may be separate from systems on premise, organizational policies should seamlessly cover both sets of systems. There may be a difference in the personnel who manage the systems and a special focus on multitenancy issues, but that should not require two sets of policies. It is okay to have too many scenarios covered in a policy, but not too few.

7.1.1 Types of Clouds

The following list explains the types of cloud services that exist. Some companies may provide a combination or hybrid of these configurations.

- **Personal cloud.** This is the term given to cloud services individuals can use to store their personal data, such as files, music, pictures and videos. This is a great convenience for individuals who only need a simple backup service, access to their content from multiple devices or a way to provide friends and family with access to their content.

- **Private cloud.** Many organizations manage their own data centers in the cloud. They may be staffed with employees or contractors. Private cloud data centers are often distributed for redundancy purposes and to reduce latency. When creating this type of cloud, organizations should be sure to lock it down so only employees and other authorized personnel can access it. Policies should also be in place to provide guidance on who can access data and how it should be processed. In general, the policies that apply to data centers on premise should apply to cloud data centers. An extra focus should be placed on protecting the communication links between cloud data centers. There should also be a business continuity plan in place if communication to the cloud data center is lost.

- **Public cloud.** Organizations will sometimes offload the responsibility of running a cloud data center to a service provider such as Amazon, Google or Microsoft. This can simplify costs, deployment time, maintenance and support. However, IT professionals should not underestimate the new risks involved with having a third party manage their cloud-based data center. They need to ensure that third parties address concerns like these:

  - Assurance that personnel live up to organizational policies

  - Effective backup procedures and handling of media

  - Proper disposal of antiquated and damaged equipment containing data

  - Restriction of visibility by other hosted companies

  - Limitation on who can access the servers and services

- **Community cloud.** This is a cloud service that is shared by multiple organizations with common concerns or interests such as compliance, security, performance or running a specific set of applications. A community cloud has the benefits of a private cloud in the restriction of access and the benefits of a public cloud such as shared resources.

7.1.2 Types of Cloud Services

The following list describes how individuals and organizations might use cloud services. Some service providers may provide a combination or hybrid of these services.

- **Storage.** The most common use of cloud services is to store information. Some individuals use a storage service for backup purposes while others use it as their main means of storage. Storage providers can typically provide the amount of storage needed almost instantly. Many cloud storage providers automatically provide backup, maintenance, upgrades and redundancy of storage systems. Storage providers may also provide encryption services for data in transit and at rest.

- **Database.** Organizations often run applications that use a database to store application data. Small businesses may not have the resources necessary to manage a database or may just want to minimize costs. Instead of managing the database itself, an organization might use a cloud service provider to manage the database. This can lower costs, improve accessibility and streamline maintenance requirements.

- **Infrastructure.** Organizations may use a cloud service to provide extra hardware such as hard drives, computer systems or web servers to run applications or augment the organization's infrastructure needs during times of traffic or seasonal increases.

- **Platform.** Platform refers to the operating systems and execution environments upon which applications are run. This is an important service for organizations and developers as it can provide not only ability to scale resources but also a means for testing across multiple platforms. Developers can test on Windows, Unix and Java platforms from a single vendor while ensuring that they have the most recent updates.

- **Software.** Individuals, developers and organizations often use software from a cloud service provider. Salesforce.com is the first and most famous of the cloud software providers. More commonly known as software as a service (SaaS), it is used to provide accounting, e-mail, photo, development and billing software.

7.1.3 Policies and Practices

Deciding to invest in cloud computing is a serious undertaking regardless of the type of cloud configuration that is being considered or the type of service that will be utilized. The most important attributes to consider are policies, practices and training. Without meaningful security and privacy policies in place and training to educate employees about those policies, cloud computing can be a ruinous undertaking. An organization's practices are a direct indicator of how it executes its policies. Before an organization selects a vendor for hosting cloud computing services, it should perform a thorough evaluation of its policies, practices and training. If the cloud computing services are provided by a separate organization, then a contract should be in place that mandates specific requirements needed by the organization. Here is a list of possible items to include in the contract:

- The contract's effective period

- Who shall have access to computer systems and servers

- Who will be permitted to configure applications

- Restrictions on sharing and usage of data from hosted company

- Compliance obligations, such as PCI or HIPAA

- How backups are performed

- Proper disposition of media

- Whether it is acceptable to use a shared computer for storage of applications or data

- What happens to computer systems once they are taken out of service

- What happens to hardware, software and data once the contract expires

Periodic audits should be performed to help ensure that hosting companies are abiding by their contractual obligations. The following sections look at privacy and security concerns to consider before investing in cloud computing.

7.1.4 Privacy Concerns

This section looks at privacy concerns that come into play when deciding to invest in cloud computing services. While many of these are common concerns that should be addressed with any data center or when using vendors to manage data, having the data in the clouds may create the additional complications of transmitting data securely, segregating multihosted data, mitigating hacking threats and dealing with personnel from multiple companies within the data center.

- **Thorough policies.** When creating privacy policies, organizations must include the risks that may occur from the use of cloud computing and hosted environments. Privacy practices must reflect the policies, and training must exist to teach employees about any additional cloud computing policies and practices.

- **Prudent contracts.** Contracts with hosting companies must cover all aspects of data handling to help ensure that their practices align with organizational policies. Regular audits should occur to help ensure that expectations are being met with regard to data-handling practices.

- **Access to data.** Special care must be taken to help ensure that employees within the cloud computing company are not inappropriately accessing organizational data. Where practical, access controls must be restricted and data must be encrypted. There will be cases where hosting employees are administrators on hosted systems. In those cases, audit logs should be in place to help track any inappropriate access to data. Hosting employees must be instructed on what data and systems they may access. Having a dedicated set of employees assigned to managing your systems is a prudent practice to consider.

- **Inappropriate usage.** Organizations providing cloud computing services may wish to use data hosted within the cloud computing environment for their own purposes. Privacy policies and contracts should be clear about how data can be used and which organization governs how a set of data can be used. A set of exceptions can be provided to hosting companies that address the need to use hosted data for security, fraud and service improvement.

- **Inappropriate sharing.** Organizations that host data in the cloud for other companies may have permission to use that data for their own purposes. However, the organization may not have the clearance to share the data with third parties. Within a cloud-hosted environment there may be a tendency to provide statistical or marketing data from the companies being hosted. Contracts with cloud-hosting companies should be clear about restrictions on sharing hosted data, including information about the companies being hosted.

The sharing of data with law enforcement and another country is something to consider when a data center crosses country borders. Understand what the hosting company's obligations are around disclosing law enforcement requests and access to data by foreign government officials. It would be prudent to keep sensitive data on premise and not subject it to these types of risks.

- **Proper separation (in a multihosted environment).** Cloud services companies often host multiple companies on the same set of servers or database. Even though members of a hosted company may not have permission to access the resources of another hosted company (such as files, groups or databases), they may be able to see the names of those resources, providing a clue that other companies are being hosted there. This could be an unwelcome revelation to some organizations and they should be aware of these types of practices. In addition, if another organization within the hosted environment runs afoul of the law and its data is seized as evidence, any data from other tenants that exists on the same hardware will also be seized.

7.1.5 Security Concerns

This following security concerns come into play when deciding to invest in cloud computing services:

- **Requirements and service-level agreements (SLAs).** This is the first-level security concern, setting the standard for all other cloud matters. There should be a clear understanding between the cloud service provider and the hosted company over the security requirements needed for the data and systems it is being entrusted with. When an issue occurs, there should be a clear understanding of the engagement strategy and how long it will take for the issue to be resolved.

- **Complacency.** Organizations should not move into the cloud services space treating it like a private data center or typical service deployment. They must take time to understand the security concerns specific to cloud computing before embarking on a cloud service deployment.

- **Physical security.** Data security relies on proper physical security. Computer systems should have restricted access. In multihosted environments, servers holding data for a particular environment should be separated from other servers with physical security. Where resources permit, a separate administrator should be assigned to each set of hosted servers.

- **Geographic location.** The country in which a data center is located will dictate the laws that apply to data stored there. There may be restrictions on what data can be collected, how it may be processed or the extent to which it may be transmitted elsewhere, especially across country borders. The risk that data or servers could be seized by a government should also be evaluated.

- **Proper access security.** Though this is a general consideration, it requires special attention for cloud environments because a hosted company may not be the organization involved in hiring employees and may have special requirements for individuals accessing its data. They may need to be of a specific nationality, have a certain security clearance or certification or need to avoid certain conflicts of interest. Organizations that have special access requirements for their data should make sure these are specified in any agreements made with the hosting company.

- **Proper encryption.** When data is hosted in a cloud environment, its encryption requirements should be maintained. This may mean adding encryption for transfer to the cloud environment. Analysis should be done in advance to ensure that the cloud services environment supports the encryption required by the data controller.

- **Data breaches.** Data breach is a major cause of data loss for organizations. While there may be a tremendous loss of data, a data breach does not necessarily equate to a privacy breach. Personal data must be involved for that designation to apply. A data breach can occur in several ways:

  - **Malicious insider.** A bad employee can easily walk away with valuable data. An employee at a cloud service provider is less likely to be loyal to the hosted company than an employee of the hosted company. Due diligence should be performed when hiring, training and auditing employees who have access to data.

  - **Poor access controls.** All data should have access controls by default. Servers for different hosted companies should have different passwords, even if the same person is the administrator of the machines, to minimize the risk of a password breach permitting access to all data in the data center. Passwords should be changed on a periodic basis to reduce the risk of misuse when a person leaves the company or a password is inadvertently revealed. When applications are being hosted by a company, access control over the application should be minimized.

  - **Lack of encryption.** As much as possible, data in the cloud should be encrypted to minimize the risk from a data breach. When data is encrypted, it decreases the ability for an individual to access it and can alleviate the need to perform a data breach notification.

- **Cyber theft.** Hackers are always looking for ways to steal data. Using encryption, strong authentication practices and intrusion detection can minimize the risk from cyber thieves.

- **Data loss.** Employees are often responsible for the loss of data due to lost or stolen laptops, thumb drives, mobile devices and backup media. Limiting what the cloud service employees can place on their devices, their ability to leave the data center with the devices and encrypting the data while it is on the devices can minimize risk from data loss.

- **Traffic hijacking.** When transferring data between an organization and the outside world, there is always the opportunity for the data to be intercepted. Encrypting the data and the transmission medium can minimize the risk from traffic hijacking. When working with a cloud service data center, ensure the hosting company is protecting all external data transfers.

- **Insecure interfaces.** When applications, databases and platforms are hosted by a cloud computing company, the hosted company needs to connect to those services in a secure manner. Below are tools that IT professionals can implement to provide secure connections to cloud services:

  - **GSS-API.**[5] An API that can be used to provide secure services. Must be incorporated by a software vendor.

  - **IP address filtering.** Permits the blocking of IP addresses to prevent specified traffic from entering or leaving a network.

  - **MAC address filtering.** Permits the blocking of devices from accessing a network based on their MAC address.

  - **Network port disabling.** Prevents connection to specified ports on a device over a network.

  - **OWASP ESAPI.**[6] An API that can be used to provide secure services. Must be incorporated by a software vendor.

  - **Protocol disabling.** Restricts the protocols that can be used over a network.

  - **Virtual private network.** Provides a secure means to connect to an organization over a public network. Usually incorporates authentication, encryption, filtering and other security measures.

- **Denial of service.** Organizations that rely on cloud services for processing of certain activities can be in a predicament when those services are unavailable due to an outage or denial-of-service attack (where a person prevents access to a cloud service by others by overloading the service with access requests). Popular websites such as Amazon.com are often subject to denial-of-service attacks, so this threat should be taken seriously.

- **Services misuse.** Shady individuals and organizations may engage in legitimate contracts with cloud service providers for nefarious purposes. For example, cloud services could be used to store stolen credit card data, network credentials, encryption keys, certificates or illicit adult material. Cloud computing power could also be used to crack encryption keys and passwords. Be certain, too, that policies governing the use of cloud services restrict any unwanted activity. All hosted sites should be audited on occasion to ensure hosted companies are complying with agreed-upon policies.

- **Storage of information by sensitivity.** Organizations hosting data for other companies should be made aware of special storage or access requirements for sensitive types of data. For example, medical, financial, trade secret and foreign national data has regulatory requirements in different jurisdictions. In addition, there may be auditing or reporting requirements that need to be addressed.

- **Proper auditing and logging.** Proper records give the hosted company a view into what is happening within a data center and can help identify inappropriate access to and processing of data. When using a hosted cloud data center run by vendors, it is paramount for compliance reasons to ensure that they are respecting their security and privacy commitments.

7.1.6 Associations and Standards

Cloud computing is a complex topic and as such has a large set of standards. The NIST Cloud Computing Standards Roadmap contains a great deal of information on cloud computing standards as well as about defining, deploying and securing cloud computing systems.[7] The Cloud Standards Wiki contains information about several organizations that focus on cloud computing standards and ways to get involved.[8]

The Cloud Security Alliance (CSA) consists of member organizations, including most large cloud providers, that work together to define best practices in security. It offers a number of useful resources, many of which are becoming de facto standards.[9] For example, the CSA Cloud Controls Matrix is a framework for implementing good cloud data center security practices.[10] It provides detailed security concepts and principles in 13 domains and coordinates with security standards.

The Storage Networking Industry Association developed the Cloud Data Management Interface standard, which defines the functional interface that applications can use to create, retrieve, update and delete information from the cloud.[11] The interface permits applications to discover the capabilities of the cloud storage offering and use this interface to manage containers and the data that is placed in them. Applications can also use the interface to apply metadata to the containers and their data elements.

7.2 Wireless Technology and Devices

"Euan, I've been reviewing the different wireless technologies that we've deployed and how the data is being used, and I'm a bit concerned about how we are inadvertently tracking individuals' movements as they traveled around during the day," said Amy "There also seem to be efforts to use biometrics to identify people for some of the POS systems that we are developing. Could you work with Bill and David to ensure that the systems are being used in accordance with our guidelines?"

"Certainly Amy," replied Euan. "I'll work with them to verify that everything is in compliance."

Wireless technology provides the ability for devices to conveniently connect to a plethora of networks, untethered, along with the thousands of services available over those wireless networks. Product payment, research sharing and communicating with friends can all happen while strolling through a mall, playing sports in a park or enjoying a mai tai poolside. The convenience of wireless connectivity also makes it easier for evildoers to sniff all communications moving between wireless devices and the endpoint to which they are connecting.

Another downside of wireless technology is that the provider of the technology can be aware of all data going across it, where it is going and who sent it. It doesn't matter if the service provider is an ISP, corporate network or telephone company—they can all see the data and its metadata unless it is encrypted.

These examples demonstrate how wireless technologies can be a potential privacy risk to users. They can cause personal data to be stolen, resulting in embarrassment, account hijacking or identity theft. Wireless technologies can also track users everywhere they go. This tracking can expose the location of a person's home, workplace or visits to a cancer clinic. Likewise, organizational and customer data transmitted over unprotected networks can be captured by those looking to steal data.

In general, wireless providers should not be seen as intending to misuse data passing over their networks. However, they can become overzealous when it comes to using data that they collect for their own purposes. Except for necessary functions such as security protection and fraud prevention, wireless providers should not feel comfortable using data on their networks for their own purposes unless an opt-out mechanism is provided to the subscriber and it is utilized. The following sections look at the different wireless technologies available to people.

7.2.1 Radio Frequency Identification (RFID)

RFID is a technology that is used quite broadly for identification of products and personnel. It is based on the ISO/IEC 18000 series of standards.[12] The technology can be deployed as a tag embedded in a sticker or identity card. The tag is a passive device that becomes activated in the presence of an RFID reader. Once activated, an RFID tag typically sends a unique identifier to the receiver. This is a great way to quickly perform product inventories. RFID tags are also used in many employee badges to identify employees and unlock entryways. When an RFID tag comes near a receiver, its code or data can be read by the receiver. The maximum range of a receiver can vary from a few inches to several feet. Anyone with an RFID receiver can easily read the RFID values from anyone in range.

When RFID technology was first introduced, there was enormous concern about the possible privacy risks since the devices are so easy to read. It was compared to the initial fear that newspapers and cameras would result in a loss of privacy. With RFID being embedded in clothing, products and new passports, there were concerns that not only would individuals be tracked, but so would their purchases. There was great resistance to RFID in passports due to possible risk to diplomats. However, after RFID tags came into wide use, the privacy fears were not realized.

There is a real threat of users being tracked by their RFID tags by a passerby or hidden RFID receiver. A person could have RFID tags attached to their clothing, shoes or other products that could be identified by an RFID receiver. One could be used to trigger the presence of a specific individual in order to signal a paparazzi or kidnapper. A thief could read the RFID tags within shipping containers to determine what to steal or copy an employee's RFID badge and walk into a secure building unimpeded.

RFID data is often collected in a database along with other personal data that could provide information about a user's identity, purchasing history or travels. Companies should be careful to restrict access to personal data, and encrypt or hash sensitive data. Companies that attach tags to their products should notify consumers that the tags exist and provide instructions on how to remove or disable them.

Individuals who are concerned about being tracked via RFID tags can remove the tags, destroy them in a microwave oven or screen them by placing them in a shielded case.

The Privacy Rights Clearinghouse in conjunction with the American Civil Liberties Union, Electronic Frontier Foundation, Electronic Privacy Information Center and others have created a framework for the proper use of RFID technology.[13] The European Commission Joint Research Centre created the document "RFID Tags: Privacy Threats and Countermeasures."[14] The Information and Privacy Commissioner of Ontario created the document "Privacy Guidelines for RFID Information Systems."[15] Organizations wishing to deploy RFID technology should be familiar with these documents and follow their guidelines.

7.2.2 Near-Field Communications (NFC)

NFC is a variation of RFID technology based on the ISO/IEC 14443 series of standards.[16] Available in many new smartphones and devices, it permits the transfer of information between NFC-enabled devices and an NFC receiver in close proximity to the device. This feature is typically used for payment purposes, transmitting credit card data to POS systems. Users are able to represent multiple credit cards with one device. This is a great feature for people looking to decrease the time spent at a checkout stand and reduce the number of cards that they carry around. However, it can also be a boon for thieves looking to steal credit card information.

Users can protect themselves from thieves looking to intercept their credit card data by disabling the NFC feature when not in use. NFC-enabled devices should also be password protected in case the device is lost or stolen.

7.2.3 Bluetooth

Bluetooth is a wireless technology based on the IEEE 802.15.1 standard, which permits devices to have two-way communication with each other.[17] The Bluetooth mouse is probably the first interaction that people have with the technology. The Bluetooth earpiece for mobile phones quickly became popular as well. Other Bluetooth devices include the keyboard, speakers, headphones and many other small devices.

Bluetooth technology permits the discovery of nearby Bluetooth devices. A Bluetooth receiver with a display can list nearby Bluetooth-discoverable devices. The display can list the name and sometimes unique identifier for the device. Figure 7-1 shows an example of how a Bluetooth-enabled Macintosh was found using the "Add a device" feature in Windows. Retail stores or individuals can use the same capability to track people carrying Bluetooth devices. If a person carrying a Bluetooth device makes a credit card purchase, the store can connect the Bluetooth identity to the purchase. When the same device is detected in the future, it can then be associated with past purchases, and recommendations or coupons could be offered to the person.

Figure 7-1: "Add a Device" Feature in Windows Displaying a Detected Bluetooth-Enabled Device

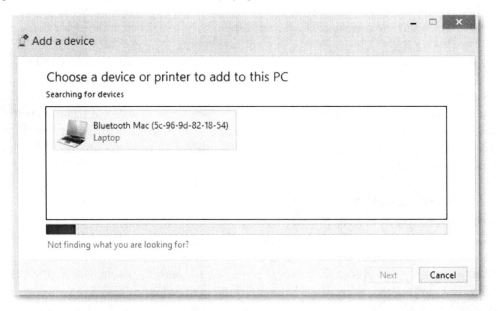

Used with permission from Microsoft.

Bluetooth devices can be hacked and communications intercepted. This can result in the copying of files being transferred or eavesdropping on conversations. Be sure to modify the default password of all Bluetooth devices and disable the Bluetooth functionality when not in use.

To avoid being tracked via Bluetooth, users can disable the Bluetooth discovery feature, turn off Bluetooth altogether or place the device in airplane mode.

7.2.4 Wi-Fi

Wi-Fi is the wireless networking technology based on the IEEE 802.11 standard that many people use to connect to the Internet.[18] It is available on computers, laptops, tablets and mobile devices. It provides the same capability as when a computer is hardwired to a network. However, because it is a wireless technology, anyone with a network sniffer can use it to see unencrypted data flowing between devices using it. This can include passwords, cookie values, credit card information and sensitive correspondence. Wi-Fi networks can also be surreptitiously connected to by any Wi-Fi device unless measures are taken to prevent such rogue connections. Once connected, the Wi-Fi device can see other devices on the network and possibly connect to them and access their files.

When deciding to connect to a Wi-Fi network, it is prudent to connect only to encrypted networks. The list of wireless service set identifiers (SSID) in a Wi-Fi control panel will normally indicate whether or not a network supports encryption. When deploying a wireless network, the following features can be used to help protect it from unwanted users:

- **Hidden network.** By not broadcasting a network's SSID, devices will not be able to connect to it unless the user knows the network name in advance. The network will either not appear in the list of Wi-Fi networks displayed by the Wi-Fi control panel or will be listed as something obscure, such as "Hidden network."

- **Password protection.** Password protection will prevent an individual from connecting to a network even when the network name is known. Requiring a password is an extra level of precaution for avoiding unwanted individuals on a network.

- **Encryption.** Using encryption on a network prevents miscreants from seeing data on the network as it passes between a device and the network endpoint.

7.2.5 Wireless Encryption Protocols

The Wi-Fi Alliance is a nonprofit association of industry companies that developed a series of wireless encryption protocols to help protect data as it is transmitted over a wireless network.[19]

- **Wired Equivalent Privacy (WEP).** This was the first encryption protocol developed by the Wi-Fi Alliance. It uses the RC4 stream cipher. WEP is a mostly ineffective encryption protocol that can be easily defeated by hackers and should not be used.

- **Wi-Fi Protected Access (WPA).** This protocol superseded WEP as a more secure encryption protocol. It uses Temporal Key Integrity Protocol and Advanced Encryption Standard for encryption.

- **Wi-Fi Protected Access 2 (WPA2).** This is the successor to WPA and is the most secure wireless protection available. When setting up a wireless network, select this protocol where possible.

7.2.6 Cellular Telephones and Tablet Computers

Cellular devices are used to connect to telephone networks, but can also connect to the Internet via the cellular carrier for the device. AT&T, Orange and Verizon are examples of cellular carriers. These networks are mostly encrypted and as such are protected from those looking to steal data that passes over those networks. The cellular carriers themselves, however, do have access to the data and could use it for their own purposes or hand it over to law enforcement agencies. There has been a lot of news lately about the National Security Agency (NSA) in the United States and Government Communications Headquarters in England using carriers to provide them with information on their subscribers.[20]

Unfortunately, the courts have not been sympathetic to the plight of mobile phone users. Not only may their location be tracked by their mobile carriers, but law enforcement can get unfettered access to a person's location history. In the summer of 2013 a U.S. Court of Appeals ruled that historical location data can be extracted from mobile phone carriers without a search warrant. That same summer a California court ruled that a user's mobile phone can be searched without a warrant. Individuals as well as IT professionals should be aware of these risks to not only personal data, but also organizational data that may be on the phone.

Mobile devices contain a range of wireless technologies that can be used to track users as they move about in public. Bluetooth, Wi-Fi and near-field communications features all give out telltale signals that a department store with wireless receivers can use to track visitors as they browse through their store. Major League Baseball has developed a wireless tracking system that permits visitors to their stadiums to control whether or not they are tracked and receive updates via a mobile application that must be downloaded from their website.[21]

Applications running on cellular devices have the ability to gather information from a device and send it to the creator of the device or any other destination. Information such as browsing history, online searches, contact lists and location can be collected by mobile apps. Users of such devices should be aware of the collection practices of the applications they use and manage those with the apps' controls, if they exist. Applications such as MobileScope can discover which cellular applications are sending data off the phone.[22] Application developers should minimize the data they collect from users, ensure users benefit from the data collection, inform users about the data they are collecting and permit them to control how that data is used.

IAPP's Mobile App Privacy Tool consists of seven mobile application guidelines, which simplifies the process of adopting best practices for application developers, platform developers, advertising networks, operating system providers and mobile service providers.[23] Each guideline takes the user through nine requirement categories: data collection, data retention, notice and transparency, choice and consent, accountability and oversight, privacy controls, security, children and miscellaneous. The tool includes input from seven regulatory bodies and industry groups on each requirement category and industry area.

7.3 Location-Based Services (LBS)

LBS can provide some of the most meaningful searches, recommendations and coupons by using location as an indicator of what the person wants. While the random delivery of items based on a person's location may seem odd when the person is sitting at home or in an office, when out and about they can be welcomed or even invaluable. Being able to use LBS to find the nearest hospital, clinic, pharmacy or gas station can be a godsend. Imagine walking the downtown streets of a foreign city and having a craving for your favorite cup of coffee. With LBS you can get the visual location of the coffee shop nearest to your current position that serves the coffee you like and get a discount coupon in the local currency.

LBS have evolved to be a valuable addition to the plethora of mobile phone apps that exist today. They can augment maps, traffic updates, photos, videos, texts and social posts as well as online searches. At the same time, however, they can expose users to being tracked because the location metadata that is embedded in content can be viewed by anyone who has access to the content. LBS also log requests such that they can have a record of a person's movements over time. While you are looking at a digital map, it is looking back at you and recording everywhere you go. That data can be passed on to advertisers and other companies looking to benefit from the data. The location setting on mobile devices should be turned off when not in use. Users of an application should have a thorough understanding of when location data is being captured, how it is used and how long it is kept. Many applications that ask for location when installed allow the setting to be disabled afterwards without affecting the use of the application. The retention of location data provides opportunities for strangers to know your whereabouts, which could enable theft, stalking or kidnapping.

7.3.1 Evolution of LBS on Mobile Phones and Personal Digital Assistants

Location-based services on mobile phones started off as simple maps. However, the ability to see where you were at any point in time was simply divine for people who traveled a lot. Getting off an airplane in a new city and being able to pull up a map was a great feature. The ability to perform address searches was a nice addition to the mapping capability. Soon maps became more elaborate, with the ability to show not only landmarks but also local shops and general information. Query functions also became more sophisticated and were able to respond to questions such as, "Where is the nearest coffee shop or Burger King?"

Foursquare brought the integration of social media to LBS. It permits people to check in at specific places and let their friends know where they are. Facebook and other applications integrated LBS as well, increasing the ability to keep in touch with friends and family by location. These scenarios represent passive uses of LBS, but application developers quickly began to find ways to interact with mobile phone users based on their location. Location-based advertising started to appear on mobile devices. Retail stores began to take notice of their visitors with smartphones and to deliver coupons that shoppers could use right away.

Personal digital assistants (PDAs) were the next services to be integrated with location-based services. Apple's Siri and Google's Now are both able to take the user's current location into account when making suggestions such as when to leave for an appointment, when a flight arrives or what interesting sites are nearby.[24] PDAs can respond to a wealth of voice commands and take several things into account before responding, including the user's demographics, past events and current location. The data collected by a PDA can be used to determine where a person is and what she is doing there. The determination of a user's actions is not limited to static attributes, but is based on intelligent analysis about users and their surroundings. For example, based on movement patterns, a PDA can determine where a person lives, works or likes to eat. If a person is at a concert hall, it can be determined who was performing at the time and the type of music the person likes.

The data collected by a PDA can be sensitive or embarrassing to a user. Users should be aware of the data being collected and disable the functionality or delete its history when no longer needed. Companies that develop the technology or collect the data from PDAs should be sensitive to the harm that misuse of personal data can cause, be careful to protect the data during storage and remove it when there is no longer a business need to keep it.

7.3.2 Global Positioning Systems (GPS)

GPS is a satellite-based system developed by the U.S. government that permits a device connected to such a system to determine its location. There are 24 GPS satellites in orbit at about 19,312 kilometers (12,000 miles) above the earth. GPS was originally developed for the military but is now used in many commercial, academic and personal applications.

GPS coordinates are typically accurate to within 3 meters (about 10 feet), but can be accurate to within 1 meter (about 3 feet). (Military GPS is more accurate, but not accessible to civilians for security reasons.) The accuracy of GPS makes it an important part of many LBS systems. Wi-Fi and cellular technologies can provide crude location capabilities where they have coverage. GPS signals can be found everywhere across the globe and can provide accurate location with the use of three orbiting satellites. At least four satellites are needed to provide altitude information.

Many companies use GPS to track vehicles and devices. Most states have laws permitting the tracking of employees, though some limit such tracking to work hours. It is not legal to use GPS to track the location of personal vehicles or devices without permission.[25] There has been resistance by employees against employers that want to track them, even to the extent of using software that provides a sophisticated means to keep up with employees' whereabouts. While using GPS to track employees and property can improve productivity and reduce theft, it can also increase stress for employees.[26] Employers should consult with legal and labor resources before deploying an employee monitoring system and set expectations with employees around monitoring.

The utility and availability of GPS have motivated companies to integrate it into many personal devices, avionics systems, and vehicles. Companies use GPS to track employees, vehicles, devices and shipments. The availability of the GPS signal on devices has led companies to develop all sorts of applications that can consume the signal. GPS for navigation systems in cars is probably the first commercial application that was available to the general public. It quickly simplified the ability to find locations without having to pull out a map. The data that is used to help drivers find their way in unfamiliar surroundings helps car manufacturers and rental companies track their cars as well. Finding lost or stolen cars or assisting individuals whose lives are in danger certainly seem like practical uses. However, what happens to that data when it is no longer needed?[27] Currently, users do not have the ability to opt out of the tracking or to have the data deleted. Manufacturers and rental companies should be open about the tracking that takes place with their vehicles and provide an opt-out mechanism where practical. IT professionals should be aware of any tracking that occurs with vehicles the company uses and the impact it may have on company policies or agreements.

When someone posts on Facebook, tweets on Twitter or takes a picture with a smartphone, the user's location may be included. Location data is often shared with applications and sent to the publisher of the application, unbeknownst to the user. Games such as Angry Birds, standalone apps such as Brightest Flashlight and communication apps such as WhatsApp require that users share their location with the applications, even though there is no obvious need for that information.[28] Many mobile apps not only collect location information for themselves, but they also share it with third-party companies along with other data.[29] This level of data collection and sharing is disturbing for many privacy advocates and regulators. Companies should be careful about being involved in these practices without the user's consent. IT professionals and individuals can use applications such as MobileScope to see what data is being transmitted from their mobile devices.[30]

The collection of GPS data beyond the control of individuals can have a chilling effect on their perceived feeling of safety, freedom and privacy. GPS data can be used to discern a person's predilection to addiction, sexual preference, religion, political leanings and social connections and to wrongly associate someone with illegal activities. Collecting GPS data can also become a legal liability for those collecting the data. IT professionals should take a close look at their company's policies concerning these collection and usage practices and work with their legal and privacy counterparts to ensure that they are taking a conservative approach to GPS data usage.

7.3.3 Geographic Information Systems (GIS)

GIS differs from GPS in that instead of depicting longitude and latitude coordinates, it consists of a computer service or application that combines geographic data along with descriptive information associated with that data. Geographic data can include elements such as coordinates, areas on a map or buildings. Descriptive information can include driving directions, topology, an employee directory or points of interest.

Geographic information systems don't merely help individuals find people, places and things; they also enlighten individuals about those locations once they are found. Metadata about locations can be augmented by a GIS on a continuous basis. The harm in this augmentation is the extent to which it includes personal data. It used to be that mapping software provided only street information. Now most mapping software comes with 3D imaging that permits someone to see the building or house you might be visiting, which could reveal information you weren't willing to share.

With GPS a person can know not only your location but also details about where you are, such as the kinds of activities that occur at the location, the history of the building you are in, what services are provided, the kind of food that is served, who may live there, the types of products that are sold there and much more. That type of information exposure can be problematic for people who do not want to publicize the types of places they are visiting.

It used to be that knowing a person's GPS coordinates or current address would not tell you much about them. However, GIS makes it easier for advertisers to take that information and apply inferences to individuals that can later be used to serve them targeted advertising. Some argue that knowing someone's location constitutes minimal risk to them. In isolation that may be true. However, GIS can provide a wealth of information about the area surrounding a location. A person could falsely be associated with a political party, abortion clinic or a life-threatening disease due to the improper processing of a location.

GIS can also provide demographic information in greater detail than zip codes can. This can permit companies to more accurately apply demographic data when determining the price for online goods, selecting a health insurance policy or making employment decisions. Some people may feel safe if they disable location tracking on their mobile device. However, they often provide their home or shipping address when interacting with online companies. Privacy protections tend not to cover data that is freely given. Applicants for services are typically told that their application information will be used when providing those services, but few details are given about the extent to which data is processed.

Geographic information systems can be an important tool for fire departments, police, delivery services and city planners. Application developers and IT professionals must be careful to gain permission before applying GIS data to individuals based on their location. Even then, unneeded and sensitive data should be filtered from the data to minimize risk to personal privacy. Additional information can be found online to help understand the concerns around GIS.[31]

It is important to note that GIS systems by themselves are fairly innocuous. It's the location data that is fed to them that can turn them into sophisticated tracking services. Limiting the location information that is available to them will limit their usefulness.

7.4 "Smart" Technologies

Smart technologies, as the term is used here, refer to the many computerized devices that are able to augment their intelligence via information that they can download off the Internet or to their ability to be controlled via an Internet connection. The "Internet of things" (IoT) is a term used to describe the many devices that are now connected to the Internet. Entertainment systems have long had connections with the outside world, starting with cable TV. Cable companies expanded their service to include telephone and Internet access as well. That, of course, permitted people to see television programs, surf the Internet, play video games and answer calls, all without leaving the couch. A great convenience, but not necessarily a good lifestyle choice.

With Internet connectivity into the home came the ability to control the entertainment devices remotely. So if a person left the house and forgot to record a show, he could record it remotely using a mobile app. The remote control ability expanded to home security systems, enabling people to monitor their homes while out for an evening or on vacation. The nanny cam was one of the biggest innovations that came out in the security system era.

Though the "house of the future" has been talked about since the 1970s, it didn't seem to come into realization until long after the Internet era was in full swing. Now people can manage their heating systems, sprinklers, lights and alarm systems, listen in on the kids and lock the doors, including the garage door, all remotely.

It doesn't stop there, of course. Shoes are connected, as are wristbands, watches and cameras. Driverless cars can be controlled over the Internet, as can traffic lights, street lights, commercial buildings, data centers and major utilities.

With all these advances comes the opportunity for people to misuse the capacities afforded by the IoT for bad purposes. One attack has been for a hacker to take over the camera and microphone of a computer or personal device and record what they see and hear. People caught in front of their cameras in the nude have been blackmailed into giving the perpetrators money in return for not posting the video on the Internet.[32] The "record" light is not a good indicator that a camera is being activated as it can be bypassed. Some people have resorted to covering the camera lens on their computer with tape when not in use, which is not a bad idea.

There is a famous case of a person logging in to a family's baby monitor and screaming obscenities at the baby just for fun.[33] The person was able to listen in on and view the baby's room as well. Two security researchers proved that the new intelligent cars can be hacked.[34] Google Glass, which is made by a company that spends a lot of time focusing on privacy and security, has been hacked.[35] Anything that is connected to the Internet or the cellular phone network can possibly be hacked by an intruder.

A special type of Internet bot, called thingbots, was named based on its attack on IoT devices. A set of thingbots was used recently to send spam and phishing e-mails from devices such as multimedia centers, refrigerators and televisions.[36] This shows that attackers are relentless in their search for new ways to launch their attacks.

It is not possible to be connected and totally protected. To enjoy the technological advances that improve our lives on a daily basis, we have to accept the fact that we will be exposed to a certain level of risk. However, there are things that individuals and device providers can do to help minimize risks, as outlined in the next sections.

7.4.1 Mitigating Hacking Risks (Users)

Auditing

- Enable the auditing feature on your devices where it exists

- Monitor the audit logs for your devices for any suspicious activity or errors

- Ensure there are limits on the amount of disk space or memory used for log collection

Disconnect

- When devices are not in use, turn them off

- If Internet connections are not needed, disable them

- Limit who can connect to your devices where possible

- Block camera lenses where practical

Encryption

- Enable encryption where possible for storage and transmission of content

- When selecting a device or service, ensure that encryption is a strong part of the equation

Internet

- When setting up Wi-Fi Internet service, enable encryption, require a password to connect, select the proper protocol and do not broadcast the Wi-Fi ID

- Control who can connect to the network if possible

- Disable the Wi-Fi Internet feature if it is not needed

Passwords

- Never use the default password that comes with software or devices

- Use a complex password

- Don't share your password

- If there is a risk that your password may have been compromised, change it right away

7.4.2 Mitigating Hacking Risks (Vendors)

Auditing

- Provide auditing capabilities for your products

- Make it easy to access auditing logs and detect inappropriate access

- Have defaults that will permit auditing without consuming an inordinate amount of resources

Defaults

- Provide defaults that help protect privacy and security out of the box

- Force setting and changing of passwords during setup

- Enable encryption by default

Encryption

- Provide a means to encrypt data and connections for devices and services

- Provide encryption for your websites

- Permit users to control the encryption key for their data

Filtering

- Provide a means to limit who can connect to a device or network by ID

- Provide a means to restrict connections to a device or network by IP address or location

Passwords

- Provide a means to enforce complex passwords

- Provide a means to expire passwords

Security Patches/Updates

- Provide ongoing support for software and services

- Provide a means to automatically update software with security patches

- Provide online or phone support to address security or privacy issues

7.5 Surveillance of Individuals

As we go about our daily lives we are, for the most part, constantly being tracked by the many cameras that exist in public, the devices we carry on our person or the computers we use at home, at work or while visiting other places such as libraries and Internet cafes. Being aware of this surveillance can help us minimize and control when the surveillance might happen and what data is collected. IT professionals have a duty to limit the surveillance of individuals and how data collected during surveillance is used.

Just knowing that an area might be under surveillance can have a chilling effect on people's ability to access services, frequent certain businesses, assemble in public, exercise their right to freedom of speech or visit public figures. The data that companies collect during surveillance of individuals may protect company assets, but it also places those individuals at risk from stalkers or overbearing governments. Organizations known to monitor individuals could be viewed negatively in the court of public opinion, causing them to lose customers and revenue.

When creating surveillance policies within the workplace they should include what areas can be placed under surveillance, who can be tracked and when, who can access surveillance recordings, how long the recordings can be kept and how they can be used. Privacy Rights Clearinghouse answers some tough questions around workplace surveillance.[37]

7.6 Video/Audio Surveillance

As we walk about the streets today in almost any city in the world, cameras can be seen watching us as we watch them. They exist in grocery stores, office buildings and athletic clubs. People have them outside their homes and in most rooms inside the home. The cameras record not only what can be seen, but what can be heard. Over time cameras have gotten smaller and incorporated into more devices.

Google Glass is a device worn on the face, like glasses, that provides a means of video surveillance. It has received a great amount of attention lately, though wearable video recording systems have been available for quite some time. Google has been the first to incorporate recording, viewing and Internet connectivity into a small wearable form. While many organizations have policies around recording and photography, some feel that Glass may need a separate policy because of the way it is worn, though a mobile device could as easily enable video recording as a person walks through the halls of a building or sits in a conference.

Surveillance cameras can now be found in smoke detectors, clocks, radios, wall outlets and even coat hooks. Google Glass is not the first type of glasses that contain a hidden camera or microphone. When developing policies for wearable technologies, policymakers should not focus on a specific product, but the type of surveillance they permit. In addition, privacy professionals need to ensure that their policies evolve along with technology. Employees should be aware when surveillance exists in the workplace or when individual employees are being tracked. Having employees find out they are being watched on their own is not the right way to generate goodwill within an organization. The European Data Protection Supervisor created a set of video surveillance guidelines that can be used by organizations looking to deploy surveillance systems.[38]

7.7 Data Surveillance

People often think about themselves being tracked via biometrics or obvious means such as GPS or wireless IDs. However, much about a person can be determined by their contact lists, whom they e-mail, whom they call and what they browse for on the Internet, which is all tracked these days, and not just by the NSA. Even all standard mail sent via the U.S. Postal Service is tracked.[39] Contact lists can be especially revealing as they can contain personal information like passwords, credit card numbers and bank account numbers.

Today many applications and services require access to much of a person's data, such as the contact list and location, when it is not needed for the application's features or to provide the service. Access to the application's or service's usage patterns is also requested, typically to improve them. Users should be wary of using such applications because of the risk of all that can be deduced from such data. A person's friends, colleagues, preferences, hangouts, vices and sensitive proclivities can be gleaned from data collected by way of one's actions. According to Aristotle, "We are the sum of our actions."[40] That is, if someone is able to know our actions, they are able to know us.

Data surveillance also occurs offline by companies that comb through public records or purchase data previously collected directly from individuals. This type of surveillance often goes unnoticed and offline companies currently do not make it easy for individuals to view or modify the data they have collected.

Individuals should be aware of the surveillance that is being done on them and the possible risks of such surveillance when control over the collection, usage and persistence of such data is not provided. It is well known that price discrimination occurs based on a person's demographics.[41] Bias can also occur when applicants are selected for insurance, loans and employment.

IT professionals should minimize risk to their organizations by being mindful of the surreptitious surveillance they perform on individuals and how that surveillance would be perceived if it became public or, worse, was misused due to a data breach. When collecting data from individuals those persons should be made aware of it, benefit from the collection and have control over the collected data.

7.8 Biometric Recognition

Biometric recognition can occur by various means, such as fingerprints, footprints, retinal scans, voice print or facial recognition. The biometric recognition that is in wide use today is typically used to provide access to secure areas, perform background checks or find criminals. The recognition that occurs is typically done in plain view with the subject's knowledge and, for the most part, consent. However, some recognition occurs without the person's knowledge.

Many video cameras that can be seen mounted in public are controlled by software that contains the ability to determine a person's identity. To identify someone, though, the software has to have access to a database of images. Unfortunately, social networks provide such a database, unbeknownst to many of their members.[42] This type of recognition can be harmful to people who are in witness protection programs, hiding from abusive spouses or just trying to maintain their privacy from people looking to benefit from identifying them, such as the paparazzi.

Facial recognition software could soon be in the hands of the general public, permitting any store that a person walks into to be able to identify them. People wearing Google Glass could instantly identify people walking past them, even if they are wearing a disguise. The video being collected by the millions of businesses across the globe could become a treasure trove for companies looking to start a business finding people who don't want to be found. Organizations should understand the sensitivity of collecting biometric data and the potential for its misuse. Even if the intent is not there, an employee could steal the data or a data breach could cause the data to become available to the public. Social networks should be careful about permitting personally identifiable information to be available to the general public by default. Likewise, individuals should review their privacy settings on a regular basis to ensure they are not sharing more information than they desire. AVG's PrivacyFix tool can help individuals manage their privacy settings across several social networks.[43]

DNA is another form of biometrics that can be used to identify individuals. As a matter of fact, it is one of the most accurate ways to identify people and even determine if people are related. The fact that it can be left on almost anything a person touches makes it easy to collect. Based on a recent Supreme Court ruling, law enforcement can collect DNA from a person arrested for a serious crime, which makes it easier to detect if a person was involved in a crime.[44]

7.9 Conclusion

"Amy, I just finished the draft of a press release on our cloud computing offerings as well as the integrated wireless services," said Filo. "I spent a lot of time crafting the privacy protections we've incorporated into both, and I would like you to have a look at it."

"I'll have a look at it today, Filo," replied Amy. "I appreciate the effort."

"Filo, did you include a mention of our downloadable privacy and security toolkit?" asked Euan.

"You bet I did! Even if people are not ready to use our services, they will be interested in our toolkit, which will help them protect their wireless data and help prevent them from being tracked as they use their wireless devices."

"I feel the work we have done in this space provides evidence that we are not a company that provides empty promises about our commitment to privacy, but shows our commitment through our actions," said Amy. "What's next on the agenda?"

Much of the digital information a person owns is either wholly stored on or backed up to the cloud. More and more people rely on cloud providers not only to keep their data safe, but also to not misuse the data. Equally important are individuals' reliance on cloud and location-based services to fulfill crucial tasks, such as making an airline reservation or scheduling a doctor's appointment. Moreover, people expect that these tasks will be accomplished in the strictest confidence and that data provided to fulfill the tasks will not be abused or shared inappropriately.

IT and privacy professionals have a special duty to help ensure the growth of Internet commerce by mitigating the risk to personal information that fuels the Internet economy.

Endnotes

1 Ramnath K. Chellappa, "Intermediaries in Cloud-Computing: A New Computing Paradigm," in *Proceedings of the INFORMS Annual Meeting* (Dallas, TX, October 26–29, 1997), www.bus.emory .edu/ram/.

2 Amazon Web Services, http://aws.amazon.com/.

3 Google Cloud Platform, https://cloud.google.com/; IBM cloud, www.ibm.com/cloud-computing/ us/en/; Microsoft Windows Azure, www.windowsazure.com/en-us/.

4 The Right Honourable Francis Maude, Member of Parliament, "The Government adopts 'Cloud First' policy for public sector IT," Cabinet Office of the United Kingdom, May 5, 2013, www.gov .uk/government/news/government-adopts-cloud-first-policy-for-public-sector-it.

5 Generic Security Service Application Program Interface, Version 2, Update 1, Internet Engineering Task Force, http://tools.ietf.org/html/rfc2743.

6 "OWASP Enterprise Security API," Open Web Application Security Project, last modified August 23, 2013, https://www.owasp.org/index.php/EASPI.

7   "NIST Cloud Computing Standards Roadmap," National Institute of Standards and Technology, U.S. Department of Commerce, July 2013, www.nist.gov/itl/cloud/upload/NIST_SP-500-291_ Version-2_2013_June18_FINAL.pdf.

8   "Cloud Standards Wiki," Cloud Standards, last modified May 13, 2013, http://cloud-standards.org.

9   Cloud Security Alliance, https://cloudsecurityalliance.org.

10 Cloud Controls Matrix v3.0 is available for download at https://cloudsecurityalliance.org/ download/cloud-controls-matrix-v3/.

11 SNIA, Advancing Storage and Information Technology, www.snia.org.

12 Information about RFID technology can be found in the RFID Journal, www.rfidjournal.com/ rfid-standards.

13 "RFID Position Statement of Consumer Privacy and Civil Liberties Organizations," Privacy Rights Clearinghouse, November 20, 2003, www.privacyrights.org/ar/RFIDposition.htm.

14 "RFID Tags Privacy Threats and Countermeasures," European Commission Joint Research Centre, 2012, http://ec.europa.eu/dgs/jrc/downloads/jrc78156_report_rfid_en.pdf.

15 Ann Cavoukian, "Privacy Guidelines for RFID Information Systems," Information and Privacy Commissioner of Ontario, Canada, June 2006, www.ipc.on.ca/images/Resources/up-rfidgdlines.pdf.

16 Information about NFC technology can be found at NFC Times, http://nfctimes.com.

17 Information about Bluetooth technology can be found at Bluetooth SIG, Inc., www.bluetooth.com.

18 Information about Wi-Fi technology can be found at QuinnStreet Enterprise, Wi-Fi Planet, www.wi-fiplanet.com.

19 Wi-Fi Alliance, www.wi-fi.org.

20 Jonathan Freedland, "Snowden fallout throws in stark relief US and UK notions of liberty," The Guardian, December 1, 2013, www.theguardian.com/world/2013/dec/02/snowden-fallout -us-uk-liberty-nsa-spying.

21 Jason Del Ray, "Major League Baseball Completes iBeacon Installation at First Two Ballparks," Re/ code, February 14, 2014, http://recode.net/2014/02/14/major-league-baseball-completes-ibeacon -installation-at-first-two-ballparks/.

22 Evidon, www.evidon.com/mobilescope.

23 The IAPP Westin Research Center, "Comparison of Mobile Application Guidelines," International Association of Privacy Professionals, https://www.privacyassociation.org/resource_center/mobile_ application_guidelines_comparison.

24 "Siri. Your wish is its Command," Apple, www.apple.com/ios/siri/; "Introducing Google Now," Google, www.google.com/landing/now/#whatisit.

25 United States v. Jones, 132 S. Ct. 949, 565 U.S., www.supremecourt.gov/opinions/11pdf/10-1259.pdf.

26 Alana Semuels, "Tracking workers' every move can boost productivity—and stress," Los Angeles Times, April 8, 2013, www.latimes.com/business/la-fi-harsh-work-tech-20130408,0,658957,full .story#axzz2pZjaaCpu.

27 Tony Bradley, "You Might Be Shocked To Learn How Much Your Old Car Knows About You," Forbes, October 31, 2013, www.forbes.com/sites/tonybradley/2013/10/31/you-might-be-shocked -to-learn-how-much-your-old-car-knows-about-you/.

28 Andrew Leonard, "Angry Birds, tracking device?" Salon, January 18, 2013, www.salon .com/2013/01/18/the_spies_inside_our_smartphones/.

29 Scott Thurm, "Your Apps Are Watching You," Wall Street Journal, December 18, 2010, http://online .wsj.com/news/articles/SB10001424052748704368004576027751867039730#ixzz18WFHX4pP.

30 Evidon, www.evidon.com/mobilescope.

31 Harlan J. Onsrud, Jeff P. Johnson and Xavier Lopez, "Protecting Personal Privacy in Using Geographic Information Systems," *Photogrammetric Engineering and Remote Sensing* 60 no. 9 (September 1994): 1083–1095, www.spatial.maine.edu/~onsrud/tempe/onsrud.html.

32 Mike Pearl, "Hackers Blackmailed a Detroit Teenager into Pawning His Mother's Jewelry," Vice Media Inc., October 18, 2013, www.vice.com/read/hackers-blackmailed-a-detroit-teenager-into -pawning-his-mothers-jewelry.

33 Chenda Ngak, "Baby monitor hacked, spies on Texas child," CBS News, August 13, 2013, www.cbsnews.com/news/baby-monitor-hacked-spies-on-texas-child/.

34 Meghan Kelly, "Prius pwned: Hackers exploit steering & brakes on 'smart' car," VentureBeat, July 29, 2013, http://venturebeat.com/2013/07/29/car-hackers/.

35 Andy Greenberg, "Google Glass Hacked With QR Code Photobombs," *Forbes*, July 17, 2013, www .forbes.com/sites/andygreenberg/2013/07/17/google-glass-hacked-with-qr-code-photobombs/.

36 "Proofpoint Uncovers Internet of Things (IoT) Cyberattack," Market Watch, January 16, 2014, www.marketwatch.com/story/proofpoint-uncovers-internet-of-things-iot-cyberattack-2014-01-16?reflink=MW_news_stmp.

37 "Fact Sheet 7: Workplace Privacy and Employee Monitoring," Privacy Rights Clearinghouse, revised January 2014, https://www.privacyrights.org/workplace-privacy-and-employee-monitoring.

38 "The EDPS Video-Surveillance Guidelines," European Data Protection Supervisor, March 17, 2010, https://secure.edps.europa.eu/EDPSWEB/webdav/shared/Documents/Supervision/ Guidelines/10-03-17_Video-surveillance_Guidelines_EN.pdf.

39 Ron Nixon, "U.S. Postal Service Logging All Mail for Law Enforcement," *New York Times*, July 3, 2013, www.nytimes.com/2013/07/04/us/monitoring-of-snail-mail.html?pagewanted=1&_ r=1&hp.

40 William J. Bennett, *The Book of Virtues: A Treasury of Great Moral Stories* (New York: Simon & Schuster, 1993).

41 Jakub Mikians, László Gyarmati, Vijay Erramilli and Nikolaos Laoutaris, "Detecting price and search discrimination on the Internet," Telefonica Research, Universitat Politecnica de Catalunya, in *Proceedings of Eleventh ACM Workshop on Hot Topics in Networks* (HotNets-X-1, Redmond, WA, October 29–30, 2012), 79–84, http://conferences.sigcomm.org/hotnets/2012/papers/hotnets12-final94.pdf.

42 Alessandro Acquisti, Associate Professor of Information Technology and Public Policy at the Heinz College at Carnegie Mellon University, led a study that showed where a simple video camera and access to Facebook could be used to identify passing strangers. Alessandro Acquisti, Ralph Gross and Fred Stutzman, "Faces of Facebook: Privacy in the Age of Augmented Reality," Heinz College, Carnegie Mellon University, in *Proceedings of Black Hat USA* (Las Vegas, NV, August 3–4, 2011), www.blackhat.com/docs/webcast/acquisti-face-BH-Webinar-2012-out.pdf.

43 AVG PrivacyFix, https://privacyfix.com/start.

44 *Maryland v. King*, 569 U.S. http://www.supremecourt.gov/opinions/12pdf/12-207_d18e.pdf.

Index

About the Author

JC Cannon is a 16-year veteran of Microsoft, 12 of those years focused on privacy. He currently works as the advertising privacy manager for Microsoft's Online Services Division, where he performs privacy reviews of all new advertising products and services. He also monitors external privacy activities from regulators, researchers, industry and competitors and develops action plans for product, policy and marketing teams. He assists with the creation of privacy policies, standards and training. He is involved in responses to regulatory inquiries, customer requests and privacy incidents. Cannon is a regular speaker on online privacy issues.

Prior to joining the Online Services Division, Cannon developed the compliance program for Microsoft's SQL Server database product, which included white papers, an SDK, client surveys and a hands-on lab. The program enabled organizations to manage access to personal data and validate compliance based on policy.

Cannon spent four years in Microsoft's Corporate Privacy Group during its formative years, leading the creation of the first version of the privacy standard for developers, privacy training and product reviews for developers.

Cannon worked on Microsoft's Identity Management team, where he developed a program that helped developers integrate the technology providing for centralized identity and profile management. Before joining Microsoft, he worked as a software consultant for companies in the United States, England, France and Sweden. He has a BS in mathematics from the University of Texas. He is also a six-year veteran of the U.S. Navy, where he fixed avionics for A6 aircraft on the flight deck of aircraft carriers.

Cannon is a member of the IAPP Publication Advisory Board, W3C Tracking Protection Working Group, the Network Advertising Initiative and the IAB Advertising Technology Advisory Board as well as past vice president of the University of Washington World Series Board. He participates in numerous privacy events. He is the author of *Privacy: What Developers and IT Professionals Should Know* and contributed to the books *Writing Secure Code* and *Windows Security Resource Kit*. He is also the author of The Euclidian science fiction books.